MW01284514

MATERNAL MEGALOMANIA

MATERNAL MEGALOMANIA

Julia Domna and the Imperial Politics of Motherhood

JULIE LANGFORD

The Johns Hopkins University Press
Baltimore

Printed in the United States of America on acid-free paper
2 4 6 8 9 7 5 3 1

The Johns Hopkins University Press
2715 North Charles Street
Baltimore, Maryland 21218-4363
www.press.jhu.edu

Library of Congress Cataloging-in-Publication Data

Langford, Julie, 1967–
Maternal megalomania : Julia Domna and the imperial politics of motherhood / Julie Langford.
pages cm.
Includes bibliographical references and index.
ISBN 978-1-4214-0847-7 (hardcover : acid-free paper) — ISBN 1-4214-0847-3 (hardcover : acid-free paper) – ISBN 978-1-4214-0848-4 (electronic) — ISBN 1-4214-0848-1 (electronic)
1. Julia Domna, Empress, consort of Severus, Lucius Septimius, Emperor of Rome, d. 217. 2. Julia Domna, Empress, consort of Severus, Lucius Septimius, Emperor of Rome, d. 217—Public opinion. 3. Rome—History—Severans, 193–235. 4. Rome—Politics and government—30 B.C.–284 A.D. 5. Motherhood—Political aspects—Rome. 6. Imperialism—Social aspects—Rome. 7. Ideology—Political aspects—Rome. 8. Political culture—Rome. 9. Popular culture—Rome. 10. Public opinion—Rome. I. Title.
DG298.7.J85L36 2013
937'.07092—dc23 2012035555

A catalog record for this book is available from the British Library.

Special discounts are available for bulk purchases of this book. For more information, please contact Special Sales at 410-516-6936 or specialsales@press.jhu.edu.

The Johns Hopkins University Press uses environmentally friendly book materials, including recycled text paper that is composed of at least 30 percent post-consumer waste, whenever possible.

To my mother,
Mary R. Langford

Her children rise up
and call her blessed
—Prov. 31:28

CONTENTS

PREFACE

Julia Domna found me at the observation table in the 2002 American Numismatic Society's Summer Seminar. Blissfully making my way through the collection, picking through tray after tray of coins, I was trying to get a better sense of what iconography and virtues were typical of Roman imperial coinage. When I flipped over an aureus of L. Septimius Severus, I suddenly found myself the object of Julia Domna's gaze (see figure 1). Flanked by her two sons, she was clearly the focus of their attention. Her direct gaze seemed to be a personal guarantee of the words in the legend: FELICITAS SAECVLI "the blessing of/for a generation." This first encounter with the empress unnerved me. I felt a bit like a voyeur whose presence is suddenly acknowledged. Julia Domna caught me looking.

The next two trays I pulled were filled with types and legends flaunting the empress's motherhood. Here she was depicted as a nursing mother, there as the Magna Mater, and in the next tray I learned that she had received the surprising title MATER SENATVS, mother of the Senate. The variety of her types and legends made it clear that she was well publicized, but I noticed that most of these types recalled Faustina the Younger, a woman quite unlike the exotic Julia Domna, daughter of the priest-king of Ba'al. It was my first inkling that these coins were designed not to honor the historical Julia Domna but to publicize the homogenized wife of the emperor and mother of future emperors.

In many ways, this study is a product of my Mormon upbringing. Growing up in Salt Lake City in the 1970s, I witnessed firsthand the political advantages in exalting the ideal of motherhood even while curtailing the influence of individual women. At the University of Utah, I became fascinated by history as tool for thinking through my own issues. I used history to explore how other women found their voices. Of particular interest to me were stories of nuns who carved out space for their own spirituality despite a dictatorial bishop's disapproval. By the time I went to graduate school at Indiana University in 1993, I had grappled with the inevitable clash between my studies and my religion and had developed a healthy disrespect for authority. But it wasn't until I studied under feminist scholars that I developed the vocabulary to express what I had experienced. Without them, I would not have been able to give words to what I saw at the observation table at the seminar.

I have been blessed with wonderful teachers, colleagues, friends, and family. Without them, this book would not have been written, nor would I have made it through the rigors of graduate school and the dissertation and tenure processes. My mentors at the University of Utah, Glenn Olsen and Lindsay Adams, kindly spent many hours helping me reconcile, rethink, and in some cases reject what I learned from my parents for what I was learning in the classroom. At Indiana University, my friend David Branscome patiently tutored me in Greek and with his wife, Elizabeth Richey, read several drafts of my dissertation chapters. Peter van Alfen and Sebastian Heath at the American Numismatic Society were excellent sounding boards. If they thought my ideas were wacky, they never let on but patiently listened, poked at them a bit, and sent me off with more evidence to consider. Nic Terranato enriched significantly my ideas on ethnicity and empire during the bus ride from Cerveteri to the American Academy in Rome. Ellie Leach, Jim Franklin, and Julie van Voorhis graciously agreed to advise me on a dissertation topic beyond their areas of specialties. They patiently waded through numismatic jargon and helped me apply what I had learned from them to Julia Domna's literary and artistic images. My dissertation was improved greatly by their observations and expertise. Julie and Ellie are still my go-to sources for things art historical.

Rubbing elbows with other Severan scholars has given me the opportunity to test my ideas, and I have been lucky to spend time with two women whom I very much respect. Susann Lusnia generously walked me through Severan Rome one summer, and together Clare Rowan and I haunted the American Numismatic Society vaults and library for several weeks. Susann's archaeological expertise and Clare's numismatic knowledge gave roots to my flighty literary ideas. Conversations with friends and colleagues also shaped and refined my ideas. For these I thank Jason Hawke, Stefanie Levecchi Rossi, Steve Tuck, Trevor Luke, Eric Kondratieff, Elizabeth Green, Heather Vincent, Liv Yarrow, Danielle Kellogg, Mike Nehrdahl, and Sheramy Bundrick. My friend and colleague Jonathan Scott Perry (bless him!) read drafts of this book. I am not sure I ever convinced him of my arguments, but he nonetheless graciously read the full manuscript and offered suggestions. Jim Anderson, Barbara Burrell, Tony Corbeill, Kristina Milnor, and Hans Friedrich Müller also read the manuscript. Their comments strengthen a number of my arguments, though of course I am responsible for all remaining errors.

Other colleagues at the University of South Florida have caused me to rethink ideas, especially Bill Murray, Eleni Manolaraki, Phil Levy, Anthony DeStefanis, Fraser Ottanelli, Gary Gebhardt, Patrick Kelly, and David Johnson. My graduate students and undergraduate researchers helped to compile, sort, and analyze the inscriptions, provincial coinage, and coin hoards examined in this study. Andrew Bird worked closely with me to identify the handful of inscriptions erected in honor of Julia Domna by military units. Joe Magliocco and Matt Warner helped proofread the manuscript.

My dear friends Liz Cass, Sarah Cox, Davina McClain, Mary Thurlkill, and Naomi Yavneh have been wonderfully supportive, remarkably insightful, and wickedly funny throughout this process. I am a better scholar and person for knowing them. Terry and Kate Johnson witnessed the beginnings of this project. By the time I finished it, Terry had moved to Chicago and Kate was completing her degree at Eckerd College. They dodged a bullet. My husband, John Myers, saw me through the most difficult and final phases of this project. He even singlehandedly planned our wedding while I was finishing the manuscript. I am grateful that he still loves me despite all this and astounded that he is encouraging me to get started on the next manuscript.

This book is dedicated to my mother, Mary Langford, who fed, clothed, and educated seven children on one civil engineer's modest income. She woke us at the crack of dawn to read scripture before we went to school, surreptitiously robbed the grocery budget to pay for our music lessons, and mended her winter coat so that she could buy us new ones. Though she initially disapproved of my decision to pursue a career in academia instead of staying home to raise a family, once she got on board with the idea, she defended it fiercely. She admits that she does not always understand what I am yammering on about, but she is sure nonetheless that it is brilliant. For these and so many other kindnesses, I thank her.

MATERNAL MEGALOMANIA

Introduction

As the historian Herodian tells it, Julia Domna singlehandedly saved the Roman Empire from dissolution and civil war. Less than a year after her sons had assumed the principate, they nearly destroyed the empire. Though the new emperors publicly touted their cooperation and harmony, in private, the young men volleyed constant attacks against each other, even resorting to assassination attempts. Eventually, they decided to abandon all pretense and to divide the empire between them: Caracalla would receive the western provinces, Geta would rule the East. Armies and senators would be distributed equally between the two. As the negotiations drew to a conclusion and the imperial advisors looked on with gloomy acquiescence, Julia Domna at last raised her voice in dissent:

> "You have discovered a way to divide the earth and sea, my sons, and to cleave in two the continents at the Pontic Sea. But your mother, how do you propose to divide her? And how am I, wretched woman, to rend myself in two and distribute myself between you? So kill me! Then each of you, after you have carried me off, bury your part near you. And in this way, I should be split along with the earth and sea." Then amid tears and lamentations, Julia stretched out her hands and clasping both her sons in her arms, tried to draw them together to her. And with everyone pitying her, the meeting adjourned and the project was abandoned. Each youth returned to his half of the imperial palace.[1]

In her efforts to preserve the integrity of the Roman Empire, Julia Domna tapped into a fundamental Roman virtue, *pietas,* which demanded an esteem that bordered on reverence for parents, country, and gods. It was *pietas* combined with a healthy dose of guilt and a dash of needling that allowed Julia Domna to save the day. These techniques were likely in the arsenal of every Roman mother. The difference between the empress and other women, however, was her proximity to imperial power, lending her influence not afforded by any constitution. This influence was not without its limits, nor did *pietas* always work in Julia

Domna's favor. Cassius Dio dramatically illustrated this point when he described how Caracalla tricked his brother into dropping his defenses by convincing his mother to arrange a reconciliation for the two sons in her own apartments. Geta guilelessly left all his bodyguards outside her chambers:

> But when they were inside, some centurions whom Caracalla had instructed earlier suddenly rushed at Geta, who, upon seeing them, ran to his mother. He hung about her neck and clung to her bosom and breasts, lamenting and crying, "Mother, you who bore me, Mother, you who bore me, help! I am being murdered!" And so tricked in this way, she saw her son perishing at her breast in the most impious fashion. She received him at his death into the very womb, as it were, whence he had been born. For she was all covered with his blood so that she took no notice of the wound she had sustained on her hand. But she was not permitted to weep or mourn for her son, though he had met so miserable an end before his time (for he was only 22 years and nine months old). On the contrary, she was forced to rejoice and laugh, as though at some great good fortune, so closely were all her words, gestures and changes of color observed. Thus, she alone, the Augusta, wife of the emperor and mother of the emperors, was not permitted to shed tears even in private over so great a sorrow.[2]

If we had only these two vignettes by which to judge the nature of an empress's power, we would be left scratching our heads. One scene presents Julia Domna as so influential that she alone was able to diffuse a situation that would have literally destroyed the empire. Though she held no defined constitutional powers, at times her maternal reproach proved more effective than the powers of the most important officials of the court. The other scene emphasizes Julia Domna's impotence as a woman and mother: she could save the empire, but not her son as he cowered in her arms. Still worse, the most powerful woman of the empire was not permitted to mourn properly for her son, even within the privacy of her home.

Fortunately, there are more vignettes of Julia Domna in a variety of media, though these hardly clarify the contradictions witnessed above. Official Severan propaganda publicized Julia Domna as the mother of the future emperors, associated her with important female deities, and even touted her as the protectress of the empire. Contemporary authors Herodian and Cassius Dio drew inspiration from these images and manipulated them to suit their own agenda. For example, in one reverse type (see figure 2), Julia Domna stands between her two sons, resting a hand on Geta's shoulder while the two young men shake hands to show their unity of purpose in ruling the empire, represented as a globe. The inscription celebrates the empress's *pietas* while the image depicts a Julia Domna whose mere presence guaranteed familial harmony. But in Herodian's twist on the official version, he paints the boys as so selfish and self-centered that they were willing to pull apart the empire to be free of one another. Only with great reluctance do they yield to their mother's reconciling embrace. In Cassius Dio's anecdote, the empress's *pietas* is no guarantee of harmony. It was through her *pietas*, after all, that she was duped into colluding in Geta's murder.

Clearly, these three portraits present conflicting evidence concerning the empress's degree of influence. Recognizing inconsistencies in portrayals of other imperial women, recent scholarship rejects similar literary portraits as being merely descriptive. Rather, scholars assert that such images were rhetorical tools used to praise or to blame the women's male relatives.[3] Among friends, the virtuous qualities of women indirectly called attention to laudable qualities in their male relatives.[4] In the hands of enemies, women's characters could likewise be proof of their men's worthlessness and depravity.

The high drama and conflicting portraits of the empress in the passages above ought to raise other concerns among historians, alerting us that here, too, we have entered the "world of declamation," where all is not as it seems, and where rhetoric is at play.[5] As is true with other prominent Roman imperial women, Julia Domna's images are a complex mixture of literary and visual narratives that, depending on the speaker's agenda, might at one moment showcase her maternal and wifely virtues, while at the next accuse her of ambition, adultery, and incest. These literary sources are not reliable in helping us locate the real Julia Domna; they cannot tell us who she was in private, what she felt about her position as a mother, or how involved in shaping imperial policy she really was.

Rather than read these passages and imperial propaganda at face value, expecting them to tell us something of the historical Julia Domna and her influence in the imperial court, I propose that we ask what they tell us about the authors and their attitudes toward the empress's male relatives.[6] By approaching the evidence in this light, we can better explain the clash of realities between the official narrative as represented by the coin and the unofficial narratives as related in historians' anecdotes. In short, rather than use these texts and images in an attempt to peek behind the curtain of rhetoric to find the real Julia Domna, I intend to examine the rhetoric itself. In the empress's portraits drawn by the imperial administration, the military, the Senate, and the populations of Rome, I find evidence not so much for the historical Julia Domna as for ideological negotiations that took place between the creators of these images.

This approach reaps immediate rewards. Even a quick comparison of the coin with the narratives above reveals that through Julia Domna and her maternity, Dio and Herodian castigated her male relatives, painting them in the worst possible light. Herodian's anecdotes depict an imperial court in such chaos and crisis that only a mother's guilt could persuade the emperors to put aside their differences and do their jobs. If examining this passage only to excavate the real Julia Domna, Herodian's point regarding Caracalla and Geta would be lost; we would see only that Julia Domna was capable of influencing imperial policy. The leap from here to proposing that Julia Domna was a powerful player in shaping imperial policy is short yet treacherous. Likewise, the appearance of Julia Domna in Cassius Dio's account heightens the drama of the scene. As despicable as Caracalla was for murdering his brother, his character is blackened even further because of the torture he inflicted upon his mother. In this passage, Dio presents Julia Domna's motivation for the meeting as rooted in *pietas* for her family and perhaps even her country; she wanted reconciliation, a motive lacking any political guile.[7] Yet this is hardly a consistent picture of Julia Domna. Elsewhere in Dio's history, Julia Domna is so hungry for political power that she even considers a bid to seize the empire and rule it alone. Dio's scene thus emerges not as a moment when the audience should feel sympathy for the empress, but as a convenient opportunity to depict Caracalla as ambitious and bloodthirsty, with a hatred that was out of control. Knowing that Dio usually portrays the empress as the masculine foil for the effeminate emperor prevents the historian from offering Geta's death scene as evidence that Julia Domna was powerless in her home. Furthermore, these authors used Julia Domna as a metaphor for the Roman Empire in order to make her sons look even worse. For Herodian, dividing the empire between two emperors would be as unnatural and macabre as tearing Julia's body in two. For Dio, the wound that Julia Domna sustained in Caracalla's attack is analogous to the *damnatio memoriae* that followed Geta's murder. The wound to the empress's hand during the attack had to be ignored, and she was forced to laugh and smile at the preservation of Caracalla. If we approach these passages asking only how powerful or influential the empress was, we might overlook these finer points that say more about Julia Domna as a rhetorical device than as a historical figure.

Scholars writing on Julia Domna thus far have shown little recognition of the importance of rhetoric in our sources, or read these literary sources as being more about the empress's husband and sons than they are about her. Seeing the empress's extraordinary maternal titles and knowing something of her remarkable life, they endowed her with a sort of power unknown to imperial women before her.[8] I believe they have been misled because they equated visibility with power.[9] Admittedly, Julia Domna was very visible, but there is simply no evidence of a consistent agenda behind her celebration that might indicate any personal control over her own images or titles.[10]

Julia Domna's prominence in monuments, inscriptions, and coinage, stems not from unprecedented personal charisma, exotic qualities, or influence. Her official advertisement shows little of the empress's most remarkable characteristics and instead homogenizes her fascinating background, rendering her virtually indistinguishable from her predecessors, at least initially.[11] Like every other imperial woman, Julia Domna was advertised in official media when it suited the propagandistic needs of her male relatives.[12] Her titles appeared at the convenience of those who wished to benefit from them. As this book demonstrates, the empress's titles boasting her maternity over the military, the Senate, or the *patria*, which scholars have taken as indicating some sort of unprecedented personal power, were nothing of the sort. Severus and the populations he addressed in his propaganda exploited images of Julia Domna when they could be politically beneficial. Those grandiose and elevated titles that claimed metaphorical motherhood for Julia Domna, a kind of maternal megalomania, were not about flattering or courting the empress at all. For Severus, they were just one of several planks in the Severan platform of propaganda that was ultimately designed to legitimate himself and his dynasty. For the populations who employed these titles when speaking to the imperial administration, they were powerful tools, used as signals to the imperial administration that they were ready to engage ideological negotiations. The ultimate goal for such populations was to obtain favors and honors from the emperor.[13]

This book explores how Septimius Severus harnessed Julia Domna's images to negotiate ideologies with important populations in the empire, especially the military, the *populus Romanus*, and the Senate. Like most successful politicians, Severus told the people what they wanted to hear. Because these three populations had very different agendas, he negotiated an ideology particular to each. Some of the negotiated "truths" overlapped between populations, while some were used as leverage in order to bully other populations. I explore these negotiations through the case study of Julia Domna—or, more accurately, through the maternal imagery of the empress. I ask what the imperial administration was saying about her maternity, contextualizing it within the overall message of Severan propaganda sent to a particular population. I then examine the responses to these messages, looking for overlap between one negotiated ideology and another. Each "conversation" or negotiation between the imperial administration and the military, the *populus Romanus*, and the Senate produced a different image of the empress, and each of these changed over time. The distinct images that emerge are sometimes complementary, sometimes conflicting, but the goal of these negotiations was always the same: to create a mutually approved interpretation of the past, present, and future that ultimately legitimized the emperor and his dynasty while simultaneously conferring benefits and honors on the population with whom he was negotiating at the moment. What will surprise and hopefully delight the reader is that none of these resulting images are what she might expect. They were certainly not what I thought I would find when I began to examine this body of evidence.

Julia Domna Who?

Julia Domna stands in stark contrast with earlier imperial women in her origin and ascent. She was born in Syria, the daughter of the priest-king of Emesa who conducted ecstatic rites on behalf of his god Ba'al.[14] Later propaganda boasted that Julia Domna's horoscope had proclaimed she was destined to marry a king.[15] At seventeen, she married L. Septimius Severus, a native of North Africa, with whom her family became acquainted after he had served in the region some years earlier. Shortly thereafter, she bore Severus two sons, Caracalla (originally named after his maternal grandfather, Bassianus) and Geta. In 193, Severus seized the Roman Empire and spent the next four years fighting two civil wars in order to maintain his position and found his dynasty. As wife to one emperor and mother of two others, Julia Domna enjoyed an uninterrupted proximity to imperial power not known since the days of Agrippina the Younger.[16] Occasionally, Julia Domna was depicted as unscrupulous and uncompromisingly ambitious. The writer of the *Historia Augusta* reported that she was to blame for the civil war between her husband and Clodius Albinus, after she coaxed Severus into attacking Albinus so that her sons could be emperors.[17] Once the civil wars were over, Severus embarked on a campaign to punish the allies of his former rivals, and he reportedly kept Julia Domna and his family by his side. With her husband, she traveled the length and breadth of Rome's territories, appearing in Syria, Egypt, Africa, Rome, and even far-flung Caledonia, later Scotland. Severus died while on campaign in Eboracum, now York, on February 4, 211. Julia Domna accompanied her sons to Rome, bringing with them Severus's ashes and his final purported advice to his sons: "Be harmonious, enrich the soldiers, and scorn all others."[18] Julia Domna soon found herself as we first encountered her, attempting to keep peace between her fractious sons. Literary anecdotes set after Geta's murder gleefully mangle the maternal imagery touted by the imperial administration to portray Julia Domna as ambitious and unscrupulous or as the dutiful masculine foil to her effeminate and capricious son. The *Historia Augusta* charged her with incest, seducing Caracalla in order to maintain her influence over him.[19] Dio reported that Julia Domna received senatorial delegations, answered imperial correspondence in Greek and Latin, and singlehandedly ran the civic half of the empire in Antioch while Caracalla frittered away precious resources in a pointless campaign against the Parthians.[20] When Caracalla was finally assassinated in 217, Dio reports that Julia Domna schemed in Antioch with her bodyguards to seize the empire and rule it herself.[21] When she realized that Caracalla's death was being celebrated in the capital (and that her chances of ruling alone depended upon his authority), Julia Domna decided to die. Dio provided two explanations: either she killed herself by starvation or she ruptured a tumor after repeatedly beating her breast, one supposes in grief and anxiety.[22] Julia Domna's life and character, if any of these stories can be trusted, must have been extraordinary.

None of the juicier details of the empress's life, however, were the stuff of politic or polite conversation. They do not appear in official media, either produced by the imperial administration or by any other official body. When those in the know savored these tasty morsels, they whispered them behind closed doors, marveled at them with fascination or horror, but never discussed them with the emperor. Official conversations about Julia Domna were limited to her wifely and maternal capacities. Even within the constraints of these topics, however, provincial municipalities, the populations of Rome, and ultimately the Senate still found much to discuss. By the time of her death in 217, Julia Domna had accrued an impressive array of unprecedented honors and titles awarded to her by a wide variety of dedicators. Nearly all these titles were concerned with maternity, either the maternity she earned by giving birth to her two sons or the metaphorical maternity of embracing the entire empire as her children.

Carving Out a Niche

The cacophony of voices attempting to define the empress in her own day is quieter now, and the once-authoritative voice of the imperial administration has fallen silent over the course of the centuries. Imperial biographies are lost, coinage is scattered, once-proud monuments and inscriptions are fragmentary. Instead of learning about the empress through official images, which is how most of her contemporaries would come to know her, modern students most often learn about her through the scandalous anecdotes in Cassius Dio, Herodian, and the author of the *Historia Augusta*. Because these sources have survived, they have taken on an air of authority, though ironically they would have been considered subversive and treasonous by the imperial administration of the day. The once-vociferous praises of Julia Domna by competing provincial municipalities and Roman *collegia* have become mere whispers, evident only in their inscriptions, coins, and sculptural images. A reconstruction of the empress's images produced and distributed by the imperial administration allows us to put them in dialogue with responses from the military, the *populus Romanus*, and the Senate. These dialogues in turn allow for an examination of the imperial negotiations between Severus and his audiences.

My inspiration for reconstructing these dialogues comes from recent scholarship concerning imperial women, numismatics, and communications between the imperial center and the peripheries. Ando in particular paints a picture of sophisticated communications between the imperial center and the provinces through the announcement of imperial proclamations and senatorial decrees, the awarding of crowns, and the dispatch of local delegations to Rome.[23] In his discussions of these communications, Ando distinguishes "propaganda" from "ideology." Propaganda consists of messages in a variety of media designed by the imperial administration to present itself in the best possible light. Sometimes tailored to a particular audience in an effort to persuade, these messages were often fictitious claims regarding Severus's heritage, the harmony of his family, and the glorious future that awaited Rome under the rule of his son. These were not all false claims; the degree of veracity varied considerably from one message to another. Propaganda is one-sided and not illustrative of the dialogues that occurred between the imperial administration and an audience. Ideology, on the other hand, is the dialogue between the imperial administration and a given population. It comprised not only propaganda but also the responses of the intended audience. The messages sent between the two entities constitute a negotiation of competing claims of reality that ultimately resulted in agreed-upon "truths." These "truths" may or may not be accurate reflections of reality, and they can vary considerably from one relationship to another. The "truths" that are agreed upon between the imperial administration and the military, for instance, may be quite different than agreements between the administration and the urban plebs. The imperial administration maintained several ideological dialogues with different populations at the same time. Often these dialogues were complementary and overlapped, but occasionally they were conflicting or contradictory.[24] Ando limits his discussion to communications between the imperial center and provincial cities, but I apply this model to relationships between the imperial center and other entities such as the Roman populace, the Senate, and the various branches of the military.[25]

New methodologies in the study of numismatics have also brought to light some exciting findings regarding propaganda. The discomfort that numismatists displayed in the face of Jones's critique of iconographic studies is a thing of the past.[26] After years of arguing about who was responsible for the types and legends on coinage or whether the man on the street might ever pay attention to them, most scholars believe that messages on imperial Roman coinage did promote the agenda of the emperor.[27] Until recently, it was difficult to determine which messages out of hundreds in the course of an emperor's reign had been given special emphasis or even whether certain messages were targeted to particular audiences.[28] Though catalogs such as the monumental *Roman Imperial Coinage* were instrumental in giving numismatists a flavor of the variety of types and legends, they were of little help in determining the frequency with which a legend or type was employed.[29] The catalogs reflected the curators' efforts to obtain samples of every known coin type; especially prized were coins known for their rarity.[30] An important methodological step in determining the frequency of coin types came in Noreña's "The Communication of the Emperor's Virtues." Noreña examined nearly 150,000 denarii in various hoards, seeking to quantify which virtues were most commonly found on imperial coinage.[31] The study provided the methodology for numismatists to discuss with new confidence the frequency of types. The scholars who capitalized on Noreña's work refined his methodology with the recognition that the quantification of types was more meaningful ideologically when examined one emperor or one dynasty at a time, as opposed to the entire span of the principate. Hoard contexts could likewise demonstrate the use of certain types and legends in an attempt to tailor messages to a particular audience. Kemmers, for example, examined Flavian hoards in military contexts around Nijmegen, and found significant differences in the types and legends distributed to the military as opposed to the general population.[32] Kemmers's study has spurred several others like it. Rowan, for instance, compiled a database of fifty-seven coin hoards to examine the role of religious imagery in the self-presentation of Severan emperors.[33] Rowan's work and particularly her Severan Hoard Analysis database have been foundational for my own work, especially in determining what messages the imperial administration sent to the military on the empire's frontiers. It is less useful in determining which coin types were in circulation in Rome and Italy because it contains only two rather small hoards, too small a sample to be representative.[34] Despite these issues, an analysis of the contents and frequency of certain types in hoards will provide some insight into which messages were tailored for a particular audience.

Complicating my efforts in this project is my choice to study the relationship between the imperial administration and various populations through the medium of an empress's coinage. Unlike their male relatives' issues, women's coinage was not dated. Without a full die study, the best that a numismatist can do is to date a woman's coinage on the basis of a rough chronological framework of her male relatives, paying special attention to the empress's titles and to the legends bearing her husband's or son's names.[35] Julia Domna's coinage lacks a complete die study, and for this reason I must resort to analyzing her coinage within broad swaths of time distinguished by a series of titles and variations in her name.[36]

My methodology consists of reconstructing Severan imperial propaganda, determining which populations the messages targeted and exploring those populations' responses to propaganda. Because Julia Domna's advertisement was only one facet of Severan propaganda, it is necessary to explore the ideologies between the emperor and a particular audience before turning to how Julia Domna figured in these negotiations. To accomplish this task, I use all available evidence, thereby spanning several specialties. I begin reconstructing Severan propaganda through an examination of imperial coinage, inscriptions, and monuments erected by the imperial administration. This is a vital exercise because, without a basic understanding of the interplay between propaganda and audience, I cannot ascertain what and how ideologies arose between the administration and important populations. Propaganda provides a useful counterbalance to the sometimes-vitriolic statements found in literary sources, but it must be contextualized and examined in the light of those same sources. Inscriptions erected by troops, municipalities, *collegia*, and individuals allow us to ascertain responses to imperial propaganda among those populations.[37] To date, over seven hundred inscriptions mentioning Julia Domna are extant. I have compiled these into a database classified by donor and location.[38] These data are useful in two ways. First, inscriptions reveal who responded to imperial propaganda. In chapter 2, for instance, I examine some twenty inscriptions found in Rome celebrating Julia Domna. *Collegia* and imperial freedmen erected the majority of these inscriptions, while the Senate erected none. Though it is dangerous to argue from a lack of evidence, I believe that this dearth of inscriptions is significant and likely indicated the Senate's reticence toward backing wholeheartedly Severus's dynastic claims. Second, inscriptions allow me to gauge roughly how enthusiastically a population responded to imperial propaganda regarding Julia Domna. One might expect, for instance, that as the Mater Castrorum, Julia Domna would be the frequent honoree of inscriptions erected by the military. In fact, military inscriptions rarely named Julia Domna as the Mater Castrorum, even when celebrating the entire imperial family. An exploration of when the title was used and by whom will demonstrate that Julia Domna was not advertised as Mater Castrorum to the military populations, nor, as a rule, was she honored as such by them. Finally, monuments erected by populations outside the administration are also useful for gauging responses. I examine the iconography and inscriptions of such monuments as the Porta Argentarii to better understand the agenda of *collegia* who erected it. The Arch of Septimius Severus will likewise shed light on the agenda of the Senate.

My work has also been informed by scholarly examinations of Roman imperial women. The nature and scope of an imperial woman's power are also difficult to determine, but too often scholars fail to define what they mean by "power" beyond a vague reference to influence.[39] With some notable exceptions, too often the manifestation of this influence is left to the reader to ascertain. Perhaps most troubling is a tendency in scholarship to equate publicity with power. True, imperial women received impressive titles, were honored as deities in the provinces, or were discussed in literary sources, but this does not mean they were "powerful."[40] Because of this flawed logic, Julia Domna has been deemed the most powerful of imperial women, even more influential than Agrippina the Younger or Livia. Yet my investigations reveal an inverse correlation between the strength of Julia Domna's influence at court and the frequency of her official advertisement in coinage. The apex of her promotion in coinage, between 202 and 204 during Severus's decennalia and the celebration of the *Ludi Saeculares*, coincides with the nadir of her power in the imperial court.[41] Dio reports that it was during this same period, the apex of her advertisement, Praetorian Praefect C. Fulvius Plautianus openly denigrated Julia Domna to Severus. While the empress withdrew from court to the solace of philosophy, Plautianus charged her with adultery and tortured the noble women of her circle for information.[42]

Though I believe that scholars have endowed Julia Domna with too much power, she was by no means powerless.[43] Her proximity to the emperors likely gave her influence over some political decisions, which her contemporaries recognized by honoring her in numerous dedications.[44] These dedications were designed to enlist her help in swaying the decisions or actions of her male relatives. Envisioning her in this way, Julia Domna resembles a Pythia who is reverenced because of her proximity to Apollo, not because she is the source of prophecy herself. Uncovering the nature of imperial women's power is far more nuanced than simply quantifying the number of consulships held or triumphs earned. In some ways, an individual woman's power was very much analogous to that held by Augustus. It was purposely undefined so that it might expand or shrink to fit her needs or those of her family, friends, or critics. When this unspecified power was wielded in an agreeable fashion, it was called *auctoritas*. When it was oppressive, it was *potentia*.[45]

The undefined nature of a woman's power allowed Roman men and women the space to negotiate relationships on the basis of their individual needs, but for modern observers, its nebulousness can be frustrating. Boatwright attempted to quantify the degree of power wielded by Trajan's and Hadrian's female relatives. She did so by measuring tangibles such as autonomy, lineage, high connections, wealth, philanthropic activities, and building projects. She also attempted to quantify instances when imperial women's influence over their spouses or male relatives successfully changed their actions. When gauging how others measured a woman's influence, Boatwright examined dedications and statues set up to these imperial women, distinguishing between those in imperial cult contexts (which she concluded were more about dynasty than personal patronage) and those erected as sole dedications to the women. Boatwright rejected state publicity as a concrete indicator of imperial women's power, saying that what was paramount was the institution of imperial marriage or the imperial house: "This did not translate into personal power for the women figuring in these institutions in either Trajan's or Hadrian's reign."[46] Other scholars attempting to quantify tangibles of imperial women have assigned a great deal of power to Julio-Claudian women, though they are ambiguous about what the nature of this power is.[47]

In actuality, the nature or amount of influence that a Roman woman wielded was of little consequence. What contemporaries found most useful about women's influence was the rhetorical power it held over her male relatives. Was she perceived to be obedient or willful? Was she rumored to be virtuous or promiscuous? The praise or blame of these women had little to do with their behavior. For Hillard, republican women appeared in literature primarily to highlight what weaklings and wastrels their male relatives were because they could not control them. He posits that Cicero's chief target in the *pro Caelio* was Clodius; Clodia was secondary and an unintended victim of this rhetoric.[48] Imperial women likewise faced charges of infidelity, incest, and poisoning. Their mere visibility allowed critics to take aim at an emperor by accusing him of an inability to control his women. How could he possibly control an empire if he could not control his own home? The most terrifying aspect of imperial women, especially for their senatorial competitors for the emperor's ear, seems to have been the very one for which they were honored: though imperial women held no office or power endowed by the state, they could interfere in masculine realms of law, politics, or the military.[49] When imperial women were reported as "interfering with male activities," it was often more to cast aspersion on the emperor for submitting to the will or wiles of a woman.[50]

With such dangers accompanying the visibility of women, why would any Roman risk his reputation by consenting to place his women before the public eye? The practice stretches back to the Republic, when Roman women who were supposedly confined to the domestic sphere were advertised because they served as connections between important men or families. Flower demonstrates this principle with Cornelia, mother of the Gracchi, who came to be important for two rival families, the Metelli and Scipiones.[51] The phenomenon was even more prominent in the Roman Empire as state art advertised these relationships.[52] The most important function for advertising Julio-Claudian women was to lend legitimacy to a successor, as Corbier convincingly demonstrated.[53] Imperial administrations had to choose carefully which women to celebrate and when. Those receiving attention had to conform to certain public expectations.[54] Pliny's sketch of Trajan's wife and sister in the *Panegyricus* provides the ideal: they were quiet, obedient, unpretentious, and most importantly did not meddle in state affairs.[55]

The tricky part for an emperor was to manage the perception that an empress influenced his decisions only occasionally and without political guile, otherwise she could severely damage his reputation. The perceived influence of imperial women could turn otherwise good emperors into tyrants. Emperors thus walked a fine line between reveling in the important dynastic connections that publicizing their women could provide and denying that their women had any undue influence over their political or military decisions.[56] Emperors and their administrations were not alone in creating portraits of imperial women. An emperor's critics could sketch as memorable an image of an imperial woman as could the emperor's supporters. The ideological needs of their creators and promulgators were paramount in shaping the literary, numismatic, and artistic portraits of imperial women. Studying the rhetoric surrounding these women can give us a better understanding of the men who created these images and their motivations for portraying these women as they did.

Severan Dynastic Propaganda and Julia Domna

To understand how the titles and images of Julia Domna reflected relationships between the emperors and important populations, we must first explore the role assigned to the images of Julia Domna in Severan propaganda. This brief discussion roughly outlines how the imperial administration modified images of the empress over time to suit its immediate needs and agenda.

Pay No Attention to the Woman behind the Curtain: Beginnings, 193–195

In the first stage of Severan propaganda, Julia Domna is more absent than present. She probably received her Augusta title in 193 or 194, soon after the Senate formally hailed Severus as emperor.[57] Shortly after Severus's accession, the new empress appeared on a handful of types minted at Rome, readily recognizable by the obverse legend IVLIA DOMNA AVG.[58] The coinage informed viewers of Julia Domna's name and association with Septimius Severus but revealed nothing of the empress's exotic origins, intelligence, or influence over her husband.

There was good reason for keeping the empress's public profile low in the early years. Cassius Dio described Severus as δεινότατος—the cleverest of the three contenders for the principate—because Severus realized that he needed the support of the Senate and set out to court it by promising to treat them with respect.[59] He understood the importance of allowing the Senate its dignity even when it could no longer claim to select emperors or control them. Severus developed a plan for winning the Senate's support and for keeping at bay his erstwhile rival Clodius Albinus. If Pliny's *Panegyricus* is a reliable indication of senatorial sentiments, the Senate preferred an adoption succession policy.[60] Severus thus hid his dynastic pretensions behind his claims that he intended to corule with the Senate and to adopt a successor.[61] Calling too much attention to the empress at the beginning of the reign would be tantamount to announcing Severus's intention to found a dynasty, which would undermine relations with the Senate.[62] Julia Domna was barely mentioned as a consort in Severus's self-presentation in Rome.

Instead, Severus portrayed himself to the world as the avenger of Pertinax. The association allowed Severus to maintain a good relationship with the Senate and the military outside Rome. Pertinax had been a respected general and popular among the armies in the provinces. His deference to the *auctoritas* of the Senate, especially toward the oldest members, was a refreshing change for those senators who had suffered under Commodus's excesses, threats, and general disrespect. Pertinax devoted himself to a policy of fiscal responsibility, consulted the Senate in day-to-day affairs and, perhaps most meaningfully, respectfully refused the titles of Augustus and Augusta that the Senate offered his son and wife. These actions signaled to the Senate his devotion to the principle of adopted succession. Thus, when Severus vowed to avenge Pertinax, he implied that he would also embrace an adopted succession policy and thus treat the Senate in the same fashion as his predecessor.

In the race to retake the city from Didius Julianus, Severus made two momentous decisions. Claiming to be an old man with children too young to rule and thus in need of an adopted Caesar, Severus petitioned the governor of Britain, D. Clodius Albinus, to be his Caesar and successor.[63] The Senate applauded this action and sent an embassy to meet Severus while he was still making his way to Rome. The new emperor also earned praise from at least a part of the Senate by dissolving the unruly Praetorian Guard, which had murdered Pertinax. Severus likely saw this action as necessary not only for his own security but as an important political statement whereby he at once avenged Pertinax and recognized the dignity of the Senate, which, if Cassius Dio can be believed, only accepted Julianus under coercion of the guard.

From entering the gates of Rome to departing three months later, the emperor's every move demonstrated his equanimity to the Senate and his generosity toward the populations of Rome. Severus required nothing less than complete consensus before turning his back on Rome and Clodius Albinus to face down Pescennius Niger, the popular governor of Syria. Niger constituted a particular threat to the new emperor well before Severus arrived in Rome; Niger's faction had staged a riot in the Circus Maximus, calling upon Niger as their savior from Didianus.[64] The support exhibited in that riot compromised the consensus so vital to Severus's security. He thus immediately devoted a great deal of thought and energy to wooing Niger's faction and the rest of the population of Rome to his side—a tactic as ideologically necessary as it was strategically sound.

According to Dio, Severus immediately met with the Senate in the Curia, where he promised to respect the Senate as coruler over the empire.[65] He next sought legitimacy by presiding over a showy funeral for Pertinax that allowed him to co-opt the legitimacy of the former emperor. In a grand display of consensus that was likely more prescriptive than descriptive, the funeral featured participants from every *ordo* of Roman society. It was accompanied by a distribution of cash to the urban plebs and a donative to the newly reconstituted Praetorian Guard. The funerary procession featured every conceivable population below the heavens. Beasts of the earth and the sea decorated the elaborate bier.

Actors wearing the *imagines* of famous, long-dead Romans walked in state while choruses of men and boys paraded past the pyre. Bronze female statues bedecked in native garb represented the provinces and subject nations as the various *collegia* of Rome—the cavalry, the infantry, and the senators and their wives—Romans living and dead, male and female, citizens and subjects, all grieved their universal loss while thanking the gods for their new emperor. Severus would have his consensus, even if it meant that he had to manufacture it himself.

Noticeably absent from this list of participants are Severus's wife and sons. According to Herodian, Julia Domna and the boys were in Rome when Severus marched upon it.[66] What role, if any, the empress and her sons played in the *adventus* of Severus or the funeral of Pertinax, however, is unknown. But while Cassius Dio might have ignored her in his description of the funeral, Julia Domna was not entirely absent from Severus's propaganda, even at this early date. The mint produced six types for Julia Domna, all featuring types and legends that had appeared on the coinage of earlier empresses.[67] The homogeneity of the types and legends seems designed to minimize the empress's individuality, influence, or exotic origins and cast her instead in the role of a good Roman matrona.[68] The imperial administration did little more than acknowledge her existence as a consort of the emperor: only two portraits survive (compared with hundreds from her later periods), and I have found scant mention of the empress in inscriptions from this period.[69] The relative lack of Julia Domna's presence in imperial propaganda is best explained by Severus's attempts to disguise his dynastic intentions.[70]

Still, for someone looking closely, imperial coinage from this period provided hints of the empress's future importance in the promotion of the Severan dynasty. Lusnia notes that the types and legends in Julia Domna's coinage from this period had all been used by the elder and younger Faustinae: Fecunditas, Iuno Regina, Magna Mater, Venus Genetrix, Venus Victrix, and Vesta.[71] Yet when the types are examined as a whole, they take on a certain daring quality, especially when advertising a woman who had no role in succession. For instance, in one denarius (see figure 3), Julia Domna sits on a throne, nursing a child while another child rests his hand on her knee; the legend celebrates her fecundity. Why would Fecunditas be an important quality for an empress who was not called upon to supply an heir? Julia Domna's other types and legends from this period, equally "traditional," present Julia Domna as the female consort of Severus (Iuno Regina), a metaphorical mother and protectress of the empire (Magna Mater, Venus Genetrix, Venus Victrix, and Vesta). These types can only be considered "traditional" for empresses required to produce a successor, and thus undermined the emperor's purported intention of adopted succession.

I suggest that the absence of the empress and her sons from Severus's grand entrance into Rome and the funeral for Pertinax was purposeful. Severus passed himself off as an emperor who would embrace the Senate and cooperate with it in terms of cogovernance and in adopted succession. For populations who chose to believe that Severus would honor his agreement with Albinus, Julia Domna's coinage during this period could be interpreted as merely showing respect for the consort of the emperor. Populations might choose to read into propaganda the messages they most want to believe. The official word was that Albinus was Severus's Caesar; Julia Domna's influence would be limited, no matter what her coinage said. On the other hand, for those looking for Severus to take control of the entire empire, the empress's coinage might have inspired hope that this would soon come about. There may even have been a third, more skeptical population that developed a wait-and-see attitude. There was no sense honoring a woman whose influence and authority, still uncertain, may never materialize if Niger were to be victorious over Severus.

Maternal Megalomania, 195–211

Julia Domna's visibility suddenly increased with the defeat of Pescennius Niger in 195. It was in this year that Severus began in earnest to create ties between his own family and that of Marcus Aurelius. Such connections not only helped legitimize his rule but also provided justification for waging war against Albinus. The first of these connections was made on April 14, 195, when Julia Domna was awarded the title Mater Castrorum.[72] She was only the second woman to receive the title; the first, Faustina the Younger, wife of Marcus Aurelius, received the honor toward the end of her life. Faustina's title was advertised on coinage in four small issues, two issued before her death and two posthumously (see figure 4). It is likely that Julia Domna's contemporaries immediately drew a connection between the two women because of this unusual title. Her contemporaries also likely assumed what many modern scholars do concerning the title: Julia Domna's metaphorical motherhood of the military indicated a particularly close relationship between the empress and the military. Material evidence, however, suggests that the close relationship never existed. Despite the fact that Severus and Julia Domna were in the East with the troops when she received the title, the traveling imperial mints that produced specie to pay the troops apparently never issued types with the Mater Castrorum title. If the title were designed to celebrate the relationship between the empress and the troops, the military seems the most obvious target for this message. As seen in chapter 1, however, this propaganda was not meant for the military. The perception of such a close relationship between the imperial family and the military provided political leverage in Rome with the *populus Romanus* and the Senate.

The second step Severus took in associating himself with the Antonines was to be adopted into the family as Marcus Aurelius's son. Around the same time, Severus changed the name of his eldest son, whom we know as Caracalla, to the name of the boy's new grandfather, Marcus Aurelius Antoninus. By the end of 195, medallions minted at Rome advertised Caracalla's new name and, more significantly, his promotion to the position of Caesar.[73]

With these connections in place, Severus turned upon his former Caesar. As Dio explains, the relationship between Severus and Albinus had long been strained:

> Before Severus had recovered from the conflicts with the barbarians he was involved in civil war with Albinus, his Caesar. For Severus would no longer give him even the rank of Caesar, now that he had got Niger out of the way and had settled other matters in that part of the world to his satisfaction; whereas Albinus aspired even to the preeminence of emperor.[74]

The ultimate defeat of Albinus gave Severus an opportunity to vent his rage at the traitorous elements in the Senate as well as to claim still tighter connections with the Antonine family.[75] Thus, when Severus returned victoriously to Rome, he gathered the Senate and efficiently ticked through the items on his agenda to his cowed "co-rulers": he formally announced his self-adoption into the Antonine house, deified Commodus, and purged the traitorous elements in the Senate by executing twenty-nine senators who were sympathetic to Albinus's cause.[76] Dio complained of Severus's remarkable capriciousness concerning Commodus in his speech before the Senate, saying "he introduced a sort of defense of Commodus and inveighed against the Senate for dishonoring that emperor unjustly in view of the fact that the majority of its members lived worse lives."[77]

Commodus's deification was useful for Severus in establishing his own dynasty. Because Severus had appointed his own seven-year-old son as Caesar and his successor, just as Marcus Aurelius had with Commodus, the new emperor had to show that his new brother was not nearly so bad as the Senate remembered him. It is significant that Severus defended Commodus by attacking the morals of the Senate; in doing so, he showed that they could not claim the moral high ground and thus robbed the Senate of their main criticisms not only of Commodus but of Severus himself. Once Commodus had been sanitized and rehabilitated—if only by comparison to the senators' behavior—the path was open to the Senate and people of Rome to accept little Marcus Antoninus as Caesar.[78]

The relationship with Commodus was only one of several familial relationships promoted in Severan propaganda. From this point forward, Severus's propaganda places a great deal of emphasis on family—his own, his Antonine heritage, and the metaphorical family of the military and the empire.[79] Julia Domna now became an important aspect of Severan family propaganda. As the biological connection between emperor and his sons, she guaranteed their legitimacy within the dynasty. Severan propaganda further employed Julia Domna's images and titles to connect Severus with the Antonines and to lend divine approval to his reign. As explained in further detail in chapter 2, through Julia Domna, Severus strengthened his claims of belonging to the Antonine family and connected himself to prominent Republican historical figures, religious rituals, and monuments in Rome. Finally, the emperor harnessed Julia Domna's *matrona* status to rebuild important cultural monuments traditionally associated with women such as the Aedes Vestae and the Temple of Fortuna Muliebris.[80] Sinking roots into Roman soil in this way allowed Severus to ignore his African heritage and suggested that he and his family were long ago written into Rome's history.[81]

Julia Domna proved useful in promoting Severus's sons as future emperors. She appeared on the obverse of coins that featured reverse types advertising the titles and busts of her sons individually.[82] Reverse types of her coinage also featured the legend AETERNIT(AS) IMPERI with facing busts of Severus and Caracalla, or busts of Caracalla and Geta (see figure 5). The legend announces and guarantees the permanence of the dynasty. As a legitimating link between generations, Julia Domna featured prominently on the reverse of Severus's coins, too. On an aureus dated around 201, Severus occupies the reverse, while Julia Domna arrests the eye of the viewer by gazing directly at him, promising FELICITAS SAECVLI (see figure 1). Julia Domna was also associated in coinage with maternal goddesses, especially Cybele, Isis, Diana Lucifera, Ceres, and Vesta Mater. These associations extended the maternal purview of the empress to universal proportions. In one case, discussed further in chapter 3, Julia Domna is even equated with the Magna Mater (see figure 6). Such claims for universal motherhood suggest that the administration was no longer content to advertise Julia Domna as the Mater Castrorum or Mater Augustorum. With this type, the imperial administration expanded Julia's maternal purview to embrace all living things. Other goddesses with whom Julia Domna was associated were slightly less expansive in their maternal purview than Isis or the Magna Mater. Instead, these connected the empress—and, by extension, her African husband and her son—with the physical location of Rome itself.

Finally, the association of Julia Domna with feminine virtues bolstered Severus's claims to *pietas*. During this period, the empress's *pudicitia* came under attack by Plautianus when he charged her with infidelity and purportedly even tortured noble women of the court to gain evidence against Julia Domna.[83] Charges of infidelity against the empress effectively undermined the legitimacy and "natural" succession of Severus's sons. Perhaps because of these charges, Julia Domna's coinage advertised *pietas* and *pudicitia* in various manifestations. I argue that these figures are not abstract virtues, or even personifications of them, but the depictions of the empress herself displaying her piety and *pudicitia*. Presenting Julia Domna as a good and faithful wife—whatever the reality of her behavior—was in the best interests for Severus's *virtus* and *pietas*. It was also vital to the success of the dynasty.[84]

During this period, the strife between Caracalla and Geta became well known outside the Palace. The relationship between the young princes was a source of genuine concern for the imperial administration as well as the subjects of the emperor. At stake was the very real possibility of civil war if the boys could not get along. Julia Domna's *pietas* types and legends might have been designed to ease anxiety in the general population concerning the gossip surrounding the fraternal tensions. Dio records that Severus also worried about the fractious pair: one reason Severus decided to campaign in Caledonia was to remove his sons from Rome in hopes of easing their rivalry and decreasing their hatred for one another.[85] It seems likely that Severus attempted to ease these fears by advertising the harmony of the imperial house on his and Julia Domna's coinage, perhaps an attempt of the imperial administration's to squelch rumors of tensions with an overall insistence upon harmony in the imperial household. The messages of these coins seemed to offer the emperor and empress as guarantors of peace. Yet literary sources reported that tensions rode high between the young princes even as the entire imperial family set out to subdue rebellions in Britain and to conquer the Caledonians. Severus died February 4, 211, while on campaign, leaving the empire to two young men who thoroughly detested one another, with only their mother to keep them from each other's throats.

Mater Augustorum, Mater Senatus, Mater Patriae, 211–217

When the news of Severus's death reached Rome, anxiety concerning the possibility of a civil war was at an all-time high. Despite shows of unity at the funeral for their father, the two new emperors seemed as intense in their mutual hatred as ever. Dio reports that the Senate voted sacrifices to be made to Concordia and other gods, for though "the two [brothers] pretended to love and commend each other, in all that they did they were diametrically opposed. Nor was it unpredictable that something awful would happen between them."[86] The Senate's sacrifice went awry, however, when the priest and the sacrificial attendants were unable to locate one another. Even more worrisome, two wolves were spotted stalking about the Capitoline, fighting in a fearsome manner. When one of them was found dead the next day, the dire omens foretelling civil war seemed confirmed and suggested that the Senate's solution would not be able to avert the impending crisis.[87]

In this tense political climate, Julia Domna received two sets of titles in quick succession upon her return to Rome: Pia Felix and Mater Senatus Mater Patriae.[88] These titles were quite different than the extravagant divine associations and expansive maternal purview evident in imperial coinage from 196 to 211. Unlike those titles, the Senate initiated and awarded the impressive and unprecedented titles to remind the empress of her duty to her family, state, and gods by maintaining peace in her household. These titles marked the apex of Julia Domna's power and influence: the most prominent men in society looked to her to protect them from her bickering sons.

The titles displayed on Julia's aureus (see figure 7) thus represent the Senate's recognition of the empress's influence within and beyond the palace. If read with an eye to the past, this recognition of the empress's domain, though not so sweeping in its grandeur as the palace's claims of universal motherhood, represents a senatorial capitulation to the influence of women—or at least this woman—in the succession process. Like every other ideological negotiation, the Senate placed its own spin on imperial propaganda and sought a particular favor in exchange for its recognition. The titles awarded by the Senate were not about succession, which was the point of palace propaganda; they were designed to flatter the empress in order to seek her assistance. Now, they seem to implore, was the time to show herself as Pia in maintaining the harmony in her family, in the Senate, and throughout the empire; all the charisma implied in Felix must be harnessed to this end.

Geta's death at the end of 211 precipitated a new ideological crisis for the imperial administration and called for Caracalla's administration to produce a new set of messages that would promote the new sole reign. Caracalla's program of propaganda was radically different than his father's, and as such Julia Domna played a small role. In fact, the power which Julia held in this period—perhaps the greatest power she or any imperial woman had held thus far—was semiofficial: she met with important men, reviewed correspondence in Greek and Latin, and forwarded only the most pressing issues to Caracalla, who campaigned while she stayed in Antioch.[89] Yet there are no indications in the official record of this semiofficial status, nor should we expect to find any. It would not portray Caracalla favorably with any audience to depict his mother as being more involved with the running of the empire than he was. Our only source for this information is Cassius Dio, who uses Julia Domna as a foil to Caracalla. He depicts the empress as diligently seeing to the affairs of government and maintaining balance by devoting herself to philosophy, while Caracalla was the glutton, out of control and emasculated by his passions.

My reading of Julia Domna as a medium for communication and ideological negotiation is strongest when examining the empress's actions after Caracalla's assassination in 217. According to Dio, she schemed with the soldiers assigned to her detail, and seemed intent on a coup until she heard of how Caracalla's death had been greeted with joy in Rome. With this news and Macrinus's order to leave Antioch, Julia Domna committed suicide. Dio reports that she died either by starving herself or as a result of beating her breasts in grief, thus rupturing the tumor in her breast. Both scenarios highlight the fleshy, feminine capriciousness of Julia Domna and strip the empress of the piety, rationality, and manly self-control that Dio had earlier assigned her. In her death throes, Dio paints the real Julia Domna falling victim to the very ideological negotiations that had created her images. She trusted too much in their transformative power. Without Caracalla to play the feminine counterpart to her constructed masculinity, however, all that was left to Julia Domna was the sex she was born with. Once Caracalla was removed from the equation, the Senate had no need of the empress it once hailed as Mater Senatus. No maternal ideology, no matter how grand, could transform Julia Domna into a serious contender for the imperial office. After Caracalla's death, Dio reverted to his typical senatorial stance regarding imperial women: they should simply butt out and let the Senate and emperor make all the important decisions. Perhaps Dio could fantasize about the repression of imperial women under Macrinus's short reign, but when faced with Elagabalus, who refused to be managed by the senatorial elite, the Senate would again welcome and celebrate imperial women, another new relationship to be negotiated.

CHAPTER 1

Not Your Momma

Problematizing Julia Domna as the Mater Castrorum

At first glance, the inscription requires little explanation:

> To Julia Augusta, Mother of the most sacred and pious Antoninus Augustus, and [Mother] of the Camp and of the Senate and the Fatherland. The First British Cohort Antoniniana, one thousand strong [dedicates this tabula].[1]

The First British Cohort Antoniniana, stationed in what is now modern Romania, honored the empress using her full complement of titles. One imagines that it was with special relish that the soldiers used the Mater Castrorum title in their dedication. The title seems to indicate an extraordinary bond between the soldiers and the empress, perhaps demonstrating the military's affection for her. A more cynical interpretation might suggest that by honoring Julia Domna, the soldiers sought to capitalize on her goodwill and influence with the emperor. Both interpretations envision the title awarded at the impetus of the soldiers. Conversely, one could argue that the imperial administration adopted the title in order to flatter the military by depicting it as a third son in the imperial family. In this scenario, the administration could maintain the military's loyalty by appealing to its sense of filial piety.[2] But these presumptions are inaccurate, incomplete, or misleading.

The soldiers who dedicated the tabula to the empress might have had a personal connection with her, but if so, it was not a typical relationship. Neither the imperial administration nor the military routinely used Julia Domna's Mater Castrorum title in creating the ideology that bound these two entities together. Individual soldiers, groups of soldiers, and veterans erected only fifty-seven of the over seven hundred inscriptions that mention Julia Domna from across the Mediterranean, less than 6 percent. Still smaller is the percentage of military inscriptions that honor Julia Domna without her male relatives, less than 1 percent.[3] Notably, six of the seven sole dedications to Julia Domna date from after Severus's death, when the administration was no longer advertising her as Mater

Castrorum.[4] So far from celebrating the supposedly close relationship the military had with the empress, the inscriptions mention Julia Domna most often in association with the *domus*; while her male relatives regularly receive their full complement of titles, only seventy-seven percent of military inscriptions employ the Mater Castrorum title, hardly an enthusiastic outpouring of esteem. Considering how little interest the military had in celebrating its relationship to Julia Domna, it is unlikely that the empress received this title from the soldiers.

Also untenable is the notion that the imperial administration awarded Julia Domna the title to flatter the military. One way the administration addressed the military was through the medium of numismatic messages distributed to the soldiers in donatives and regular salary. While the administration produced coins in the Roman mint from 196 that advertised Julia Domna's Mater Castrorum title, they did not extend the practice to eastern traveling mints that produced the specie distributed to the troops as salary or donatives.[5] The dearth of Mater Castrorum coins aimed at the military suggests that the title was not used by either of the parties to congratulate the other on a warm, familial relationship. Clearly, there was something behind the Mater Castrorum title other than a simple call and response between the military and imperial administration. In this chapter, I attempt to ascertain what the title meant, who awarded it, who used it, and what it can tell us about the relationship between the imperial house and the military. To answer these questions, we must begin with a more general examination of the relationship between imperial women and the military.

Women and the Military

In the minds of ancient authors, military camps were masculine spaces free from the enervating influence of women. Recent scholarship problematizes this image by demonstrating that women of all classes occupied military spheres; Raepsaet-Charlier, for instance, found ninety-five attestations of senatorial women who accompanied their male relatives to the provinces despite the dangerous conditions they might encounter there.[6] Allason-Jones and Allison have uncovered material evidence of the presence of lower-class women and children in military camps. Artifacts found in excavations of camps in Britain that were earlier assumed to be masculine have recently been reclassified as belonging to women or children. These scholars' findings suggest that lower-class women likely lived within the camps as slaves, prostitutes, or merchants.[7]

These realities were largely ignored by ancient authors, however, who instead envisioned the camp as being an exclusively masculine space. Here *disciplina militaris*—obedience and punishment, efficiency and organization, and physical training to withstand hardship—reigned supreme.[8] An important quality that contributed to *disciplina militaris* was *virtus*, loosely translated as "manliness" or "courage" though its semantic range encompasses mastery of one's body and physical impulses. For the Romans, *disciplina militaris* was a national trait, one that explained their military success over those less in control of their bodies, emotions, or political affairs, especially women, slaves, barbarians, and lower classes of men.[9] Like *virtus*, *disciplina militaris* was difficult to gain and remarkably easy to lose. "Sleep, wine, feasts, baths, idleness and sexual indulgence were all features of the life of luxury" and were antithetical to *disciplina militaris*.[10] Such luxuries were generally associated with the lack of control typical of individuals with insufficient *virtus*—that is, women, slaves, and barbarians.[11] Exposure to enervating activities or characters who embodied luxury, greed, or capriciousness could bring about the loss of a Roman's *virtus* and *disciplina*. Literary sources often explained Roman military failures as a loss of *virtus* or *disciplina*, either on the part of the soldiers or their commanders.[12] It was for the sake of maintaining *disciplina militaris* that Phang explains Augustus's ban on marriage for soldiers: just as Augustus "restored" morality in civilian life with his various family laws so, too, did he "restore" *disciplina* and *virtus* to the military by prohibiting his soldiers from mixing with the emasculating influence of women. Though politically motivated, this ban hardened into tradition through the second century and was only overturned by Septimius Severus.[13]

Ancient authors expressed anxiety on the part of the soldiers, their commanders, and the emperor when women entered the masculine realm of the camp. In the Roman Republic, literary sources depict lower-class women and camp followers as the biggest threat to discipline among the rank and file.[14] During the civil wars of the late first century BCE and from the establishment of the principate, however, literary sources depict upper-class and imperial women as the greatest threat to *disciplina militaris*. In her survey of literature regarding senatorial women in military camps, Raepsaet-Charlier identified three points of anxiety: extortion brought about by the "natural" greediness of women, nosey wives who interfered with military affairs or distracted their men from their duties, and senatorial women who violated social conventions by engaging in adulterous relationships with the rank and file. Ancient authors portrayed women who undertook any aspect of command in the camp as "monstrous, associated with civil war, sedition, or tyranny."[15] These depictions have much in common with those of women meddling in political affairs: women were not the targets of abuse in these narratives so much as their male relatives, who could not or would not control them.[16] Charges of impropriety against the behavior of senatorial and imperial women were aimed at their husbands rather than the women themselves.

This phenomenon is perhaps most clearly seen in Plutarch's depiction of Fulvia in *Life of Antony*:

> She was a woman who took no thought for spinning or housekeeping, nor would she deign to bear sway over a man of private station, but *she wished to rule a ruler and command a commander*. Therefore Cleopatra was indebted to Fulvia for teaching Antony to endure a woman's sway, since *she took him over quite tamed, and schooled at the outset to obey women* [emphasis mine].[17]

In echoing the Augustan propaganda that attacked Marc Antony's *virtus* and *disciplina*, Plutarch taps into fears of women usurping their husbands' official power. The perception that Marc Antony yielded to his wives at home in turn damaged the perception of his *virtus* in the public arena. Still more seriously for his soldiers and the state was the suggestion that he had let slip his *disciplina militaris* by allowing his women to run his military affairs. Cassius Dio goes even further than Plutarch. He depicts Fulvia as usurping the commander's role by strapping on a sword and leading a rebellion of veterans at Perugia.[18] Fulvia's reported gender inversion—neglecting her feminine duties for a foray into the masculine realm of the military—played upon the fears of Roman men whose *virtus* stemmed from their ability to control themselves and others. Like Fulvia, the Cleopatra of Octavian's propaganda was a strong and domineering woman and, like his first wife, the Egyptian queen would prove disastrous to Antony's reputation in civilian and military life. Octavian's partisan Calvisius charged Antony with shamelessly abandoning his judicial duties to read aloud love letters from Cleopatra; he also leapt from his tribunal and deserted a trial in order to pursue Cleopatra's litter as it was carried through the forum.[19] These sketches of his relationships with his wife and mistress reduce Antony, an experienced and capable general, to a dominated, love-struck adolescent, one much better at obeying his women than demanding their obedience. Such distractions damaged Antony's reputation in a civil context, but in the field, they could literally cause his and his army's destruction. In fact, as Plutarch presents it, Antony yielded to Cleopatra's wishes at Actium to engage Octavian on the sea rather than on land, despite his advisors' pleas to retreat and reengage in a land battle.[20] This rhetoric convinced Romans that the presence of women in the camp undermined the *virtus* and *disciplina* required of a commander.

Surviving literature gives little hint of women taking part in military affairs again until after Augustus's death, during the reign of Tiberius. Surprisingly, however, literary sources depict these women in a positive light. Suetonius reports that under Tiberius, Livia joined the effort to save the Temple of Vesta from a fire, likely by enlisting the help of the paramilitary Vigiles. Significantly, Tacitus couches Livia's activities within a larger complaint regarding the empress's intrusion into masculine spheres of activity:

> Vexed at his mother Livia for alleging that she claimed an equal share in the rule, he shunned frequent meetings with her and long and confidential conversations to avoid the appearance of being guided by her advice, though in point of fact he was wont every now and then to need and to follow it. He was greatly offended too by a decree of the Senate, providing that "son of Livia," as well as "son of Augustus" should be written in his honorary inscriptions. For this reason he would not suffer her to be named "Parent of her Country," nor to receive any conspicuous public honor. More than that, he often warned her not to meddle with affairs of importance and unbecoming a woman, especially after he learned that she had been present at a fire near the temple of Vesta and had urged the people and soldiers to greater efforts, as had been her way while her husband was alive.[21]

What does it say about an emperor who needed his mother's help from time to time (*tamen interdum et egere et uti solebat*)? As the context of the report on the Temple of Vesta makes clear, Tiberius saw Livia's interference as undermining his authority. Her actions and her proposed title called attention to the influence that she might have over Tiberius. Perceptions of womanly influence over sons and husband—regardless of whether they were accurate perceptions—had the effect of emasculating their men in the minds of their contemporaries. Tiberius desperately needed his mother to stay away from the masculine realms while he established his own *auctoritas*. In this anecdote, Suetonius employed a positive depiction of Livia to harm the reputation of the emperor. Suetonius's agenda to portray Livia in this masculine realm was not to praise her so much as to impugn Tiberius, who needed her guidance. The "complimentary" comments concerning Livia in fact hamstrung Tiberius and called into question his *virtus* and his effectiveness as a leader.

Agrippina the Elder's actions in Germany provided another positive depiction of an imperial woman mingling with the military. Tacitus reported that she and her children accompanied Germanicus to the frontier, where he traveled to quell a military revolt following Tiberius's ascension to the principate. When the soldiers refused to follow Germanicus's orders, Agrippina stepped forward to calm the troops. Later, to punish the recalcitrant soldiers, Germanicus showily sent Agrippina and her children to safety, far away from the camps and unruly rank and file. The chastened soldiers immediately promised to mend their ways. When Germanicus was campaigning across the Rhine, rumors spread that the Romans had been routed, and the soldiers remaining in camp clamored to tear down the bridge, preventing both friend and foe from crossing the river into their camp. Agrippina took matters into her own hands. She, a woman of enormous spirit (*femina ingens animi*), calmed the troops' panic by staving off the proposal to destroy the bridge across the Rhine at Vetera. She even greeted and thanked the troops upon their return.[22] By labeling Agrippina as *femina ingens animi*, Tacitus surprisingly seems to applaud her courage rather than condemn her for brazenness. This positive picture of Agrippina commanding soldiers sits uncomfortably beside the negative judgment of Fulvia, yet it also damaged the reputations of her male relatives.[23] Though Agrippina's actions could easily be interpreted as emasculating Germanicus, Tacitus distracts his viewers from such a conclusion by focusing upon Tiberius's reactions to Agrippina's behavior. He places us within the mind of the emperor, where distinctions between what Agrippina actually did and what her actions meant are murky at best.

> [Agrippina's] action sank deep into the soul of Tiberius: The commanding officer's job is a sinecure when a woman inspects units and exhibits herself before the standards with plans for money distributions. As though it were not pretentious enough to parade the commander's son around in private soldier's uniform and propose to have him called "little boots" Caesar! Agrippina's position in the army already seemed to outshine generals and commanding officers; and she, a woman, had suppressed a mutiny that the emperor's own signature had failed to check. Lucius Aelius Sejanus aggravated and intensified his suspicions. He knew how Tiberius's mind worked. Inside it, for the eventual future, he sowed hatreds. They would lie fallow, but one day bear fruit abundantly.[24]

In the list of her offenses are a bevy of actions that Tacitus had not mentioned earlier and, like Tiberius, we have no way of distinguishing rumor from event, intention from expediency. Without context, it is easy to interpret Agrippina's distributing money to the troops and parading "Caligula" before the troops, calling him "Caesar," as attempts to promote herself and her family while undermining Tiberius's *auctoritas*. Had a man done such things—even, I suspect, the beloved Germanicus—he would have been disposed of immediately and without question. Distributing donatives to the troops, for example, was the sole prerogative of the emperor. The fact that the troops seemed not to resent Agrippina's actions only worried Tiberius more.

Livia and Agrippina were not the only examples of upper-class women mingling with the military in Tiberius's reign. Tacitus also records—in a far more disapproving manner—the meddling of Plancina with the cavalry in Syria. He places Plancina's influence over the soldiers within a more general description of her husband's lack of rigor and *disciplina militaris:*

> On reaching the army in Syria, he [Piso] was lavish with gifts, bribes and favors even to the humblest soldiers. He replaced company-commanders of long service and the stricter colonels with his own dependents of bad character. He allowed the camp to become slack, the towns disorderly and the men to wander in undisciplined fashion round the countryside. The demoralization was so bad that he was popularly called the "father of the army." And Plancina went beyond feminine respectability by attending cavalry exercises and insulting Agrippina and Germanicus. Even some of the better soldiers were misguided enough to support her because of secret rumors that the emperor's approval was not lacking.[25]

The final sentence invoking the emperor is significant because it draws Tiberius again into the nexus of Livia's influence, the persecution of Germanicus and Agrippina, Plancina's behavior as a *femina militaris*, and Piso's *indisciplina.* This last idea was particularly damaging to the emperor, considering that Tiberius's military prowess was his one unassailable imperial quality. Furthermore, the meddling of Plancina and Agrippina was probably the unnamed exempla that gave force to Aulus Caecina Severus's speech before the Senate in 21 AD:

> Caecina Severus moved that no magistrate who had been allotted a province should be accompanied by his wife. He explained beforehand at some length that he had a consort after his own heart, who had borne him six children; yet he had conformed in private what he was proposing for the public; and, although he had served his forty campaigns in one province or other, she had always been kept within the boundaries of Italy. There was a point in the old regulation which prohibited the dragging of women to the provinces or to foreign peoples; in a retinue of ladies there were elements apt, by luxury or by timidity, to retard the business of peace or war and to transform a Roman march into something resembling an Eastern procession. Weakness and a lack of endurance were not the only failings of the sex; give them scope and they

> turned hard, intriguing, ambitious. They paraded among the soldiers; they had the centurions at beck and call. Recently a woman had presided at the exercises of the cohorts and the maneuvers of the legions. Let his audience reflect that whenever a magistrate was tried for maladministration, the majority of the charges were leveled against his wife. It was to the wife that the basest of the provincials at once attached themselves; it was the wife who took in hand and transacted business. There were two potentates to salute in the streets; two government houses; and the more headstrong and autocratic orders came from the women, who, once held in curb by the Oppian and other laws, had now cast away their chains and ruled supreme in the home, the courts, and now the army itself.[26]

Valerius Messalinus led the rebuttal to Caecina's apparently old-fashioned position. He argued that times had changed, that not all women behaved badly, as perhaps they had in the past. Messalinus asserted that "it was vain to label our own inertness with another title: if the woman broke bounds, the fault lay with the husband," a pithy statement concerning the manner in which a high-spirited wife might damage her husband's reputation.[27] Finally, Drusus, the emperor's own son, revealed that he took his wife on campaign and pointed to an indisputable exemplum: even the divine Augustus had his Livia as a traveling companion.[28]

Significantly, the authors who wrote depictions of women mingling with soldiers were particularly hostile toward Antony, Tiberius, and Piso. Despite the sometimes-positive depictions of these women, the context of the passages makes explicit that women taking leadership roles in the military injured the reputation of their male relatives' *virtus* and the soldiers' *disciplina militaris.* When ascertaining the attitudes of the rank and file, one must recognize that these authors were impugning the women's male relatives, rather than describing how the soldiers felt about imperial and senatorial women in their midst. This recognition resists an interpretation that would emphasize the women's relationship with soldiers or that would imply women had undue power in the military camp. But other questions remain. Did common soldiers embrace the rhetoric promulgated by these authors? How did Praetorian praefects feel about imperial women and their influence? Did the opinions of the Praetorian Guard differ from the legionaries or legionaries from veterans? If the military was in fact conservative and traditional in supporting inherited succession, as some scholars have claimed, why not celebrate imperial women as a legitimating device for an inherited successor? In fact, why not make soldiers the target of dynastic propaganda?

Faustina the Younger: The Mother of All Mothers of the Camp

Considering the anxiety that characterized ancient authors' depictions of imperial and senatorial women mingling with the military, the title Mater Castrorum requires explanation.[29] Why would an emperor be willing to let his wife be linked with the military when every instance of their interaction in the past had the ultimate effect of damaging the emperor's reputation? In order to understand the meaning of the title, we must explore the agency behind awarding it. Who awarded Faustina with the title Mater Castrorum—the military or the emperor?

Unfortunately, ancient authors offer no simple answers to these questions. As Cassius Dio tells it, Faustina's title was connected to the Battle of the Rain Miracle against the Quadi in 173 or 174 somewhere in Pannonia. After lingering over the details of Romans quenching their thirst from the heaven-sent rain while the Quadi either surrendered to the refreshed troops or were slashed to ribbons by them, Dio states:

> He [Marcus] was now saluted *imperator* by the soldiers for the seventh time, and although he was not wont to accept any such honor before the Senate voted it, nevertheless this time he took it as a gift from heaven and he sent a dispatch to the Senate. Moreover, Faustina was hailed as Mother of the Camp.[30]

The scholar looking for answers to the Mater Castrorum phenomenon finds no satisfaction here. The title seems like an afterthought to the dramatic rain miracle and leaves questions of motive and agency unanswered. One could argue that the juxtaposition of honors implies that the Mater Castrorum title was connected to Marcus's seventh acclamation as imperator. If so, perhaps the title really was awarded at the hands of the military, just as it was also the soldiers who awarded acclamations. But this explanation poses problems: the imperial administration often prompted acclamations as political events, especially if the awarding of the Mater Castrorum title were a part of the acclamation.[31] Considering the prominence given to the rain miracle in numismatic types and official art, it is possible that the imperial administration saw the event as an opportunity to promote the emperor's divine approbation and, by extension, the security of the state.[32] The administration might have designed the acclamation and title to call attention to the miracle rather than the other way around. Grammatical analysis suggests another possibility: Cary translates the adverb μέντοι in the announcement of Faustina's title to imply that it occurred at the same time as the acclamation. It is just as correct to translate μέντοι adversatively: while the rain miracle and the acclamation that followed were accepted before the Senate approved them, the Mater Castrorum was not by acclamation, not approved by the Senate, nor brought about παρὰ θεοῦ. By this interpretation, it was Marcus himself who awarded the title. Nevertheless, this evidence is too inconclusive to answer satisfactorily the questions of agency and motive behind the Mater Castrorum title.[33]

The account in the *Historia Augusta* (*HA*) offers the most complete explanation regarding all the major questions surrounding the title:

> In the village of Halala, in the foothills of Mount Taurus, he [Marcus Aurelius] lost his wife Faustina who succumbed to a sudden illness. After she had been praised in eulogy, he asked the Senate to decree her divine honors and a temple although she had suffered grievously from the reputation of lewdness. Of this, however, Antoninus [i.e., Marcus Aurelius] was either ignorant or affected ignorance. He established a new order of Faustinian girls in honor of his dead wife, and expressed his pleasure at her deification by the Senate. *Because she had accompanied him on his summer campaign, he called her Mother of the Camp.* And besides this, he elevated the village where Faustina died to a colony, and there built a temple in her honor [emphasis mine].[34]

This passage identifies agent and motive: Marcus gave the title to Faustina for accompanying him on campaign. We must use caution here, however, because there is a clear conflation of events. The placement of the title in relation to the other details regarding Faustina suggests that the title was awarded after the empress's death. Yet bronze coins minted in Rome prove that the empress received the title before she died.[35] Despite the general unreliability of the *HA*, and although this detail calls into question the accuracy of the other details, most scholars have accepted its explanation for the Mater Castrorum title, that she accompanied Marcus on campaigns. Some have even assumed that Julia Domna received the title for the same reason.[36] Yet it seems unlikely that accompanying Marcus was the only (or even the main) reason Faustina received the award; other imperial women who mingled with the troops had the opposite effect, being used to make the emperor look foolish or weak.[37] There must have been more of a motive for the Mater Castrorum title than simply honoring the empress for accompanying her husband to the frontiers.

The Military and the *Domus Augusta*: All in the Family?

As Boatwright saw it, the Mater Castrorum title was an anomaly within the history of imperial women, especially with regard to Faustina, whose appearances on coinage were intensely domestic and maternal.[38] Faustina did not receive the title of Augusta until the birth of her first child even though she had been advertised on her own coinage even as a girl.[39] This suggests that her importance to the state was in providing legitimate heirs for the principate. Faustina was also useful in legitimizing Marcus Aurelius; depictions of their marriage are accompanied by the legend VOTA PVBLICA (see figure 8). This marriage was a state affair, as is apparent from the social and political position of the bride and groom and the public nature of the couple's marriage vows. Whereas Antoninus Pius provided one variety of legitimacy to Marcus through adoption, a type of legitimacy that was particularly compelling for the Senate, Faustina provided another type through family ties; she allowed him to lay claim to a sort of dynastic charisma through an inherited succession. Boatwright notes that Faustina's advertisement was intensely domestic, at least until Marcus granted her the Mater Castrorum title shortly before her death. It was only the military and political crises as well as the imperial family's need to perpetuate itself that can explain the awarding of the title.[40]

The VOTA PVBLICA coin is but one example of the emphasis that Antonine propaganda placed on the imperial family. Coins of Faustina also advertise intimate moments with her children, in some cases even depicting the empress in the act of breast-feeding. Other coins tout her *pudicitia* (see figure 9) and *fecunditas* (see figure 10).[41] It is remarkable that the empress's sexual behavior and her reproductive abilities would be openly discussed not in rude graffiti or in tabloids but on state coinage. To offer a modern comparison, how shocking would it be for a British coin to feature Queen Elizabeth II breast-feeding Prince Charles? There is a ready explanation for presenting these intimate moments on coinage: when succession is inherited, the empress's sexual behavior and her ability to produce children become a matter of state security. If the next emperor were to spring (to borrow Pliny's term) *e sinu uxoris*, the general public would want reassurance that the child destined for the principate was in fact the emperor's legitimate son. Likewise, it would be comforting to know that, should there be a need, the empress could produce another heir.

Advertisement of the family's private life essentially threw open the doors of the palace and allowed the viewer holding the coin to envision himself as being closely connected with the imperial family and personally invested in the dynasty. The success of advertising the harmony in the imperial couple's relationship was evident in the public response to these intimate moments and seems to have inspired imitation of the concord advertised in the imperial family. Upon Faustina's death, the Senate voted for silver images of Marcus and Faustina to be set up in the Temple of Venus and Roma. Their marriage became something of an exemplum for Roman couples, as evidenced by the altar erected nearby "whereon all the maidens married in the city and their bridegrooms should offer sacrifice."[42]

Yet official propaganda did not extend the family metaphor evident in Faustina's new title to the rest of the imperial family. A quick glance at the coinage of Marcus Aurelius, Lucius Verus, and Commodus, for example, reveals no attempts to paint these emperors as familial figures with respect to the military.[43] This lack of familial imagery in propaganda tailored to the military did not prevent Herodian's Commodus from inserting it in a speech he attributes to the new emperor before the legionaries immediately after his father's death. Herodian's Commodus created an image of the imperial family in which the military acted as his older brother and another child of Marcus Aurelius:

> My father loved all of us alike. Indeed, he preferred to call me "fellow soldier" rather than "son," because he thought that the title of son was one simply conferred by nature, whereas "soldier" showed that we all shared in his excellence. When I was a small boy he used to bring me with him and entrust me to your care. So I am optimistic that I shall win your complete loyalty without difficulty. The older ones among you owe me this service as your protégé; as for the young men I might reasonably claim that we were fellow pupils in arms, since my father loved us all alike and taught us all our virtues.[44]

Here, Marcus is the father of Commodus *and* the military. More importantly, Commodus presents himself as sharing a bond of brotherhood with the soldiers. The metaphorical relationship between Commodus and the soldiers invited the military to view the empire as a kind of family business. In this context, the adoptive succession employed by earlier emperors seemed impersonal and unnatural and, just as in a family business, it seemed only right that a son should succeed his father. This was the idea upon which Herodian's Commodus relied in order to gain the support of the military for his succession:

> Fate has given the empire to me as (my father's) successor, not as an adopted heir like my predecessors who prided themselves on the added power they gained but as the only one of your emperors to be born in the palace . . . If you

> consider it in this light, you are more likely to accept me, not so much as a ruler who is presented to you but as one who is born for you.[45]

The military as family imagery seems to be an invention of Herodian, not the imperial administration. Aside from the Mater Castrorum types, I find no numismatic evidence that makes any reference to family propaganda aimed at the military. Even the extraordinary Mater Castrorum title seems to have been little advertised, at least during the empress's lifetime, and certainly not among the troops.[46] Furthermore, there is scant evidence that the military responded to Faustina as Mater Castrorum.[47]

Herodian may be the key to understanding the puzzle of imperial family propaganda and the military. His version of Antonine family propaganda—though it bears little resemblance to what the Antonines were actually promoting—might be more representative of what the civilian population understood. Perhaps the most significant aspect of the speech that Herodian attributed to Commodus is the revelation that Herodian and other civilians believed there was a familial connection between the military and the imperial house. For Herodian, the ideology that developed between the Antonines and the military was rooted in family propaganda. It was the family propaganda combined with a generous donative, he suggests, that caused the military to support Commodus upon Marcus's death.[48] Yet as Rubin noted, Herodian is little informed of military matters and probably had no idea what legionaries knew of family propaganda.[49] But the real targets of the Mater Castrorum propaganda—presumably the civilian populations of Rome and the West—would see these coins, remember the overall thrust of imperial family propaganda, and assume that the coin represented a genuinely close relationship between the military and the empress.[50] They might assume, I suggest, that the bond between the imperial family and the military was more personal than in fact it was.

It would certainly be advantageous to the imperial administration for civilians to assume such a relationship existed. If the civilian population believed that the military viewed the imperial family as its own family, they might also believe that the military—as his "brother"—would support Commodus and his accession with all the loyalty and fierceness implied in the bond of brotherhood. Such a notion would help discourage any dissent among those critical of Commodus or inherited succession.

Severus and the Mater Castrorum Title

Severus knew the value of managing the relationships he shared with the Senate, provincial cities, and military by controlling the flow of information he sent to them. Ando illustrated this awareness through an examination of when, where, and to whom the emperor advertised his first Parthian campaign. Severus did not wait for the Senate to grant him the victorious cognomina "Arabicus Adiabenicus" and "Parthicus Arabicus Pathicus Adiabenicus" before using the titles with other populations.[51] He communicated the news of his victories and his as-yet-unauthorized titles to the cities in Italy and to the provinces with the expectation that they would celebrate his successes by sending him a crown or money, the *aurum coronarium*.[52] Likewise, Severus advertised his fictive adoption into the Antonine clan by 194 to legions in Lower Pannonia, where the new connection with Commodus probably received a hardy reception, but the adoption remained unpublicized on coins from the Roman mint until 195. The news would surely not have been welcome there after Commodus had suffered a *damnatio memoriae*.[53] Dio, a senator living in Rome during this period, first mentions the adoption when Severus returns to Rome after defeating Clodius Albinus in 197, which might well have been when he had first heard of it.[54] What emerges from Ando's discussion is not simply his main point—that is, that emperors had real incentive (i.e., *aurum coronarium*) to keep information flowing to their provincial subjects—but also that Severus carefully tailored information to target audiences in order to evoke a favorable reaction. His management of Julia Domna and the Mater Castrorum title was no different.

The timing and motivation for Julia Domna's title are both more and less problematic than Faustina's. Epigraphic evidence securely dates the award to April 14, 195, though the reasons for its conferment are still contested.[55] While the date is handy to know, the sources are silent about how Julia Domna's title was awarded and who offered it. Most scholars simply apply the explanation the *HA* gives for Faustina's award to Julia Domna; she received it because she accompanied her husband on campaign.[56] Some see a propagandistic connection between the conferral of the Mater Castrorum title and the self-adoption of Severus into the Antonine household. Both, they say, were attempts to legitimize the dynasty.[57] I find the second explanation more convincing but it requires some refining. The title was certainly intended to promote the nascent Severan dynasty, though the target audience for the Mater Castrorum propaganda was not the military. Instead, Severus used the Mater Castrorum title as a tool to pressure civilian audiences to support his dynastic ambitions.

When Julia Domna received the title, she was in the East, likely at the side of Severus, who was completing his struggle against Pescennius Niger.[58] Coins minted at Rome from 195 advertise the empress's Mater Castrorum title but, significantly, the Eastern traveling mints that supplied the troops with their pay did not.[59] If the troops were the intended target of this propaganda, there would presumably have been coins distributed to them that advertised Julia Domna's title.[60] An analysis of fifty-seven hoards from around the Mediterranean dating from the third century, however, shows that the Mater Castrorum title rarely appeared on coins found in military zones.[61] If the title were given at the impetus of the troops, inscriptions erected by the military would likely have appeared on the epigraphic record that regularly and enthusiastically celebrated the empress as Mater Castrorum. Though there are instances of such examples under Severus's reign, they almost always appear within the context of a dedication to the entire *domus*.[62] Furthermore, the Mater Castrorum does not always appear in military inscriptions from this period. Julia Domna would have to wait until Caracalla's reign to be celebrated in her own right by the military.[63]

Though the military appeared less than enthusiastic about the Mater Castrorum title, inscriptional evidence shows that civilian audiences responded positively. When Kettenhofen surveyed some 450 inscriptions securely attributed to Julia Domna, he identified the Mater Castrorum as the most common title attributed to the empress besides Augusta. Because the military erected so few of Julia Domna's inscriptions, Kettenhofen suggested that the title was conventional, that it simply echoed imperial propaganda.[64] In light of these new findings, however, it seems more likely that civilian inscriptions advertised Julia Domna as Mater Castrorum because it was to these populations that she was marketed as such.

Much like the familial propaganda of the Antonines, Julia Domna's Mater Castrorum coins gave the impression to civilian audiences that the emperor and his family had a close relationship with the military. It was so close, the coins seem to say, that that the military saw the empress as a mother to whom filial piety was owed. This is significant because it suggests that in cases of civil strife the army would side with Severus. The notion of a military that thinks of the empress as mother could be read either as a comforting statement that guaranteed continuity in rulers or as a warning to those who might oppose the emperor. Thus envisioned, the coins and the Mater Castrorum title functioned as tools of the imperial administration to persuade or coerce civilian populations to support the emperor.

The timing of the award further supports this interpretation: in 195 and 196, Severus needed civilian populations to believe that he had the military's loyalty, especially because he was not certain that the population of Rome would support him in the imminent civil war. Dio reports that the populace openly lamented the upcoming conflict with a demonstration in the Circus Maximus during Saturnalia. The audience broke out into synchronized chants: "How long are we to suffer such things?" and "How long are we to be waging war?"[65] Dio saw this as a clear indication that the crowd had been divinely inspired. Portents of lights that resembled fire appearing in the northern sky and a white drizzle falling upon the Forum of Augustus also plagued the city and foretold disaster.[66] The Senate remained quiet during all these omens, Dio tells us, except for those few who openly supported one side or the other.[67] The advertisement of Severus's close relationship with the military could not have come at a more opportune time to convince the populace to stand behind their emperor.

Severus, the Military, and Julia Domna

On his deathbed, Severus reportedly gave his sons advice on ruling the empire: "love each other, enrich the soldiers and despise all others."[68] This attitude combined with important changes that Severus made to the military structure led Gibbon to identify Severus's rule as the beginning of the end of the Roman Empire.[69] Though scholars since have ceased to blame Severus for the empire's demise, they unanimously acknowledge that he substantially altered the military during his reign.[70] Shortly before he entered Rome in 193, Severus dissolved the Praetorian Guard that had treacherously executed Pertinax and sold the empire to the highest bidder. He then reformed it, increasing its numbers and recruiting from a more ethnically diverse pool.[71] The legionaries were also affected by his reforms; soldiers received their first pay increase in nearly a century. Severus rescinded the ban against soldiers marrying, which seems to have been tantamount to giving legal recognition to what scholars now perceive as a widespread practice.[72]

Though Severus might not have been responsible for the increasing militarization of the empire, as Gibbon claimed, he nonetheless had come to power on the backs of his soldiers and he owed his position to them. In recognition of the Legio XIII Gemina Martia Victrix, with whom he had seized Rome, Severus celebrated their contribution on coin reverses of all denominations. The fifteen other legions that had lent him support were likewise advertised on denarii.[73] Dio reports that several senators resented their new emperor for "placing his hope of safety in the strength of his army rather than in the good will of his associates in the government [i.e., the Senate]."[74] This evidence suggests a comfortable and supportive rapport between the emperor and his military, especially because he seemed to privilege this relationship above all others.

Yet the relationship between the emperor and the military is not so easily characterized. Part of this difficulty lies in the recognition that the military, though a community, was made up of several groups whose agenda and priorities varied considerably.[75] The interests of the emperor's pampered and preferred Praetorian Guard would naturally be different than those of the rank and file. The priorities of veterans and the concerns of paramilitary units such as the Vigiles in Rome varied widely from each other as well as the guard or the legionaries. Our ability to characterize Severus's relationship with the military is also complicated by inconsistencies in literary sources. For instance, Dio portrays the soldiers accompanying Severus on his initial march on Rome as festivalgoers, milling peacefully about with the inhabitants of Rome despite being fully armed.[76] Dio, however, undermines this characterization with an offhanded aside in his narrative of Octavian returning to Rome with his legions after the Battle of Actium. There, he reports that after Severus had seized the city, his soldiers terrified both the senators and the emperor by demanding a donative that was equivalent to what Octavian had given: one thousand sesterii. The *HA* provides the further detail that soldiers made this demand after surrounding the Curia while Severus was speaking to the Senate. In all but the first of these characterizations, the emperor's accompanying forces are fully aware of the role they played in his rise to power and believe they should be compensated for their efforts.[77]

In fact, the rank and file had every reason to support Severus. The restructuring of the Praetorian Guard allowed greater career mobility for the talented and ambitious. It seems likely that they also appreciated his frequent donatives, the increase in pay, and the legalization of marriages. The emperor's relationship with the Praetorian Guard, however, was more complicated. As the self-proclaimed avenger of Pertinax, Severus had little choice but to address the Praetorian Guard's mutiny that led to the murder of Pertinax. Thus, just before he entered Rome in 193,

> Severus . . . inflicted the death penalty on the Praetorians who had taken part in the slaying of Pertinax; and as for the others, he summoned them, before he came to Rome, and having surrounded them in the open while they were ignorant of the fate in store for them, uttered many bitter reproaches against them for their lawless deed against their emperor, and then relieved them of their arms, took away their horses, and banished them from Rome. Thereupon the majority of them proceeded reluctantly to throw away their arms and let

> their horses go, and were scattering, wearing only their ungirded tunics; one man, when his horse would not go away, but kept following him and neighing, slew both the beast and himself, and it seemed to the spectators that the horse, too, was glad to die.[78]

Dio's sympathetic tone concerning the punishment of the Praetorian Guard is surprising, especially considering that these were the very men who had created considerable chaos in the capitol by murdering Pertinax, the Senate's champion. In the ensuing chaos, the guard notoriously offered the empire for sale to Didius Julianus.[79] Up to that point, according to Dio, the guard had been limited to soldiers from Italy, Macedonia, Noricum, and Spain, "men of more respectable appearance and of simpler habits."[80] Severus's new Praetorians could be drawn from any legion, with the main criterion for membership being bravery in action. Yet some fractious senators found fault even in this gesture, as Severus had forced the former guardsmen "to brigandage and gladiatorial fighting." These senators, and apparently Dio himself, considered the new guard to be "a throng of the most motley soldiers most savage in appearance, most terrifying in speech and most boorish in conversation."[81]

The grievances voiced by senators concerning the newly reconstituted guard betray the Senate's jealousy of the close relationship between the emperor and his bodyguard. Although it was surely apparent to the Senate that the old guard as a whole had to be punished for its behavior, senatorial rhetoric cast Severus in the role of a tyrant for first promoting such unruly characters and then allowing them to terrorize the city. This depiction suggests that the emperor was more interested in promoting his bullyboy friends and henchmen than in creating a respectful relationship with the Senate or protecting the city. In all likelihood, by depicting the guard as uncouth and uncivilized, the senators were suggesting that Severus was, too, because of his association with them.[82] Thus envisioned, senatorial complaints concerning the barbaric origins of the new guard and Severus's treatment of the former guard were politically motivated rather than descriptive and should probably be chalked up to the rivalry between the two bodies.

This cozy relationship between the emperor and the Praetorians, however, was highly influenced by the praefect, C. Fulvius Plautianus, a kinsman and old friend from his hometown of Lepcis Magna, whom Severus appointed perhaps as early as 193. In this position, Plautianus would have accompanied Severus on all his campaigns. By every indication, the friendship between Severus and his praefect grew stronger over time, and the emperor's favor was eventually expressed in a political and familial fashion.[83] By June 197, Severus gave Plautianus consular status, and in 202 agreed to a marriage between Caracalla and Plautianus's daughter, Plautilla. In 203, Plautianus shared his first consulship with Geta, though he was permitted the honor of COS II in his titulature, suggesting that the consular *ornamenta* were the equivalent of holding the actual office. These actions surely further ignited the rivalry some senators felt toward Plautianus. By betrothing Caracalla to Plautilla, Severus squashed any hope of the senatorial families to grow closer to the imperial family by offering one of their own daughters. Perhaps more galling, however, was the fact that Severus had degraded the dignity of the consular designation by equating the *ornamenta* with the actual completion of the duties of the office.[84] Disregarding senatorial sensibilities, Plautianus blithely mixed his honors: "not only did he wear the broad strip on his toga, but he wore a sword at his side and on his one person wore the badge of every rank."[85] Indeed, Severus showed such preference for Plautianus that Dio claimed the praefect's power equaled even the emperors themselves. His statuary and images were even more numerous than the imperial family's, and his flatterers referred to him as the fourth Caesar in official correspondence.[86] Levick cannily observed, "secondary politicians who depend on an autocrat are as likely to be rivals as allies."[87] This principle was apparent in Dio's reports that Severus was not permitted to enter Plautianus's presence with his own bodyguard. Another time, when Severus ordered a case to be brought forward, the clerk replied, "I cannot do so, unless Plautianus bids me."[88] The position that Plautianus had schemed to obtain put him in direct competition not only with Severus's sons, but also with Julia Domna and even Severus himself.

Before Plautianus dared to rival Severus, however, he found a more natural rival in Julia Domna. By the early 200s, Severus favored Plautianus over his wife to the point of allowing the praefect to criticize her in his presence. Plautianus even accused the empress of adultery before the emperor.[89] Dio's description of Plautianus's attacks against Julia Domna bespeaks the senator's outrage. He contrasts her measured, philosophical response to the indignities she suffered with Plautianus's gluttony and intemperance:

> He used to conduct investigations into her conduct as well as gather evidence against her by torturing women of the nobility. For this reason she began to study philosophy and passed her days in company with sophists. As for Plautianus, he became the most sensual of men; for he would gorge himself at banquets and vomit as he ate, as the mass of food and wine that he swallowed made it impossible for him to digest anything; and though he made use of lads

> and girls and notorious fashion, yet he would not permit his own wife to see anybody or be seen by any person whomsoever, not even by Severus or Julia to say nothing of others.[90]

Dio's characterization may be something of a surprise because, as described in the introduction, senatorial courtiers were no fans of imperial women, who represented impediments to their own influence over the emperor. Still, in this instance, Dio sees Plautianus as the greater threat and ascribes to him gluttony, sexual perversions, and secrecy, the traditional set of tyrannical traits. Dio's characterizations of the empress and the praefect invert gender norms that associate self-control with men and capriciousness with women: where Julia Domna turns to the lessons of moderation in philosophy, Plautianus lacks the ability to control himself either sexually or physically. Despite these persecutions, the empress does not hide from the public eye, but Plautianus keeps things which should be seen—that is, his wife—hidden. The contrast between the two could not be more pronounced. That this praise of Julia Domna is meant to harm the reputation of Plautianus (and likely Severus, who did nothing to stop Plautianus's unjust charges against his wife) is apparent later in Dio's account. He will drop this sympathy for the empress as soon as she is no longer a useful foil to one of his own enemies.

Considering that commanders notoriously shaped the opinions of their men, it should come as no surprise that the guard under Plautianus's leadership was hostile toward the empress. They expressed this rather obliquely in 199 while Severus was campaigning in Mesopotamia, retaking territory that had been seized by the Parthians while he was prosecuting the wars against Niger and Albinus. His siege of Hatra accomplished little, Dio says, except "to destroy his own siege engines, sacrifice his men and wound many others."[91] After his unsuccessful attempt on the city, Severus shifted his position and tried again. This time, the Romans broke through the first wall of the city's double walls. Severus chose that moment to signal retreat, perhaps hoping that the inhabitants of Hatra would sue for peace. But on the following day, when no embassy was forthcoming and the breach in the wall had been rebuilt overnight, Severus ordered his troops to renew the siege. Dio suggests that Severus's poor management angered his "European" troops:[92]

> But the Europeans, who alone of his army had the ability to do anything, were so angry that not one of them would any longer obey him, and the others, the Syrians, who were compelled to make the assault in their place, were miserably

> destroyed. Thus the god that saved the city first caused Severus to recall the soldiers when they could have entered the place and in turn caused the soldiers to hinder him from capturing it when he later wished to do so. Severus, in fact, found himself so embarrassed by the situation that, when one of his associates promised, if he would give him only 550 European soldiers, to destroy the city without any risk to the other troops, he said within the hearing of all: "And where am I to get so many soldiers?" referring to the soldiers' disobedience.[93]

In the midst of this revolt, Julius Crispus, a tribune of the Praetorian Guard, uttered two lines from the *Aeneid:* "So that Turnus may marry Lavinia, we are all perishing unheeded."[94] Severus executed Crispus for this slight and replaced him with Valerius, the soldier who had accused Crispus of this apparently treasonous comment. The surprisingly harsh reaction of the emperor requires some context. The literary setting of Crispus's quote comes from book 11 of the *Aeneid*, as the Italian chief Drances pled before the assembly of Latin allies to abandon the conflict with the Trojans. Drances insisted that the conflict between the Trojans and the Latin allies came down to a personal feud between Aeneas and Turnus over the hand of Latinus's daughter. The *Aeneid* depicts Turnus as effeminate, foreign, and lacking *felicitas*—the support and approval of the gods. In contrast, Severus had worked hard to promote himself as emphatically Roman, masculine, and beloved of the gods. Comparing Turnus to Severus was treasonous because it revealed the emperor's self-promotion as a tissue of lies and misrepresentations. Yet there is more behind the quote than simply an attempt to personally embarrass the emperor.

Implied in Crispus's comparison of Turnus and Severus is another between Lavinia and Julia Domna. Crispus's quote modified the original Virgilian passage to include Lavinia's name, calling attention to the woman who inflamed Turnus's passions. In doing so, Crispus (or perhaps Dio) invited the audience to envision the parallel between the ancient Lavinia and Julia Domna—the contemporary one. Not surprisingly, Julia Domna is found lacking. Unlike Virgil's Lavinia, the empress was hardly silent or modest, even at this early date in her husband's reign. In fact, the *HA* reports that Julia Domna had such an influence over her husband that she convinced him to wage civil war against Clodius Albinus.[95] Both women were closely associated with the disputed lands; winning Lavinia's hand for Aeneas also meant conquering the territory in which she lived. The proximity of Hatra to the empress's hometown of Emesa, in combination with the worship of Ba'al in both cities, might have invited her association with the disputed territory. The "European" soldiers also might have equated Julia Domna with the purported prize and impetus for the war against Hatra. The imperial couple looks bad in the analogy of Turnus equaling Severus and Lavinia equaling Julia Domna because it violates the will of Jupiter and the fates. Turnus had fought impiously against these forces, but he did not win Lavinia's hand because it was foreordained that she should marry Aeneas. But if Severus is like Turnus, the marriage between him and the woman associated with the lands he was attempting to conquer should never have taken place. That the two married anyway could be interpreted as impiety on the emperor's part. Julia Domna also fails to live up to her predecessor. The bodies of Lavinia and Julia Domna were to bring forth important posterity; Lavinia bore the Roman race, whereas Julia Domna was the vessel and guarantor of legitimacy for the future emperors Caracalla and Geta. Unlike the revered offspring of Aeneas and Lavinia, however, the Severan children were the product of an unnatural and cursed coupling, of a contemporary Turnus and Lavinia. In Crispus's comparison, it was not a marriage to the blushing Lavinia for which the European troops were fighting. This contemporary Lavinia, a twisted and conniving version of the original, was the cause of Severus's passion; her influence emasculated and maddened the emperor. The lands, body, and marriage of this modern Lavinia were not worth dying before the walls of Hatra.

If this interpretation of the Crispus incident is correct, Julia Domna emerges as a source of resentment for the Praetorians specifically and for the military in general. It is worth remembering that the Praetorian praefect accompanying Septimius Severus in Hatra was Plautianus, whom Dio claimed had developed a hatred for the empress early in his career. Reports of the praefect's hostility toward Julia Domna can be explained best by his jealous competition with her for the emperor's ear. Scholars often note that enlisted men tended to adopt their officers' attitudes toward politics. Perhaps it was Plautianus's special dislike of the empress that fueled the spark of Crispus's comment. The perception that Julia Domna was interfering in masculine affairs of the state would only have made more palpable the guard's resentment.

About Face!

Sometime in the very short period between Severus's death and Geta's murder (April 4, 211, to late December 211), soldiers serving in Dura-Europos erected an inscription in honor of Caracalla, Geta, and Julia Domna:

> The faithful soldiers of the Antonine European vexillation [dedicated this] to the majesty and divine will of the Imperator Caesar, son of the divine Septimius Severus Pius Felix Arabicus Adiabenicus Parthicus Maximus Britannicus Maximus [[[—]]] grandson of the divine Marcus Aurelius Antoninus Pius Germanicus Sarmaticus; great grandson of the divine Antoninus Pius; great-great-grandson of the divine Hadrian; great-great-great-grandson of the divine Trajan Parthicus and the divine Nerva [[— to Publius Septimius Geta]] and to Julia Augusta Pia Felix mother of the Augustus and of the Camp and the Senate and the Fatherland.[96]

These men, presumably the same unit as those who refused to fight some thirteen years earlier below the walls of Hatra, might have felt it necessary to assert their loyalty to their new emperors. Their titulature strikingly conforms with what the imperial administration had been using in Rome. Geta was celebrated as the most recent emperor of Antonine heritage, while his mother was honored not only with the Mater Castrorum title but with titles bestowed by the Senate after the death of Septimius Severus.[97] This inscription demonstrates that even at the edge of the empire, its dedicators knew the most up-to-date titulature. Their motivation for erecting the inscription might also indicate that the troops were closely following current events. The dedication raised by the *vexillatio Antoninianorum Europaeorum* might well have been motivated by anxieties concerning the new emperors' ability to get along.

So what happened between the mutiny of 199 and this surprisingly flattering and official-sounding celebration of the new emperors and Julia Domna? It is likely that Severus learned a lesson from the insubordination of Plautianus and installed a Praetorian praefect better in sync with his own imperial objectives. Just as Plautianus poisoned the well against Julia Domna and her sons, so a new praefect loyal to the Severan dynasty policy could effect a change of attitude among his men. Certainly, Messius Atticus, a centurion of the Seventh Praetorian Cohort, seemed earnest in his dedication to Julia Domna as the Mater Augustorum and Castrorum sometime between 209 and 212.[98] Imperial propaganda's new emphasis on the promotion of the dynasty as a whole might have been the reason why Atticus was willing to honor the empress late in Severus's reign, when he had withheld any mention of her in two earlier inscriptions honoring her husband and sons.[99]

In addition, there are a number of signs suggesting the imperial administration learned more discretion when bringing imperial women within the sphere of the military, perhaps a response to the hostility exhibited toward the empress in 199. Herodian recalls that when Julia Domna accompanied Severus and her sons to Britain in 209, she kept her distance from the front lines, opting instead to stay with Geta, who performed civic duties rather than campaigning with his father further to the North.[100] Julia Domna was permitted to accompany Severus when he met the Caledonian chieftain Argentocoxus to negotiate a treaty but, significantly, she was left to discuss cultural matters with the chieftain's wife while the men negotiated the more important political and military details.[101] Analysis of fourteen British hoards suggests that the administration never ceased actively promoting Julia Domna there; however, the most common types in these hoards associated her with domestic virtues and goddesses.[102] Hoards from Britain reveal the empress's most common reverse types minted between 196 and 211: VENVS FELIX, PIETAS PVBLICA, and VESTA SANCTA. Most of these goddesses bespeak family and fertility, but PIETAS PVBLICA stands out as an important exception. Julia Domna's *pietas*—her devotion to family, state, and gods—takes on a particularly public quality with this ubiquitous type (see figure 11). The empress, shown raising her arms and hands in an attitude of prayer over a lit altar, suggests that Julia Domna's *pietas* was somehow involved in the maintenance and preservation of the empire, the *res publica*. Her piety, as explained in greater detail in chapter 3, was of special concern to the inhabitants of the empire toward the end of Severus's life. I suspect that this type was designed to soothe anxieties caused by the contentious brothers.

Under Caracalla's administration, however, the emphasis shifted slightly in favor of Diana Lucifera, Vesta, and Venus Genetrix. Yet the military continued to celebrate the empress's *pietas* after Caracalla had abandoned it. Two inscriptions erected after 212 by cohorts in Britain under the care of the legate C. Julius Marcus celebrate the empress *pro pietate ac devotione communi numini eius.*[103] The *pietas* and *devotio* mentioned in the inscription imply an awareness of one's place in the universe, honoring those institutions such as family, state, and the gods. Significantly, earlier inscriptions in the same area under the care of C. Julius Marcus failed to mention Julia Domna, perhaps because he and his men underestimated the need for the empress's piety until after Severus died.[104]

These inscriptions suggest a rethinking by legionaries and the Praetorian Guard concerning the empress's role in ideological negotiations. The ubiquitous PIETAS PVBLICA type assigned Julia Domna a semiofficial position suggested that her *pietas* was sufficient to maintain the harmony between the private sphere of her household and the public entities such as the military, Senate, and *populus Romanus*. Epigraphic evidence suggests that the military did not consider the empress's piety particularly important before Severus's death. The response to the PIETAS PVBLICA propaganda evident in these inscriptions only appears under the joint reign of Caracalla and Geta but continues throughout Caracalla's reign. The PIETAS PVBLICA type was abandoned by the administration after Severus's death. The military's insistence on celebrating the empress's public piety propaganda was thus out of step with Caracalla's presentation of his mother. Simply put, it was only after the imperial administration tailored its advertisement of the empress to be more domestic and kept her away from the camp and battlefield tactics that she became a talking point for the military when communicating with Caracalla. Whether the empress ever influenced military matters is highly speculative, but what mattered most was the appearance rather than the actuality of an imperial woman's involvement in military affairs. When Julia Domna's influence over military affairs was less apparent, her popularity with the troops improved.[105] The appeal to the empress's public piety in these inscriptions, however, might have sprung from the same anxieties that beset the civilian population. The military, much like civilians, might also have been looking to Julia Domna to maintain harmony between her sons. Perhaps it was because of Geta's impious murder, however, that both military and civilian populations felt that it would be best for the empress to maintain her concern for the public harmony between the imperial house, the gods, and the various components of the state. For the military, the desire for Julia Domna's public *pietas* was even more pronounced in Caracalla's sole reign.

Conclusion

Julia Domna's Mater Castrorum title was awarded for similar reasons as Faustina's: it was designed not to flatter the military or to build ideology between the army and the emperor, but to convince civilian populations in Rome and throughout the provinces that the emperor had the army's unflinching support for his reign and the establishment of his dynasty. Early in Severus's reign, the military likely regarded Julia Domna as an intrusion into the masculine sphere of the camp, probably because she seemed to wield undue influence over the emperor. Rumors of her influence in political and military matters and the endowment of the Mater Castrorum title by the administration would only have hardened this resentment. The Praetorian Guard was highly influenced in its attitude toward the empress by the hatred its powerful praefect had for her. Plautianus's resentment combined with Julia Domna's perceived influence over Severus and his military goals might have added fuel to the fire of the army's frustrations at the siege of Hatra. The exclamation uttered by Julius Crispus, I suggest, was an expression of this frustration that treasonously struck at the heart of the emperor's self-presentation. Not only did Crispus's comment strip Severus of his carefully constructed Roman ethnicity and his special relationship with the gods, it suggested that the empress had undue influence over the emperor's actions. The pithy little utterance cost the Praetorian his life. Severus and his imperial administration probably learned a great deal at Hatra, and thereafter managed the empress's movements and advertisements to avoid any impression that she had influence in military matters. It was only once the empress was needed to maintain the harmony between brothers that the military celebrated her and her maternal influences.[106]

CHAPTER 2

Romancing the Romans

Julia Domna and the *Populus Romanus*

In his description of the *adventus* of Severus in Rome in 193, Cassius Dio carefully dissected the social classes that crowded into the streets to greet their new emperor.

> After doing this [i.e., dismissing the Praetorian Guard], Severus entered Rome. He advanced as far as the gates on horseback and in cavalry costume, but there he changed to civilian attire and proceeded on foot. The entire army, both infantry and cavalry accompanied him in full armor. The spectacle was the most brilliant of any that I have witnessed. The whole city had been decked with garlands of flowers and laurel and adorned with richly colored stuffs and ablaze with torches and burning incense. Men wearing white robes with radiant countenances sang many praises. The soldiers too were conspicuous in their armor as they moved about like participants in some holiday procession. Finally, we [senators] were walking about in state. The crowd chafed in its eagerness to see him and to hear him say something, as if he had been somehow changed by his good fortune. Some of them held one another aloft, so that they might catch sight of him from a higher position.[1]

His classifications reveal a senator's vision of the three main power brokers an emperor must please to secure and maintain his position: the military, Senate, and urban plebs. As Aldrete notes, "[the urban plebs] were raised to the same level as the senate and army by being classified together with them as the main groups whose acclamations were necessary to assure the legitimacy of the emperor."[2] These three populations jockeyed for the emperor's favor and its accompanying benefits. Ancient authors sympathized with the Senate and its rivalry with the Roman populace for the emperor's ear. Because of this, they painted the Roman populace with broad strokes, often neglecting to acknowledge important distinctions within this socially and economically diverse group. Unless the Roman populace acted in accordance with the wishes of the Senate, ancient authors accused it of greed, capriciousness, and superstition.

This chapter explores the ideology negotiated between Severus and the populations at Rome, especially in terms of the maternal imagery of Julia Domna. Though Severus had taken the city without bloodshed, he knew that its loyalty was tenuous, easily forgotten once he was out of sight. Severus needed the support of the *populus Romanus*.[3] He thus strove from his first encounter with the urban plebs to win its support for his reign (and eventually for his dynasty) through a series of strategies, including games, shows, and distributions of money.[4] More creatively, Severus attempted to solidify his power by exploiting the superstitions that supposedly characterized the urban plebs. He bolstered assertions of divine favor for his rule through Julia Domna, for instance, by advertising her horoscope that foretold her marriage to a king.[5] In addition, Severus used claims concerning the empress's metaphorical maternity and her connections to the Antonines in order to give him, a native of Lepcis Magna, roots in the topography, history, and rituals of Rome. Julia Domna's image was useful in promoting family propaganda that discouraged political dissent. Once an emperor and empress were known as the father and mother of the empire, to rebel against them constituted impiety at best, patricide at worst.[6] The responses of the urban plebs to Severus and his general policies concerning the city were enthusiastic, while responses to Julia Domna's maternal propaganda were mixed. Though inscriptions erected within the city mentioned the empress, the population was by and large less interested in the real or imagined maternity of Julia Domna than with what the emperor could provide them. Perhaps aware of these priorities, Severus gave the people what they wanted: peace (eventually) and prosperity. Inscriptions suggest that the *populus Romanus* enjoyed the fruits of what the emperor had promised them and thus largely approved of Severan policies irrespective of the ancient authors' censorious assessments of his reign.

The Nature of the Sources

To examine the relationship between Severus and the populations of Rome, we must consider literary and material evidence, especially in the form of coinage, inscriptions, and monuments. Each type of evidence represents its own challenges.

Like his predecessors, Severus was loath to leave the interpretation of his reign to hostile senatorial authors. So he penned an autobiography that both Herodian and Cassius Dio described as filled with the dreams, omens, and portents foretelling his rise to power. This autobiography is no longer extant, but through ancient testimonies, we can make some general observations about its contents and intended audience. Unfortunately, references to the autobiography are couched within the biases and judgments of the ancient authors and must therefore be treated with caution. Herodian reports that several ambitious men composed histories and poems exaggerating Severus's deeds and lending credence to the emperor's dreams and *omina imperii* (omens foretelling his ascension to the throne) in the hopes of winning his favor.[7] Cassius Dio openly admits to being one of these men.[8] Probably not long after Albinus was defeated, Dio presented a pamphlet on the history of the civil wars that brought Severus to power. He reports that the emperor approved of the pamphlet, which is not surprising because Dio included stories of the *omina imperii* that imperial propaganda was circulating. When writing his larger history of the Romans, Dio included portions of that pamphlet, though this was not simply a cut and paste hack job. He modified select passages to more closely reflect his later and franker assessment of Severus and his reign. Resulting passages in the epitome of Dio's history are jarringly uneven, recounting divine approbation of Severus's reign immediately followed by snide, subversive jabs at the emperor. Interpreting such passages is challenging.

Imperial coinage was plentiful during the period and rich with propagandistic messages. A glance through the catalogues of modern coin cabinets reveals an impressive variety of types that boast Julia Domna's real and metaphorical maternal purview. Yet this evidence is problematic. Modern coin cabinets and their catalogs are not representative of the quantities of coins that were produced. They cannot answer questions of where certain types were distributed or how they circulated.[9] Coin hoards can prove a useful metric by which to ascertain what propagandistic messages were targeted for a particular audience.[10] Ironically, it is far more difficult to ascertain which messages were meant for particular audiences in Rome and Italy than in the provinces. Out of fifty-seven published hoards from the Severan period, only two come from Italy and of those, only one from Rome. The hoard found in the Via Tritone is therefore precious but problematic. It likely represents a glimpse of what was circulating within the city sometime after 244,[11] when Severus's coinage reached its peak circulation, but alone it is virtually useless, because it is too small a sample size to be representative.[12] It is thus unwise to rely too heavily upon the Via Tritone hoard in determining which messages the administration directed toward the urban plebs. It is no sounder methodology, however, to ignore the many types and legends that populate the coin cabinets and catalogs because we are not certain of their circulation or intended audience. Without more hoards from Rome and Italy, one cannot say with any certainty which types or how many of each type were distributed there. Yet the proportion of Julia Domna's coins to Severus's in the Italian hoards (1:2.5 in the Via Tritone hoard) suggests that though the empress had fewer types, the size of her issues in Italy was larger than in most provinces (1:1.89 to 1:2.38).[13] This seems to indicate that a proportionally greater number of Julia Domna's coins circulated in Italy and the Western continent than in areas maintaining a large military presence.[14] The sample sizes of hoards in the provinces compared to those in Rome and Italy are huge: for example, the Danubian region boasts a sample of well over 1.5 million denarii from nineteen hoards, while the Via Tritone and Vicenza hoards combined have only 938 denarii. The tiny sample size of the Italian coin hoards means that whatever evidence might be culled from them is likely skewed. Curiously, the most common types of Julia Domna from the Via Tritone hoard are the same as those found in the frontier hoards.[15] This raises an interesting question, because the *RIC* records fifty-four types of Julia Domna minted in Rome under Severus; 55 percent of these address Julia Domna's literal or metaphorical motherhood.[16] Where are all those coins advertising the empress's maternity? I can think of two possible explanations for their absence in hoards. In the first, the Roman mint produced a very limited number of the maternity coins, and consequently they are poorly represented in all hoards across the Mediterranean. In the second, the maternity types received regular issues but their distribution was limited to Italy. In this scenario, the coins do not appear in the archaeological record because we have such a small and biased sampling of hoards in Italy. Considering the healthy sample sizes of hoards on the empire's frontiers, the best explanation is that the maternal coins were distributed in Rome and Italy to civilian populations. This is an imperfect methodology, but at the moment it is the best we can do.

Severus's building program within the city was another point of ideological negotiation with the populations of Rome. In his own and his family's names, Severus refurbished important monuments through the city and built new structures. The placement of Severan monuments within the Forum Romanum effectively wrote Severus into the heart of Roman history, as Lusnia most recently demonstrated.[17] Severus was an outsider who lacked Roman roots, a point noted by his rivals and critics. For instance, we hear in the *Historia Augusta* of the embarrassment Severus must have felt because his sister could speak no Latin; it was whispered that Severus himself spoke with a pronounced African accent well into his old age.[18] But with each new monument or refurbishment, Severus erected inscriptions celebrating his contributions to the city and thus linking himself to the prominent figures of the original dedicators.[19] I explore two such inscriptions that are useful in determining the role that was assigned to Julia Domna's maternity in these ideological negotiations.

Because of the limitations of the literary sources in gauging the responses of the urban plebs to Severan propaganda, I turn to inscriptions erected in honor of the imperial family in Rome to better understand the relationship between segments of the population and Severus. The *collegia* erected dedicatory inscriptions to honor Severus and his sons, occasionally mentioning the empress but only as a member of the imperial family. Freedmen, perhaps imperial freedmen, erected inscriptions dedicated solely to the empress. These freedmen likely had a different motivation for doing so than the *collegia*, as they were likely meant to flatter Julia Domna personally as opposed to seeking favors larger than she alone could grant, as was likely the case with *collegia* dedications.

These scraps of epigraphic, numismatic, and archaeological material will supplement the literary evidence and will be employed to explore the negotiation of Julia Domna's maternal ideology between Severus and the *populus Romanus*.

The Princeps and the Plebs

One of the most important moments for the creation of ideology between an emperor and the Roman populace was the face-to-face interaction that occurred in games, public rituals, and libations. Herodian describes Severus's attempts to woo the Roman populace, who despite the emperor's gifts still viewed him warily:

> His [Severus's] subjects submitted from fear rather than affection. He did try, however, to do what would please the people (τῷ μέντοι δήμῳ); he staged costly spectacles of every kind, killing on numerous occasions hundreds of animals of every species collected from all parts of the empire and from foreign lands as well, in connection with which he distributed lavish gifts. He held triumphal games for which he summoned dramatic actors and skilled athletes from every quarter.[20]

The imperial administration put a great deal of planning into the encounters between emperors and the populace at Rome. In spectacles such as triumphs, funerals, or games, the emperor's perspective was privileged above all others because he shaped and controlled what was seen. In games, he was quite literally the editor, both in the ancient and modern sense of the word; he decided upon the content of the games and by doing so shaped his own version of reality. An emperor presented within the arena "truths" about himself and his character as *princeps*, the extent of his power and his ability to wield the empire's resources, the populace, and its role in the empire. In some ways, the emperor was like a republican orator only much, much more powerful. According to Quintillian, particularly talented orators employed φαντασία, the rhetorical strategy of summoning up images in the minds of their audience through their words. Considered an especially effective rhetorical tool, φαντασία evoked emotional responses that could move the audience even to act contrary to its best interests. In order to do so, however, the orator had to display convincingly the same emotions that he wished his audience to feel.[21]

Much like an orator, the emperor modeled the emotions that he wanted his subjects to feel. He displayed *civilitas*, an important quality that allowed him to be considered a part of the society (though hardly an equal), rather than simply ruling it.[22] Unlike an orator, the emperor had no need to summon φαντασίας to move the emotions of his people and persuade them to think and act as he wished. He placed the "real" thing before their eyes. The spectacles found in the arena, triumphal processions, and funeral and imperial speeches were factories of ideology in which carefully constructed ideas and political relationships were presented as being real and natural. Perched upon his triumphal chariot or looking upward from his imperial box in the Colosseum, the emperor was visible to all. He also saw all. His physical position and disposition, sponsorship of the display, and the role assigned to his various subjects all worked in tandem to create the illusion that the emperor controlled all he and the crowd saw, that he quite literally controlled reality.

Encounters between the emperor and the urban plebs were social dramas in which both parties reconfirmed their positions within the hierarchy.[23] As Gunderson asserts, the arena "can be taken as an apparatus which not only looks in upon a spectacle, but one in which its organization and structure reproduces the relations subsisting between observer and observed."[24] Spectacles were also important opportunities for Roman populace to voice opinions or complaints. By the reign of Tiberius, republican popular assemblies were closed entirely, and imperial spectacles such as triumphs, speeches, games, and theater events became the arena for the disenfranchised populace to make its will known to the emperor.[25] Ironically, the loss of *libertas* inherent in the closing of the assemblies allowed the populace a much freer exchange of ideas than might be found among senators in the Curia: shouting out a comment during an emperor's speech from the midst of the anonymous crowd engendered a kind of candor unknown in assemblies.[26] On the other hand, organized seating in theaters and amphitheaters constituted a "careful and comprehensive map of Roman society."[27] Thus it was possible for the emperor to identify at a glance a certain segment of society and learn how it reacted to what it saw. Groups captured the emperor's attention through rhythmic and unified chants, sometimes mixed with clapping or stomping feet in time.[28]

Ironically, the careful planning of political events that privileged the emperor's realities and perspectives could be thoroughly undone in a moment. The interactions allowed subjects to make demands of the emperor, ask him questions, or simply pit their own interpretations of "truth" or "reality" against his. Because of this polyvocality, the emperor was in constant danger of losing control of his interpretive monopoly on what constituted reality. Suetonius captured the frustration an emperor might feel when an audience failed to echo Caligula's vision of reality: "Would that the Roman populace had only one neck!"[29] Despite several instances recorded by literary sources of clashes between the emperor and the urban plebs, popular critiques of the emperor and his depictions of reality were relatively rare, more often the exception than the rule. The interactions between the Roman populace and the emperor usually solidified the power of the emperor, strengthened the bond between them, and "reaffirmed the power and the status of the groups bestowing the acclamation."[30]

The Roman Populace, Public Demonstrations, and Divine Inspiration

Cassius Dio recorded several instances just prior to and during Severus's reign in which populations of Rome took advantage of the nature of spectacles to make their opinions known. In each of these instances, Dio inserted the supernatural into his account, either by denigrating the supposed superstition of the crowd or by attributing divine inspiration or foreknowledge to it.[31] His word choice in describing the urban plebs provides clues to his approval (or disapproval) of its behavior and attitudes. Ancient authors are seldom consistent in their terminology regarding the *populus Romanus,* but Yavetz notes that Cassius Dio used δῆμος and πλῆθος as neutral terms, the first being the equivalent to the *populus Romanus*—that is, the entire Roman people including all its various classes—while πλῆθος refers to the urban plebs. Dio chose the more derogatory ὅμιλος or ὄχλος in order to cast aspersion on the actions of the plebs.[32]

In the passage that opens this chapter, Dio inventoried the different classes of the *populus Romanus* who gathered to witness Severus's first *adventus.* The description of the urban plebs is particularly memorable:

> Men (ἄνθρωποι) wearing white robes with radiant countenances sang many praises (πολλὰ ἐπευφήμουν). The soldiers too were conspicuous in their armor as they moved about like participants in some holiday procession. Finally, we [senators] were walking about in state. The crowd (ὅμιλος) chafed in its eagerness to see him and to hear him say something, as if he had been somehow changed by his good fortune (ὥσπερ τι ὑπὸ τῆς τύχης ἠλλοιωμένου). Some of them held one another aloft, so that they might catch sight of him from a higher position.[33]

Dio does not say whom he meant by ἄνθρωποι, but their stately robes and restrained behavior suggest that they were of the upper classes. By contrast, Dio depicted the urban plebs as rambunctiously holding one another aloft, an action that apparently lacked the dignity of the ἄνθρωποι or the senators. His disapproval of this behavior is marked by his terminology, ὅμιλος. Equally significant is Dio's depiction of the crowd's *superstitio:* they imagine (falsely, apparently) that Severus's τύχη had changed. Rubin believes this passage originally appeared in Dio's political pamphlet because it paints a far rosier picture of emperor's *adventus* in comparison with passages from Herodian and the author of the Vita Severi in the *Historia Augusta.* In those passages, the crowd is also interested in the fortune of Severus, but they fear his arrival. Rubin suggests that in the transfer of this passage from the pamphlet to the larger history, Dio added a cynical twist to an otherwise positive depiction with that one phrase, ὥσπερ τι ὑπὸ τῆς τύχης ἠλλοιωμένου. This jab reflects the historian's jaded view of the *adventus* from hindsight. Rubin notes that throughout his history, Dio denigrated emperors who trusted in Fortune while praising those who embrace Virtue, a characterization that was a hallmark of senatorial histories.[34] Yet Dio also recognized the positive side of τύχη. He related a dream in which a δαιμόνιον appeared to him and commanded him to write history. Τύχη gave him strength to continue the task when he was weary or wanted to quit.[35] Yet in the *adventus* of Severus, the urban plebs would not have looked for evidence of the emperor's τύχη, a Greek concept laden with both positive and negative connotations, so much as *felicitas,* a wholly positive trait that signifies a certain blessedness and, by extension, divine favor. I know of no word in Greek that captures the sense of the Latin *felicitas*; τύχη is the closest equivalent. Dio's little jab seems to suggest that Severus lacked *felicitas* before his *adventus.* Had he made such an observation to the emperor directly, Dio likely would have been charged with *maiestas*—treason. Severus was known to kill men for such statements.[36] Notably, however, Dio projected his cattiness onto the observations of the rowdy urban plebs.

Such manipulation of the plebs and its understanding of divine will and the supernatural is quite common in Cassius Dio's history. Some scholars see Dio's interest in supernatural phenomena as a mark of his own credulity or as a shift in society's understanding of the role of the supernatural in everyday life.[37] I reject these assertions. Dio was trained in rhetoric, and with his political pamphlet he demonstrated a willingness to place the supernatural at the service of a political agenda.[38] As the passages below illustrate, Dio's claims of divine inspiration and the supernatural promoted his agenda and added weight to his own interpretations, thus providing himself with greater *auctoritas.*

In making this assertion, however, I do not wish to suggest that Dio did not also believe that the supernatural manifested itself in a variety of ways around him. Still, as Harris points out, "there was belief and belief." In exploring to what degree Romans "believed" in dreams and other supernatural phenomena, Harris posits that it is not sufficient merely to cling to the now-tired dichotomy of orthodoxy versus orthopraxy. He notes that although belief was certainly present in the writings of Plato, Aristophanes, Hellenistic authors, and Cicero, readers ought to take into account the range of behaviors or inactivity that accompanies it. In inviting scholars to consider the "propensities to action in both public and private life" of ancient authors, Harris cites the behavioralist philosopher Gilbert Ryle:

> Beliefs, like habits, can be inveterate, slipped into and given up; like partisanships, devotions and hopes they can be blind and obsessive; like aversions and phobias they can be unacknowledged; like fashions and tastes they can be contagious . . . belief might be said to be . . . "propositional"; but this, though not far wrong, is too narrow . . . [belief] is a propensity not only to make certain theoretical moves but also to make certain executive and imaginative moves, as well as to have certain feelings.[39]

As discussed below, Dio's "belief" translated into behavior, but not in a reverential manner so much as a self-interested one.

Shortly before Severus marched on Rome, a crowd of onlookers heckled Didius Julianus as he prepared a sacrifice to Janus near the entrance of the Curia. The populace (ὁ δῆμος), whom Dio had earlier described as openly sullen toward Julianus, took advantage of the opportunity to shout "as if by agreement" (ὥσπερ ἐκ συγκειμένου τινός) that he was a "robber of the empire and a parricide" (τῆς τε ἀρχῆς ἅρπαγα αὐτὸν καὶ πατροφόνον). When Julianus tried to calm the crowd by offering them a liberality, they shouted, "We don't want it! We won't take it!" (οὐ θέλομεν, οὐ λαμβάνομεν).[40] The violence that Julianus then ordered the Praetorians to unleash upon those standing nearest did little to quell the crowd's outrage, and the city erupted with demonstrations. In Herodian's version of the event, he identified the Circus Maximus as the location where the people (τὸ πλῆθος) gathered to make their opinions known. There the crowd bemoaned how wretchedly they were treated.[41] Dio's δῆμος, however, was less peaceful; they resisted the guard in clashes throughout the city and eventually armed themselves and spent the night and the next day in the circus without food or water. They invoked the names of various provincial governors to come to their aid, but in particular they called upon Pescennius Niger, governor of Syria. The riot was quelled only by the exhaustion of its participants.[42]

Strikingly, Dio and Herodian use words with neutral meanings, δῆμος and πλῆθος, to describe an armed mob clashing with the Praetorian Guard, raging through the streets, and finally seizing and occupying a major public space traditionally associated with public demonstrations. In choosing these innocuous words, Dio and Herodian signal their approval of the crowd's persecution of a man depicted by both authors as a tyrant and poor successor to the beloved Pertinax. Dio is particularly subtle in his attempts to shape his audience's judgment of the crowd and its actions. He described its initial monovocal communication with Julianus as "as if by agreement" (ὥσπερ ἐκ συγκειμένου τινός). Because Dio coyly offered no further explanation, he invites his audience to believe that the crowd's wondrous apparent ability to chant in time is a result of divine guidance. Dio's uncharacteristic failure to mention any social or economic strata within this crowd presents it in elevated terms, removing its actions from the sordid world of political maneuvering.[43] Rather than acknowledge that the crowd was likely incited by political agents for provincial governors, Dio introduced an element of the marvelous with his phrase "as if by agreement," inviting readers to consider the mob's actions as resounding with righteous indignation and reflecting divine disapproval of Didius Julianus. Yet despite Dio's reticence, the fact that the mob knew on which provincial commanders to call in order to save them from the injustice of Julianus means that Dio's interpretation was politically motivated.

In another passage concerning public demonstrations and Plautianus, Dio explicitly ascribed foreknowledge to the crowd. In doing so, he gave authority to the voice of the mob in order to add weight to its chastisement:

> On Mount Vesuvius a huge fire blazed up, and there were bellowings mighty enough to be heard in Capua, where I live whenever I am in Italy. I have selected this place for various reasons, and particularly for its quiet in order that

> when I have leisure from my duties in the capital I may write this history. In view, now, of what happened on Vesuvius, it seemed probable that some change in the state was about to occur, and in fact there was an immediate change in the fortunes of Plautianus. This man had in very truth grown great and more than great, so that even the populace (δῆμος) in the Circus once exclaimed, "Why do you tremble? Why are you pale? You possess more than do the other three." They pretended, to be sure, that they were saying this of him in another connection, but by "the three" they meant Severus and his two sons, Antoninus and Geta. Plautianus was always pale and trembling because of the kind of life he lived, the hopes he entertained and the fears he felt.[44]

By drawing a connection between the eruption of Vesuvius and Plautianus, Dio shaped this event to promote his political agenda. He presented himself as a local authority on the area and, by extension, on the meaning of the eruption and the demonstration. Significantly, Dio never explained what the "other connection" (ἄλλως) was for which the crowd pretended to chant at Plautianus. He veiled the less-favored interpretation from his readers by failing to expound upon it, thus giving primacy to his own. Dio's use of the neutral term δῆμος signaled his approval of the crowd's actions. From his descriptions of Plautianus's behavior, it is clear that Dio was no fan of the Praetorian praefect; as covered in chapter 3, he championed (at least in his histories) the empress against Plautianus's accusations of adultery. Still, we need not turn to other passages to detect Dio's hatred of Plautianus because his superlatives say it all: the praefect had become great and in truth, beyond great (μέγας μὲν γὰρ ὡς ἀληθῶς ὁ Πλαυτιανὸς καὶ ὑπέρμεγας ἐγεγόνει). This statement on the tyrannical behavior of the praefect combined with the urban plebs' shocking address to someone other than the emperor signals that Dio believed that Plautianus's demise was not only foretold but also foreordained. The very fact that the urban plebs addressed the praefect would have been considered threatening to the emperor and would have indicated that they considered him at least as powerful as the Augusti.[45] Such a suggestion may well plant resentment in the heart of Severus and raise his suspicions concerning his Praetorian praefect.[46]

In another demonstration, Dio explicitly described the crowd as moved by divine inspiration. The demonstration occurred in the Circus Maximus during the lull between the first Parthian expedition and Severus's showdown with Albinus. The chants of the crowds here, however, are more challenging to interpret:

> Then, while the entire world was disturbed by this situation [i.e., the rivalry between Severus and Albinus], we senators remained quiet, at least as many of

> us as did not, by openly inclining to the one or the other, share their dangers and their hopes. The populace (δῆμος), however, could not restrain itself, but indulged in the most open lamentations. It was at the last horserace before the Saturnalia, and a countless throng of people (τι χρῆμα ἀνθρώπων) flocked to it. I, too, was present at the spectacle, since the consul was a friend of mine, and I heard distinctly everything that was said, so that I was in a position to write something about it. It came about in this way. There had assembled, as I said, an untold multitude (τι χρῆμα ἀνθρώπων) and they had watched the chariots racing, six at a time (which had been the practice in Cleander's day) without applauding any of the contestants at all, as was their custom. But when the races were over and the charioteers were about to begin another event, they first enjoined silence upon one another and then suddenly all clapped their hands at the same moment and also joined in a shout, praying for the good fortune for the public welfare (εὐτυχίαν τῇ τοῦ δήμου σωτηρίᾳ). This was what they first cried out; then applying the terms "Queen" and "Immortal" to Rome, they shouted, "How long are we to suffer such things?" and "How long are we to be waging war?" And after some other remarks of this kind, they finally shouted "So much for that" and turned their attention to the horserace. In all this they were surely moved by some divine inspiration; for in no other way could so many myriads of men (μυριάδες ἀνθρώπων) have begun to utter the same shouts at the same time, like a carefully trained chorus, or have spoken the words without a mistake, just as if they had practiced them.[47]

In this passage, Dio gives his audience several clues that he is not being completely candid. He goes out of his way to explain why he would attend such a gathering. Perhaps this was an issue of class posturing, that a senator ought not enjoy attending the games.[48] In doing so, he suggests that his presence at the games was some anomalous activity. Yet elsewhere in his history, Dio indicates that he had attended many such events, at least in the days of Commodus.[49] He would have been quite familiar with the rhythmic chanting he attributed to the crowd (ἄνθρωποι). Such chants were relatively simple to execute and required little planning in order to pull off convincingly. Even large crowds could chant in unison with little or no practice by changing a few key words in well-known songs, poems, or phrases. Notably, scholars view Cassius Dio as an important source for exploring the mechanics of crowd demonstrations.[50] Dio's approval of the crowd's sentiments is again marked out by his choice of positive words. These men (ἄνθρωποι) are no mere rabble; they are respectable, much as those men who looked upon Severus's *adventus* with gleaming countenance, not like the ὄχλος who held one another aloft to see the emperor and ascertain his *felicitas*.

The omen of the chanting crowd in the Circus Maximus seems an odd choice to include in Dio's pro-Severan political pamphlet if it originally appeared there, as Rubin suggests. The point of the anecdote seems to indicate an overall divine disgust with Rome's political affairs, perhaps even with Severus himself. As Rubin sees it, however, Dio "deliberately blurred" the importance of this omen by failing to articulate when and under what circumstances it occurred. Unlike other easily interpreted *omina imperii* that highlighted Severan propaganda of divine approval, this one sounds like an overall divine condemnation of the political situation. Yet this is clearly not the whole story: Severus won the war against Albinus, proof positive for many Roman minds of his *felicitas* and of his *virtus*. In an attempt to make sense of this omen, Rubin examined evidence of Severus's whereabouts during the demonstration and found that the emperor was likely in Rome at the time along with several legions. He reads the crowd's invocation of "Queen" and "Immortal" Rome as a plea for the legitimate power (i.e., Severus) to quickly restore order to the state. For Rubin, "so enthusiastic a support of Severus on the part of the populace would be easily explicable by the presence of Severus and his soldiers in the city. Divine inspiration was conjured up by the army."[51] Perhaps Rubin is too cynical. That Dio left out key elements in his narration of the demonstration shows his politically motivated manipulation—or perhaps more generously, a "reinterpretation"—of the omen.

In two omens that immediately follow the narration of the Saturnalia demonstration, Dio again placed himself in the center of the action as an eyewitness. In the first, the appearance of a great fire in the sky made the entire city look like it was burning; in the second, a fine "silver" rain descended upon the Forum of Augustus. Dio tells us that after it had fallen (he does not claim to have witnessed the "rain" fall himself), he plated some bronze coins with the silver rain. The coins retained their silver appearance for three days before the substance rubbed off.[52] For Rubin, both omens foretold Albinus's defeat. The second omen, however, was worth noting for its ingenuity. Rubin interpreted the silver rain to be an indication of the temporary nature of Albinus's reign: the semantic range of the Greek word for "silver" (ἄργυρος), which is the basis of the word "silver-like" (ἀργυοειδῆς), includes "white," a play on Albinus's name. The rain occurred in the Forum of Augustus because it represented a contest for the position of Augustus. The coating only lasted for three days—Albinus was Severus's Caesar for three years—and the temporary nature of the coating suggested that just as the "silver" coating was counterfeit so, too, was Albinus a counterfeit Caesar. In his clever anecdote of the silver rain, Dio implicates himself in the manipulation of *omina* by claiming to have personally experienced the counterfeit coating on bronze coins.

Finally, in Dio's account of Severus's first *adventus*, the senator attributes to the urban plebs an interest in the emperor's fortune. Modern scholars have often accepted without question what Dio hinted at, namely that supernatural "evidence" was more convincing to common people than to the aristocracy. Following the contours of ancient testimony, Harris divides his chapter on Roman opinions concerning the truthfulness of dreams by social orders.[53] As he concludes, we should be wary of too close an association between the common people and a willingness to believe supernatural evidence. Indeed, the most vibrant ancient testimonies for dreams and divine intervention come from the elite: Philostratus's *Vita Apollonii* or Aelius Aristides's *Hieroi Logoi* provides evidence that at least some of the elite trusted in dreams. Surely there were people from every socioeconomic background who recognized that dream interpretation was subject to manipulation. Scholarship as a whole, however, has failed to acknowledge this manipulation and as a profession, we have blithely allowed ourselves to accept the ancient snobbishness of attributing superstition to the plebeians. But as Harris points out, "publication" of Dio's political treatise meant copying the manuscript and sending it around to important men—his apparent audience—who seemed every bit as interested in the τύχη of Severus as the crowds who lined the streets at his first *adventus*, holding one another aloft to see how or whether his fortunes had changed. "Belief" in the supernatural seems to be the elite's elephant in the room during this period, much as the popularity of the games was in the Late Republic; though senatorial authors claimed that they despised the games, we never hear of their reserved seats left empty.[54] People can and often do simultaneously believe contradictory things; they make room for the inconsistencies and ambiguities whenever convenient. These intellectual acrobatics can spring from desperation—such as a cancer patient seeking alternative medicine or a former atheist praying in a foxhole—or from seeking political advantage—such as an earnest young senator seeking the goodwill of a new emperor—or from circumstance—no one believes in ghosts until it grows dark and strange noises are heard. There is no reason why Dio, for instance, cannot claim seriously that in a dream Severus instructed him to write or that he was visited by his own personal Τύχη, who encouraged him to embellish or manipulate Severus's "genuine" dreams. The fact that Dio wrote this treatise for important men suggests a world in which senators can at once believe and not believe. Herodian perhaps captures the point most vividly when speaking of Severus's dreams and the reactions his contemporaries had to them: "These prognostications are all believed to be absolutely true when in actual fact they turn out well."[55] Still, it must be recognized that all these passages point to the fact that Dio's accounts of the urban plebs and the supernatural arc politically motivated, in no way "harmless" as Millar posits.[56] As such, they must be treated with caution.

Severan Propaganda and the Urban Plebs

M. Tullius Cicero famously outlined four qualities vital for the success of a Republican *imperator*: *scientia rei militaris*, *virtus*, *auctoritas*, and *felicitas*.[57] As the ultimate *imperatores*, emperors also embraced these qualities. It is therefore not surprising that Severus advertised his prowess in each quality of the Ciceronian canon to important populations via coinage, monuments, literature, and paintings. He did not celebrate all these qualities at the same time, however. In the *adventus* passage, for instance, Dio reports a particular public interest in his τύχη or *felicitas*. The coinage minted for Severus that year concerns itself less with his *felicitas*, however, than with the other virtues in Cicero's canon, particularly his *virtus* and, even more prominently, his knowledge of military affairs.[58] For his subjects, Severus's victories over his enemies were proof that he possessed these qualities. The Roman mint's output in 193–194 is also notable for the emperor's attempts to target his most important audiences. Types celebrating the legions that had thrown their lot in with Severus are therefore prominent.[59] The other major population that Severus sought to appease was the urban plebs, and the *Liberalitas* type served to remind the viewer of monetary distributions that Severus handed out during his first brief stay in Rome. The legend SAEC(VLO) FRVGIF(ERO) CO(N)S(VL) on another denarius (*RIC* 4a.19, 93) referred not simply to the prosperity that Severus promised, but it also implies the emperor's pledge to maintain the *annona*. The type features a personification of Saeculum Frugiferum, radiate, holding a winged caduceus and trident. The mention of grain combined with the reference to the sea with the trident suggests a promise that Severus will look after the grain supply to Rome. In fact, Severus took over the management of the *annona* immediately after he seized power and managed it so efficiently that he left behind a seven-year surplus upon his death.[60]

All four of the Ciceronian virtues are present in coins from the Via Tritone hoard, the only roughly contemporary published hoard found in Rome. The find spot suggests that the types and legends of the coins found within the hoard contained messages likely intended for the Roman populace.[61] The latest dated coin of the hoard was minted in 244, and of the 828 denarii, some 214 were minted for Severus during his lifetime, most in Rome (203). Table 2.1 lists the best-represented types in the hoard along with their dates, *RIC* reference number, reverse legend, and reverse type.

Several types from the hoard indirectly celebrate the emperor's *scientia rei militaris* through a celebration of the peace that Severus won through his various military campaigns. Thus the legend PACI AVG(VSTAE) in *RIC* 4a.37, 96 acknowledges the peace Severus won through war, while *RIC*.4a.88, 101 does so more obliquely by featuring the goddess Pax holding a branch and scepter.[62] The two types explicitly link Pax with the emperor through the adjective AVGVSTA and by encircling the goddess with the emperor's titles. The coin type with the highest frequency in the hoard, *RIC* 4a.167, touts the emperor as the RESTITVTOR VRBIS. While scholars sometimes interpret this coin as referring to the extensive building projects that Severus undertook within Rome, a closer look invites another reading.[63] The military and religious iconography of Severus leaning on his spear and standing before an altar implies that the emperor was able to restore the city through his military efforts and his relationship with the gods, his *felicitas*. Another prominent type (*RIC*.4a.211, 118) features Victory standing with her foot on a globe, inscribing a shield set on palm tree. The iconography anticipates the victory over the tribes of northern Britannia while reminding the viewer that the peace that Rome now enjoyed was maintained by the emperor's military campaigns.

Prosperity and abundance were the fruits of the emperor's hard-won peace, and these were manifest to the *populus Romanus* in the form of the *annona*. Pera interprets *RIC* 4a.266, 125, which features the legend INDVLGENTIA IN CARTH, as the shorthand expression of several reforms that Severus undertook in Africa. These reforms included the reordering of the province, imperial oversight over trade in order to better manage the *annona,* and the distribution within Rome of grain, oil, and possibly wine from North Africa.[64] If the reading is correct, this coin type would be particularly relevant for the urban plebs, not only those who enjoyed the benefits of the *annona* but also those who profited from their role in supplying the city. Severus's handling of the *annona* also finds prominence in the personification of the dole, standing with ears of corn, and cornucopiae representing abundance. The modius, a unit of measurement, implies not only equitable proportions but careful management.

The spectacle of Severus's Parthian triumph in 202 expounded upon the numismatic themes of Pax as a result of the emperor's military prowess. In these celebrations, Severus was careful to limit the scope of his victories to his Parthi-

TABLE 2.1
Most frequent types of Severus minted at Rome in the Via Tritone hoard

Number	Date	RIC	Reverse legend	Reverse type
6	194	37	PACI AVGVSTI	Pax seated l., holding branch and cornucopiae
5	196–197	78	FORTVNAE REDVCI	Fortuna seated l., holding rudder on globe and cornucopiae; under seat, wheel
6	196–197	88	P M TR P V COS II P P	Pax, seated l., holding a branch and scepter
6	196–197	96	VOTA PVBLICA	Emperor, veiled, standing l., sacrificing out of patera over altar
5	197–198	113	MARTI PACIFERO	Mars standing l., foot on cuirass (?), holding branch and spear reversed
6	197–198	117	P M TR P VI COS II P P	Sol, radiate, standing l., raising r. hand and holding a whip in l. hand
12	201	167	RESTITVTOR VRBIS	Severus in military dress, standing l., sacrificing with a patera over tripod, holding a spear
6	205	196	P M TR P XIII COS III P P	Jupiter, naked, standing l., holding thunderbolt and scepter; at feet, an eagle
5	206	200	P M TR P XIIII COS III P P	Annona standing l., holding ears of corn and cornucopiae; at feet, left, modius
7	207	211	P M TR P XV COS III P P	Victory standing r., foot on globe, inscribing shield set on palm tree
6	202–210	265	FVNDATOR PACIS	Septimius veiled, standing l., holding branch and roll
7	202–210	266	INDVLGENTIA AVGG IN CARTH	Dea Caelestis riding r. on a lion, holding a thunderbolt and scepter; below, waters gushing from a rock
7	202–210	308	VOTA SVSCEPTA XX	Severus veiled, standing l., sacrificing with patera over altar

Source: These data are culled from the Severan Hoard Analysis database compiled by Clare Rowan and are available through the Severan Database Project.
Note: The first column lists the number of occurrences of that particular coin type in the Via Tritone hoard.

an campaigns, passing over in silence his struggles against Pescennius Niger or Clodius Albinus.[65] In the triumphal procession, the emperor employed the usual arsenal of images, including paintings depicting the various sieges he conducted against the Parthians. Significantly, Herodian mentions the τύχη of Severus in connection with his military victories and the triumph:

> Thus, more by luck than good judgment, Severus won the glory of a Parthian victory. And since these affairs turned out more successfully than he had any

> reason to hope, he sent dispatches to the Senate and the people, extolling his exploits, and he had paintings of his battles and victories put on public display.[66]

The spectacle of these images allowed the emperor's Roman subjects to participate in Severus's victories and to revel in his claims of peace and prosperity. In order to make the recollection of the triumph and the benefits derived from his campaigns more present in his subjects' minds, Severus ordered these paintings to be displayed publicly. Some scholars posit that these images were the model for the grand panels on the Arch of Septimius Severus in the forum, a tantalizing notion.[67]

The last of the Ciceronian virtues, *felicitas,* is also apparent in the types of the Via Tritone hoard. Though this quality did not appear in Severan coinage minted at Rome until 196, it was ubiquitous in a variety of media thereafter.[68] It is worth considering the subtleties of *felicitas*. The *Oxford Latin Dictionary* lists the most common meaning of *felicitas* as "good fortune, luckiness" with a secondary definition of "successful outcome of one's activities; success, prosperity and specifically, blessedness."[69] Scholars have explored the political implications of *felicitas*, particularly with regard to Late Republican strongmen.[70] They envision *felicitas* as something that, at least partially, found its origins in divine favor toward the *imperator* in question. This same quality came to be highly prized in the *statio principis*, as well, as is apparent from the abundant instances of the legends FELICITAS and FORTUNA on imperial coinage from Trajan onward.[71]

Several types from the Via Tritone hoard advertise the special relationship Severus shared with the gods in terms of his *felicitas* or divine favor. Seven of the thirteen most frequent types in the hoard advertise the emperor's piety in sacrificing to the gods or associate him with the gods. Severus stands before an altar, often veiled, and sacrificing in *RIC*.4a.96, 102; *RIC* 4a.167, 113; and *RIC*.4a.308, 129. The legends VOTA PVBLICA, RESTITVTOR VRBIS, and VOTA SVSCEPTA all invite the viewer to see the emperor as a man of his word, one who fulfills his duties and obligations to the gods and his subjects, and does so because he enjoys the blessedness of divine favor. In a rather indirect manner, Severus celebrated his *felicitas* on the reverse of *RIC*.4a.78, 100: the legend FORTVNAE REDVCI refers to the emperor's safe return to Rome in 196–197. But when paired with the iconography of Fortuna, a rudder, globe, and cornucopiae, the overall message implies that the gods smiled upon Severus's efforts outside of Rome, that Fortune and the gods accompanied him throughout the civil wars and saw to his safe return. The cornucopiae round out the full meaning of *felicitas* by referencing the fecundity and prosperity that Severus's rule has brought the empire.

If Dio's report of the people's interest in Severus's τύχη (or more likely *felicitas*) on his arrival in Rome in 193 is accurate, the imperial administration was a little late in advertising it. Once he began to promote his *felicitas* and *fortuna* after deposing Clodius Albinus, however, Severus did so with enthusiasm. For instance, it was likely about this time that the emperor supplemented the numismatic messages with the publication of his autobiography. As Dio tells it, the autobiography was replete with dreams, portents, and oracular responses that claimed divine approval for the emperor's rise to power.[72] Herodian reports only one dream, "the most important and most recent which was also a declaration of his highest expectations":

> At the time of the announcement of Pertinax's succession, Severus made the sacrifice publicly and took the formal oath of allegiance to Pertinax as emperor. Then he returned to his house and after he had fallen asleep that night, he dreamt that he saw a fine, large horse wearing the imperial trappings carrying Pertinax down the middle of the Sacred Way in Rome. As it came to the entrance of the Forum at the point where popular meetings used to take place in Republican days, the horse appeared to shake off Pertinax and throw him down. While Severus was just standing there the horse got down under him and carried him off on its back without mishap, until it stood right in the middle of the Forum, where it held him up on high for everyone to see and honor. Today there is still a huge bronze statue on that spot to commemorate the dream.[73]

In both the dream's setup and within the dream itself, Severus portrayed himself not as a usurper (which he arguably was) but as a subject loyal to Pertinax. In real life, Severus had sworn his oath of allegiance to Pertinax without hesitation. Likewise, in the dream, Severus made no move to capture or tame the horse (a metaphor for the empire), even when it had thrown Pertinax from its back. Severus's message comes through Herodian's redaction quite clearly: Severus did not choose to be emperor; Rome chose him. Herodian was careful to give background information on the location of the dream so that his Greek audience might understand the significance of the setting: it took place in the forum, the place in which the *populus Romanus* met during the Republic. A Roman audience, however, would require no such explanation, for it would understand the historical significance of the setting and its accompanying implied claims. By locating Pertinax's fall and Severus's rise to power there, within the former *comitium*, the emperor specifically referred to his acceptance by the *populus Romanus.* If the people were permitted to choose their own leader—and in the emperor's dream, the people did just that in the form of the horse—the people would select Severus. Thus envisioned, the erection of an equestrian statue of Severus on the spot was as much about honoring the *populus Romanus* for its support of his reign as it was about Severus's *felicitas* and divine approbation.

Dio records other dreams that also situate Severus within Rome's history and landscape. Topographical references to monuments and the Forum Romanum within the dreams suggest that Severus intended these to be especially meaningful for the *populus Romanus,* likely in an attempt to win its support.[74]

> The signs that had led Severus to hope for the imperial power were as follows. When he was admitted to the Senate, he dreamed that he was suckled by a she-wolf just as Romulus had been. When he was about to marry Julia, Faustina, the wife of Marcus, prepared their nuptial chamber in the temple of Venus near the palace.[75]

These dreams and signs allowed Severus not only to claim divine favor and approval for his reign, but also to construct for himself an emphatically Roman heritage. This construction is most obvious in the first of these dreams, as it ties the emperor to the physical city of Rome and its earliest founders. By positioning himself shoulder to shoulder with Romulus, suckling at the teat of the she-wolf, Severus claimed a place for himself within the heart of Rome and its origins. His presence at the founding of Rome quieted questions regarding his Roman ethnicity, and the emperor's dream invited its audience to envision Severus's rise to power as fateful and as divinely approved as that of the first king of Rome. Furthermore, the dream associated Severus with the prominent and revered landmark, the *ficus ruminalis.* This fig tree, under which the she-wolf nursed the founders of Rome, remained an important and honored location within the city. I explore more fully the dream of marrying Julia Domna in chapter 3, but it is sufficient to note here that Severus again emphasized his place within the physical topography of Rome by locating his wedding chamber in the Temple of Venus near the imperial palace. In doing so, he connects himself to Augustus, whose progenetrix was Venus; this interpretation is supported by the further clarification of the Temple's location near the imperial palace. These dreams thus strengthen the connection between Severus and the physical location of the city while propping up Severus's claims to Roman ethnicity and Rome's foundation. In this way, Severus promoted himself as more Roman than the families of the bluest blood, as a leader whose elevation was foretold and foreordained while at the same time claiming and courting the support of the *populus Romanus*.

Roman Matrona, Mother, and Protectress

Severus used the images of Julia Domna in Severan propaganda aimed at the *populus Romanus* to link him with important Roman historical monuments and figures. This in turn reinforced Severus's claims of Roman ethnicity. She also received attention as the physical manifestation of the legitimate relationship between her husband and her sons so necessary for the establishment of Severus's dynasty. Although the first of these purposes seems counterintuitive—for how could a Syrian woman provide Roman roots to her African husband?—Severus and the administration cleverly played upon Julia Domna's status as wife and mother to accomplish both aims. Evidence of these strategies is found in literary sources, as well as in monuments, coinage, and inscriptions that originated with the imperial administration.

In Dio's redaction of the dream in which Severus was about to marry Julia Domna, Faustina the Younger acted as their *pronuba* (loosely translated as matron of honor). Because the mother of the bride was the usual choice for a *pronuba*, Severus invited his audience to see Julia Domna as the daughter of Faustina.[76] In doing so, the emperor strengthened the connection between the two empresses beyond their sharing of the Mater Castrorum title. This totally fictional relationship between dead and living empresses further underlines the connection that Severus advertised between his own family and the Antonines. The location of the marital chamber in the dream was also significant because, according to Cassius Dio, this same temple housed the silver statues of Marcus Aurelius and Faustina the Younger, which by decree of the Senate were erected beside an altar. It was upon this altar, Dio explains, that Roman brides and their intended husbands offered sacrifices.[77] This dream scenario unfolded in the shadow of the former Antonine (now Antonine-Severan) imperial palace, where the family connections claimed in the dream came to fruition.

None of these topographical subtleties would have been lost on a Roman reader. Furthermore, if readers of Severus's autobiography envisioned their wedding ceremony, they would likely envision Severus and Julia Domna clasping hands in *iunctio dextrarum*, the typical pose in numismatic types of married couples or those in the process of marrying. The viewer would have been most familiar with these types from Antonine coinage and thus might have envisioned the well-advertised domestic bliss of Antoninus Pius and Faustina the Elder joined in *iunctio dextrarum* (e.g., figure 12). Or perhaps the visualization would evoke more recent issues of Faustina the Younger that featured her and Marcus clasping hands with her own mother and *pronuba* presiding (see figure 8). The emperor's dream marriage to Julia Domna allowed for rich and meaningful connections to the landscape, imagery, and history of Rome, as well as to the last generation of the beloved Antonines.

Severus also used Julia Domna to bolster his claims for divine favor by advertising her horoscope:

> After he had lost his wife, Severus wished to marry another woman and he made inquiries about the horoscopes of marriageable women, being a very skilled astrologer himself; and when he learned that there was a woman in Syria whose horoscope predicted that she would wed a king (I mean Julia, of course), he sought her for his wife, and through the mediation of his friends secured her. By her, presently, he became a father.[78]

This report casts Julia Domna as the darling of fate. It was written in the stars that she was to become empress and she awaited only the right man, the one destined by the fates to become emperor. By seeking out his foreordained bride, Severus proactively fulfilled his destiny to become emperor; he does not do so with the ambition of a usurper, but as a pious man obedient to the will of Fate and the gods. When he married Julia Domna, according to the logic of this anecdote, Severus proved his *felicitas,* that he was beloved and chosen by the gods.[79]

Severus sought to sink deeper roots into Roman soil by evoking Julia Domna's name in his restoration of prominent monuments and rituals. The imperial administration erected three extant inscriptions in Rome that mention her name, but none of them call attention to Julia Domna's Syrian heritage. Instead, they present her as an ideal Roman *matrona* and they connect her, and by extension her husband and sons, to revered ancient cults. In the fragments of the *cippae* that describe the events of the Ludi Saeculares of 204, Julia Domna is recorded as leading 109 other *matres familiae* in prayers, feasting, and ceremonial dances.[80] The *sellisternia* they performed honored the important feminine deities Juno Regina and Diana.[81] Her participation was surely meant to associate the empress with Juno Regina—and likely also Diana Lucifera—both of whom figure prominently on her reverse coin types during this period.

Julia Domna also finds mention on the dedicatory inscription of what was most likely the Temple of Fortuna Muliebris, located about four miles southwest of Rome on the Via Latina.[82] This historically significant building was particularly associated with women and their contribution to the state. Livy reported that the temple initially honored the women who saved the city from the warrior-turned-traitor Coriolanus. He had abandoned Rome because of his unjust treatment at the hands of the tribunes and popular assemblies. Refusing to parley with his former friends and countrymen, he attacked his homeland with the help of Volscan troops, the very tribes he had earlier helped to conquer. His mother Veturia, his wife Volumnia, and a group of *matronae* received permission from the Senate to meet with the angry hero and to beg his mercy. Livy's Veturia shamed her son for his treachery and as a result, he abandoned his siege. The *matronae* wanted to celebrate their victory by creating a temple to Fortuna Muliebris. Livy's account couches the building and dedication of the temple in terms that reveal the tensions between the sexes in Augustan Rome:

> Roman husbands lived at that time [i.e., in Coriolanus's day] free from the disparagement of others' glory and did not begrudge their wives their praise or their monument; a temple to the Fortuna Muliebris was built and dedicated.[83]

Presumably, Livy felt this was worthy of mention because, during his own lifetime, husbands did begrudge their wives glory or praise. The observation takes on new significance when we examine the inscription that likely graced the temple:

> Livia, daughter of Drusus, wife [of Caesar Augustus built? restored? this] | The Imperatores Caesares Severus and Anto[ninus Augusti and most noble Geta] | and Julia Augusta, mother of the Aug[usti restored [it]].[84]

For some scholars, Livia places more emphasis on her role as the daughter of Drusus than as the wife of Augustus by mentioning her father before her husband. They see Livia's self-identification as exerting a degree of independence from Augustus and his agenda.[85] The juxtaposition between Julia Domna and Livia calls attention to the difference in how the two imperial women are portrayed.[86] Julia Domna appears almost as an afterthought, tacked on behind the titles of Severus and his sons. Given the interpretation attached to Livia's daring inscription, however, this placement was likely intentional. Severus literally contextuated Julia Domna within the family on the dedicatory inscription in order to emphasize her *pietas* and obedience: in the inscription above, Julia Domna is a mother, one whose role was to support the dynastic claims of her husband, not compete with him for prominence as Livia seems to have done with her inscription.

Severus did not as a rule omit Julia Domna's Mater Castrorum from inscriptions. It appears in another tabula found in the Forum of Trajan, where Julia Domna is listed as the sole dedicator:

> Julia Augusta, Mother of the Augusti and of the Camp restored [this] for the matrons. Sabina Augusta [erected? this] for the *matronae*.[87]

The context for the inscription has been lost, but on the basis of the designation of *matronis* as the dedicatees, scholars have speculated that the inscription originally graced either the *conventus matronarum* or the *senaculum mulierum*.[88] The inscription need not have been attached to a building however. It could just as easily have been placed on a statue base or monument.[89] While Gorrie obliquely suggested that this dedication might be interpreted as initiated by the empress and thus an expression of Julia Domna's autonomy, Lusnia convincingly illustrates how all Severus's building projects fit into an overall agenda of legitimizing the dynasty; the restoration of Sabina's project was likely not the empress's pet project. Why, then, was Julia Domna's name allowed to stand alone on this inscription but not on the Temple of Fortuna Muliebris? I suspect that Severus understood Livia's inscription in much the same way as Purcell interpreted it. It was a show of independence that Severus would not afford his wife. In the case of Sabina's inscription, however, there was no such challenge to Hadrian's authority. Likewise, because this project seemed not to challenge Severus's authority, he permitted the use of her full complement of titles and to be sole dedicator.

Imperial coinage provides the most abundant and explicit testimonies of the advertisement of Julia Domna and her maternal imagery. Severus employed well-known and novel associations with Roman goddesses and virtues in the empress's types and legends. For instance, VESTA was common legend on earlier empresses' coinage; Severus used this legend as well as the novel VESTA SACRA and VESTA MATER types on Julia Domna's coinage. The last of these allowed him to link the foundational Roman cult of Vesta with the maternal imagery of his wife.[90] This association is in line with the larger mission of Severus's imperial propaganda: he had gone out of his way to depict himself as a native of the city of Rome.[91] The connection of Julia Domna to the cult of Vesta simply provided his wife and sons the same sort of native connections that he sought for himself.[92]

The Roman mint produced celebrations of Julia Domna's literal maternity on her own and Severus's reverses (e.g., figure 5).[93] Most of the empress's coinage, however, highlighted metaphorical motherhood, associating Julia Domna with maternal goddesses such as the Magna Mater, Isis, Diana Lucifera, Ceres, and Vesta Mater.[94] These associations suggested divine patronage but also broadened the maternal purview of the empress to universal proportions. The motivations behind such associations are often best explained as dynastic in nature. Thus Julia Domna's legend, SAECVLI FELICITAS, though similar to Severus's aureus explored earlier (see figure 1), features a new type. Here the empress is associated with Isis, who is depicted with one foot on a ship's prow while nursing the infant Horus (see figure 13). The fecundity behind *felicitas* may well point to Julia Domna's actual role as a mother because Isis is depicted nursing Horus. On the other hand, Isis was a patron goddess for sailors, a point celebrated by the prow upon which her foot rests. The goddess's naval aspect combined with her Egyptian origins may indicate that the *fecunditas* had something to do with Severus's revamping of the *annona*.[95]

The association with prominent mother goddesses becomes far more insistent between 196 and 211. Though the Magna Mater had appeared in the earliest phase of Julia Domna's coinage, from 209, the Magna Mater and the empress were equated. It was in this year that Geta was promoted from Caesar to Augustus, a promotion that earned Julia Domna a new title totally her own: Mater Augustorum (usually abbreviated as MATER AVGG in coinage and inscriptions). Accompanying this legend are types of the Magna Mater enthroned upon a lion-drawn carriage, resting her left arm on a tympanum and extending a branch in her right hand (see figure 6). The nominative case of the legend implies that this is no mere association with the mother goddess. It is assimilation and equation: Julia Domna *is* the Magna Mater. The legend simply labels and identifies the Magna Mater type as the Mater Augustorum. In identifying Julia Domna as the Magna Mater whom Lucretius had dubbed *magna deum mater/materque ferarum et nostri genetrix*, the empress takes on a sort of universal motherhood.[96] With this type, the imperial administration promoted the empress as the mother of all living things. Contemporaries surely saw these statements as hyperbolic. Even the best-advertised empresses—Faustina the Elder and the Younger—were never equated to the Great Mother. I call this insistence on the universal mother of Julia Domna "maternal megalomania." Yet it was not Julia Domna who was megalomaniacal; it was her husband in his determination to use his wife's images to help him legitimate himself and his sons.

Imperial coinage also touted qualities highly valued in Roman women, *pietas* and *pudicitia*. Numismatists often equate the personifications of these virtues with the emperor or empress advertised on the obverse. In some of these types, Pudicitia/Julia Domna is portrayed *en face* (see figure 14), an unusual numismatic aesthetic that was quite rare before the Severans. In the hundreds of coin types minted by Severus and Caracalla, I have found roughly seventy such types, all but one associated with Julia Domna.[97] *En face* depictions violate the expectations of the viewer and demand special attention to the message transmitted through the legend; it seems likely that the administration would use this aesthetic in order to drive home the most important messages to its audiences. The *en face* Pudicitia/Julia Domna, who arrests the viewer's gaze, parallels the aesthetic depiction of Julia Domna on Severus's SAECVLI FELICITAS aureus discussed earlier (see figure 1). In Severus's aureus, Julia Domna seems to speak directly to the viewer, to engage him and to personally guarantee the legend's message with her direct and unflinching gaze. In the Pudicitia/Julia Domna type, we again encounter the direct gaze of the empress, but the effect is less startling because we see her entire figure, not just a bust; her gaze, though less intense, nonetheless demands her viewers' attention. It seems likely that the administration reserved *en face* depictions for the most urgent and important messages. The historical realities behind the decision to render Pudicitia/Julia Domna in this fashion might have been to squelch rumors of the empress's sexual impropriety. The administration needed a response to Plautianus's charges of infidelity, which undermined the legitimacy of Severus's carefully constructed naturalism of his nascent dynasty.[98] If Julia Domna were unfaithful, her sons' legitimacy would be called into question, and Severus would simply not stand for his dynasty to be undermined.[99]

Thus far, the evidence I have examined for maternal imagery on Julia Domna's coins comes from *Roman Imperial Coinage*.[100] Yet catalogues are ineffective in indicating the frequency of particular types or their circulation. A look at the Via Tritone hoard shows some interesting patterns, though the same caveats concerning this hoard apply here as mentioned above.[101] Of the 828 denarii of this hoard, seventy-five coins feature Julia Domna on the obverse, the vast majority minted under Severus. The most frequent coin types and legends are listed in Table 2.2.

The most notable examples of the administration's claims for Julia Domna's universal motherhood are less pronounced here than they appear in coin catalogs. Types advertising the empress's sons on the reverse do not make an appearance on this list, nor do the ideologically loaded types MATER AVGG, which featured the Magna Mater, nor MAT(ER) AVGG(VSTORUM) MAT(ER) SEN(ATVS) M(ATER) PATR(IAE), the significance of which will be discussed in chapter 3. Instead, the emphasis of the types in this hoard is on *pietas*, *felicitas*, and *pudicitia*.[102] In other words, the maternal megalomania evident in the types listed in the *RIC* were not so well circulated in Rome as were the types and legends that emphasized the empress's calming, maternal influence over her family. True, types of important maternal goddess are represented here, but the qualities

TABLE 2.2
Most frequent types of Julia Domna minted at Rome under Severus in the Via Tritone hoard

Number	Date	RIC	Reverse legend	Reverse type
6	193–196	536	VENERI VICTR	Venus, naked to waist, standing r., holding apple and palm, resting l. elbow on column
7	196–211	551	FELICITAS	Felicitas standing l., holding caduceus and scepter
5	196–211	556	HILARITAS	Hilaritas standing l., holding long palm and cornucopiae
10	196–211	574	PIETAS PVBLICA	Pietas, veiled, standing front, head l., by altar, raising both hands
4	196–211	575	PVDICITIA	Pudicitia *en face,* veiled, seated l., head front, holding scepter in l. hand, r. hand on breast
4	196–211	576	PVDICITIA	Pudicitia veiled, seated l., r. hand on breast, l. arm resting on chair
4	196–211	580	VENVS FELIX	Venus standing front, head l., holding apple, drawing drapery from her shoulder
4	196–211	587	VESTAE SANCTAE	Vesta standing l., holding patera and scepter

required of her literal motherhood—*pietas*, *felicitas*, and *pudicitia*—are far more pronounced.

Severus, the *Populus Romanus*, and the *Collegia*

Overall, the nonelite inhabitants of Rome had every reason to be happy with Severus's reign. He put the city's inhabitants to work by mounting an ambitious building program, the likes of which had not been seen since Domitian.[103] Severus also saw to the city's entertainment with various games, the most notable of which celebrated his decennalia and the impressive Ludi Saeculares in 204.[104] These special occasions were particularly ideologically significant events for Severus:

> On the occasion of the tenth anniversary of his coming to power, Severus presented to the entire populace that received the grain dole and to all the soldiers of the Praetorian Guard gold pieces equal in number to the years of his reign. He prided himself especially on this largess, and in fact, no emperor had ever before given so much to the whole population at once. The total amount spent for the purpose was two hundred million sesteres.[105]

One of the most important ways in which Severus won over the *populus Romanus* was by facilitating the importation of staples into the city, expanding the *annona* to include rations of olive oil, and distributing liberalities. The *HA* reports that he took control of the *annona* and managed it admirably, even adding a regular distribution of olive oil.[106] This was a welcome change from the *annona*'s poor management under Commodus that led to riots and the eventual execution of Cleander. Severus thus revamped it considerably. His love of efficiency was never so apparent as in the *Historia Augusta*'s testimony that, at his death, the emperor left a seven-year surplus of grain for all of Italy. Stores of olive oil were also abundant, as archaeological evidence confirms.[107] Though Lo Cascio sees the *HA* claims as wildly exaggerated, he does not deny that the *annona* was more efficiently run and was likely to have "almost entirely covered the urban population's need of the staple food commodity."[108]

Severus sought the help of a number of *collegia* in order to manage successfully the feeding of the city. Though modern scholars still debate the nature and activities of *collegia*, there can be no doubt of their prominence in Severan Rome and their interest in imperial favor. *Collegia* provided opportunities for the Roman elite to become patrons and to lavish favors upon nonelite groups of Rome. The offices and honors of these voluntary associations provided their nonelite members with their own sort of *cursus honorum*, in which they might express excellence and obtain social distinction. The *collegia* as a whole, not simply the ones named after professions, constituted an important component of the local economy. These groups received gifts from patrons for their maintenance, but these funds could be used for other activities, including dining and funeral funds. As Liu has recently demonstrated, endowments from patrons might have also served as sources of credit, which the *collegia* might use to loan to others. Some *collegia* even evolved into financial organizations in their own right.[109]

Inscriptional evidence reveals a wide range of *collegia* in Rome and Ostia, many of whom erected honors for Severus and his family.[110] The motivations behind these honorary inscriptions were likely to thank the imperial family for granted or anticipated favors. When one considers the building activities that Severans sponsored in Rome, it comes as little surprise that the *collegia* of the timber workers honored the entire imperial family.[111] The *collegium fabrum tignariorum* (construction workers) were more specific, honoring only Caracalla.[112] *Collegia* associated with supplying the city with food staples and grain for the *annona* also erected inscriptions honoring the imperial family, specifically the bankers and cattle merchants (*argentarii* and *boarii*) salt carriers (*saccarii salarii*), and the *acceptatores* and *terrarii*.[113] The fishermen and divers (*piscatores et urinatores*) thanked their equestrian patron because he had set up statues of Caracalla and Julia Domna, as well as given the *collegium* money and distributed *sportula* to its members.[114] Such dedications reveal the honor and glory wealthy elites enjoyed from patronage and reflects the wisdom of these same upper classes in honoring the imperial family. The patron gains the honor and respect of his social inferiors while courting the favor of the imperial family who, if pleased with this gift, could reward the elite patron in a variety of ways. Elites erected other dedications to honor *collegia* members. M. Aelius Rusticus probably saw the power that the measuring officials of the dole wielded and thus honored them in an inscription he erected.[115]

The *collegia* of the *argentarii* and *boarii* additionally erected a fascinating monument in honor of the imperial family in 203. The Porta Argentarii (also known as the Arch of the Argentarii) was erected in the Forum Boarium and likely served as an entrance into the *schola* of the *collegia*.[116] When describing this monument, scholars have rightly seen echoes of Severan propaganda in its inscription, panels, and ornamentation. The *argentarii* and *boarii* were likely motivated by the expected or received benefits from Severus's attention to the economic life of the city and thus were careful to produce a monument that would be pleasing to the imperial family.[117] The monument exhibits fine attention to detail and an attempt to keep up with changes in the imperial family, as the scars of two different of *damnationes memoriae* demonstrate. Scholars are nearly unanimous in reconstructing the participants of the central panels. The western pier featured Caracalla in the act of sacrificing (still extant), while the two figures that were beside him were his father-in-law Plautianus and his wife, Plautilla, now the victims of *damnatio memoriae*; the eastern pier depicted Severus, veiled and sacrificing, and Julia Domna with her hand raised in a hieratic gesture and holding a caduceus with the no-longer-extant Geta standing beside her (see figure 15). Though most scholars agree that all the family members in the central panels were mentioned in the original text of the inscription, the debate continues as to when particular titles were awarded, especially Julia Domna's titles Mater Senatus and Mater Patriae.[118] Scholars also disagree regarding the identity of the worn figures on the front exterior frieze of the monument. Some argue for the consuls for 203 (one of whom was also the urban praefect), while others see the patrons of the *collegia* as a more likely choice.[119]

Desnier and Elsner made an important step in the interpretation of this monument, however, when they shifted the focus from the Severans to the *collegia*. For Desnier, the monument was as much about the *collegia* as it was about the imperial family. The monument's location and rich ornamentation, he argued, proved the importance of the *collegia* within the city's economic life. In order to erect the monument, the *collegia* would have had to receive the support of the urban praefect and perhaps even negotiated in person with the imperial family. He interprets the supposed error in the tense of the monument's inscription, *invehent* instead of *invehunt,* as intentional because it implies a future commitment to the life of the city. Elsner capitalized upon Desnier's shift of emphasis and took it a step further by examining the monument from the perspective of the viewer instead of seeing it as a mine of Severan propaganda. This approach allowed Elsner to consider the sacrifices depicted upon the Porta Argentarii as "a visual construction of religious narrative."[120] He recognized that the monument attempted to control the viewer's interpretation of sacrifice by ignoring the melee of state sacrifice and focusing on the key actors. The central panels invite the viewer to participate in the sacrifice, particularly through Julia Domna's *en face* depiction that seems to reach out to the viewer and draw her into the historical moment of the sacrifice. While the viewer is of course free to dissent from the reality presented in the panels, it is nonetheless apparent that the monument attempts to control her perceptions. Elsner cannily notes that the panel depicting the *boarii* in the lower register of the exterior west pier moves in the opposite direction of the other panels, which center upon victory and sacrifice of the imperial family. He interprets this opposing movement as an invitation to read the monument as the viewer wishes. For Elsner, the monument argues against a univocal reading because it "actively encourages a range of readings across surfaces, around piers horizontally and up and down them vertically. It uses narrative, generalized allusive symbolism and iconism emphasised by frontally; and it challenges the viewer by arranging its decor to affirm an intersecting and not always unitary thematics."[121]

To Desnier's and Elsner's excellent analysis of the monument, I add only a few comments. The Porta Argentarii is unique in that it represents not one response to Severan propaganda, but several over the course of the years. Its evolving response is particularly apparent in the various stages of the inscription that faithfully echoed whatever the imperial administration was saying at the time. I agree with Desnier that the future tense of the inscription was intentional and that such a reading reinforces the willingness of the *collegia* to modify the inscription to accommodate the evolution of Severan propaganda. The *argentarii* and *boarii* were committed not only to their role in the city, but also to the imperial family, and as the demands of the imperial family changed, so, too, would they. The lower register in the exterior friezes also echoes the interaction between the *collegia* and the imperial family. The frieze on the west pier depicts a cowherd, apparently driving his cattle in a direction opposite to the one in which the soldiers move with the Parthian captives. The frieze on the east pier was built into the wall of San Giorgio in Velabro and is not accessible, but I believe that the answering panel on the east pier likely depicted the activities of the *argentarii.* With these panels, the *boarii* and *argentarii* wrote themselves into the larger narrative of the Severan dynasty. True, the majority of the monument's baroque ornamentation calls attention to the martial and sacrificial activities of the imperial family, but this official narrative is literally built upon the backs of the *boarii* (and presumably the *argentarii*). The placement of these panels suggests that the success of the imperial family would have been impossible without the foundational support of these groups.

And Julia Domna?

An analysis of the roughly twenty inscriptions I found that specifically mention Julia Domna in Rome indicates that the imperial administration was not always consistent in using all the titles the empress had been officially awarded (Table 2.3). Out of the three inscriptions that can be securely attributed to Severus's administration, only two employ all of Julia Domna's official titles.

The seventeen other inscriptions that mention Julia Domna in Rome were erected between 195 and 218 by a variety of dedicators: professional *collegia* (four); religious *collegia* (one); priests or priesthoods (three); freedmen (six); and paramilitary groups—that is, *vigiles* and the *princeps Castrorum perigrinorum* (three).[122] As mentioned previously, the *argentarii* and *boarii* scrupulously maintained Julia Domna's official titles, though probably not so much to honor her as to respond to the emperors' new propaganda apparent in the various *damnationes memoriae.* This was clearly not true of all the inscriptions erected by the *collegia.* Neither the fullers nor the *piscatores-urinatores* referred to the empress's official titles, while the *kalatores* (sacrificial assistants?) did. The entry for the *kalatores* inscription in the *CIL* described it as a large marble tablet that likely occupied the *schola* of the *kalatores.* The expense incurred with this inscription is borne out by the care taken to get the titles of the entire family correct. The two inscriptions erected by the Arval Brethren that mention Julia Domna are inconsistent; they did not use the Mater Castrorum title while Severus lived, but after his death, the full complement of titles appeared, though in an unusual order and with a misspelling of *Felicis*: IVLIAE AVG(VSTAE) / PIAE FELI<C=O>(IS) M(ATRIS) IMP(ERATORIS) ANTONINI AVG(VSTI) N(OSTRI) SENATVS CASTRORVM ET PATRIAE. Regarding the Arval Brethren's senatorial status, see chapter 3. The six inscriptions erected by freedmen are a mixed bag: three employ all of Julia Domna's official titles, while three do not. Finally, the Fourth

TABLE 2.3

Inscriptions from Rome mentioning Julia Domna

Date	Citation and location	Donor	Julia Domna's titles
198–209	*CIL* 06 00883 Temple of Fortuna Muliebris	imperial family	[IVLIA] AVG(VSTAE) MATER AVG[G(VSTORVM)[1,2]
204	*CIL* 06 32328-9 Pighi IV. 9–V.30.8 Ludi Saeculares	administration	[IVLIAE] AVG(VSTAE) MATRI CASTROR(VM) [IVLIA AVG(VSTA)] / CONIVGE IM[P(ERATORIS)]; IVLIAE AVG(VSTAE) MATRI CASTROR(VM) CON[IVGI AVG(VSTI)
209–211	*CIL* 06 00997 = *ILS* 00324 Conventus Matronarum?	administration	IVLIA AVG(VSTA) MATER AVGG (VSTORVM) ET CASTRORVM[3]
209–	*CIL* 06 01040	Collegium of Dendrophoroi	IVLIAE AV[G(VSTAE) MATRIS AVGG(VSTORVM) ET CASTRORVM ET SENATVS ET PATRIAE] NB: Most of these titles have been reconstructed
203; 205? 213?	*CIL* 06 01035[4]	Collegia of Argentarii, negotiantes boarii	IVLIAE AVG(VSTAE) MATRI AVG(VSTI) N(OSTRI) ET CASTRORVM ET SENATVS ET PATRIAE[5]
212–218	*CIL* 06 01872	Collegia of Piscatores and Urinatores	IVL(IAE) / AVGVSTAE DOMINAE NOSTR(AE) (NB: Caracalla is called domini nostri here)[2]
212–218	*CIL* 06 09428 = Waltzing 01034	Collegium of Fullers	EX INDVLGENTIA . . . [ET IVLIAE AVGVS]TAE MATRIS AVG(VSTI) ET CAS[TRORVM][2]
195–211	*CIL* 06 36932 = *AE* 1900 00086 statue bases	Collegium of Kalatores	(IV)LIAE AVG(VSTAE) / (M)ATRI AVG[G?] (VSTORVM) ET / (C)ASTRORVM
198–209	*CIL* 06 30763 = *CIL* 06 00419 = *Merlat* 00234	Priests of Jupiter Optimius Maximus Dolichenus?	IVLIAE AVG(VSTAE) MAT(RIS) / AVG<G?>(VSTI) ET <<CASTRORVM SENATVS ET POPVLI ROMANI>>; these titles probably replaced Plautilla's name and titles[5]
214	*CIL* 06 02103 = *AFA* s. cic ff. = *ALI* 00272	priests/colleges, Arval Brothern	IVLIAE AVG(VSTAE)[2]
Post-212	*CIL* 06 02086 = *CIL* 06 32380 = *CFA* 00080 = *CFA* 00099a = *D* 00451 = *D* 05030 = *D* 05041 = *AE* 1998 00113	Arval Brothern	IVLIAE AVG(VSTAE) / PIAE FELI<C=O>(IS) M(ATRIS) IMP(ERATORIS) ANTONINI AVG(VSTI) N(OSTRI) SENATVS CASTRORVM ET PATRIAE
Post-195	*CIL* 06 02149	freedman? watermen?[6]	IVLIAE AV/G(VSTAE) DOMINAE / MATRI CAS(TRORVM)[3]
198–209	*CIL* 06 30760 = *CIL* 06 00410 = Merlat 00191-CCID 00372	imperial freedmen Semnus lib avgg	ET / IVLIAE AVG(VSTAE) ET S(ENATVS) P(OPVLI)Q(VE) R(OMANI)[2]

continued

TABLE 2.3 *(cont.)*

Date	Citation and location	Donor	Julia Domna's titles
198–209	*CIL* 06 00180 = = *D* 03703	imperial freedman Antoninus Proximus a libellis	/ ET IVLIAE AVG(VSTAE) MATRIS / AVGG(VSTORVM) [[[ET PLAVTILLAE AVG(VSTAE)]]][2]
213	*CIL* 06 40646 = *AE* 1965 00338 = *AE* 1983 00028	imperial freedmen and *conliberti*	[IVLIAE AVG(VSTAE) MATRIS] SENATVS ET CA[STRORVM ET PAT]/[RIAE ET MATRIS] DOMINI NOSTR[I ANTONINI AVG(VSTI)]
212–218	*CIL* 06 36935 = *AE* 1911 00178	(imperial?) freedmen Acilius, Stephanus	IVLIAE AVG(VSTAE) PIAE / FE[LICI] MATRI / IMP(ERATORIS) M(ARCI) A] VRELI / ANTO[NINI] PII AVG(VSTI) E[T] CASTR[OR(VM) E]T SENATV[S] / ET [PAT]RIAE[3]
212–218	*CIL* 06 01071 = *CIL* 06 36883 = *CIL* 06, 40641	imperial freedman Eutychus	IVL (I) AE [AVG (VSTAE)] / MATRI(S) AVG(VSTI) ET CASTROR[VM] / TOTIVSQVE DOMVS DIVIN[AE][2]
198–205	*CIL* 06 00220 = *D* 02163 = *AE* 2004 +00181	Cohort IV Vigiles, who received the dole	IVLIAE AVG(VSTAE) MATRI AVGG(VSTORVM) ET CASTROR(VM)[5]
March 15, 212	*CIL* 06 01063 = *CIL* 05 00429, 017 = *D* 02178	Cohort I Vigiles	ET IVLIAE AVG(VSTAE) MATRI AVG(VSTORVM) N(OSTRORVM) [ET] / CASTRORVM[2]
209–212, post-212	*CIL* 06 00354 = *D* 02218 = *SIRIS* 00370 =	Princeps Castrorum Peregrinorum, L. Ceius Privatus	ET / IVLIAE AVG(VSTA) MATRIS AVG(VSTI) <<N(OSTRI)>> / ET / CASTROR(VM) ET <<SENATVS ET PATRIAE>>[5]

[1] NB: The stone breaks off after "mater Aug" and could have included the Mater Castrorum title.
[2] Official titles awarded to Julia Domna at the erection of the inscription were not used.
[3] Julia Domna was the only Severan family member mentioned.
[4] Titles given here are what are currently visible on the arch, not the originals. Cf. *CIL* 06 01035 (p 3071, 3777, 4318, 4340) = *CIL* 06 31232 = *D* 00426 = Caro 00034 = *AE* 1993 00118 = *AE* 2002 +00148 = *AE* 2005 00183 for reconstructions of original text.
[5] Inscription modified in order to conform to *damnationes memoriae*.
[6] Williams 1902, 295n2–3 inexplicably identifies these dedicators as "watermen." *CIL* 06 02149: IVLIAE AV/G(VSTAE) DOMINAE / MATRI CAS(TRORVM) / IT(VS) IM(M)VNIS.

Cohort of the Vigiles erected two inscriptions and, like the freedmen, one is consistent with Julia Domna's official titles and the other is not. Notably, the correct inscription bears the scars of the *damnationes memoriae* of Plautianus, Plautilla, and Geta. This inscription was carefully prepared and maintained to keep up with changes in the Severan *domus*. The same is true of an inscription erected by the Princeps Castrorum Peregrinorum, L. Ceius Privatus, who added SENATVS ET PATRIAE after Julia Domna's titles in order fill the space left by the erasure of Plautilla's titles.

Perhaps the most interesting and certainly the most unique piece of evidence concerning the reception of Julia Domna by the populations of Rome comes in the form of an articulated ivory doll found in the tomb of the Vestal Virgin Cossinia (see figure 16). The "ancient Barbie," as she was dubbed in the Italian press, has the hairstyle and features that look much like Julia Domna's, particularly from the period of Severus's reign.[123] The clothing on the doll, if there was any, has long since decayed, but gold jewelry seems to say something of both the owner and the model for the doll. The owner was likely from a wealthy family and, being a Vestal Virgin, she certainly knew the most powerful and prestigious people in the empire, though this may not have been true when she first acquired the doll. The depiction of the empress is certainly not the maternal figure that the imperial administration so vigorously promoted in Rome. As other commentators have noted, it does not invite or teach its owner to cuddle or nurture it. Instead, the bracelets and sophisticated coiffure bespeak an elegant lifestyle in which beauty and poise are the most valued qualities.[124] The doll offers little evidence that she has or will bear, suckle, or nurture children, as we see on the bronze coinage of Julia Domna that was distributed in Rome (see figure 3). This doll—if it was meant to be a representation of Julia Domna—bears no trace of the empress to whom the administration ascribed universal motherhood. Instead, it allows us to see Julia Domna through contemporary female eyes. The girl (and eventually woman) who owned this doll was a Vestal Virgin, someone who rubbed shoulders with powerful men and women. She might well be the elusive woman whose response to imperial portraiture Wood once wondered about.[125] She certainly would have seen images of the empress on the coins and monuments liberally scattered through Rome and would have heard stories about Julia Domna's maternity. Yet the image of the empress that she held in her hands was not any of these. This doll might well have emboldened Cossinia to embody those other qualities of Julia Domna that were not touted by the imperial administration, the ones perhaps whispered about and even admired by upper-class *matronae.* And that would be its own kind of response to—and rejection of—maternal megalomania.

But What Does It All Mean?

The literary, numismatic, and epigraphic evidence suggests that Severus was keen to present himself to the populations at Rome as an emperor who enjoyed the approval of the gods, who had secured peace through the prosecution of war, and who—most importantly—attended to the needs of the city's inhabitants. Literary accounts of Severus's interactions with the *populus Romanus* show a willingness of the emperor's subjects to accept his constructed realities, with no sign of resistance against him or his policies during his reign. He achieved the consensus of the populations at Rome not just through the usual methods of liberalities, games, and shows, but also through the reorganization and expansion of the *annona* as well as with his building projects. Inscriptional evidence supports the literary accounts in this regard.

In his negotiations with the *populus Romanus*, Severus used Julia Domna in an effort to bolster his claims for divine approval, to bind him more closely to the Antonine dynasty of which he claimed to be a part, and to provide legitimacy for the accession of his sons to the *statio principis*. The Roman population's response to these claims was mixed at best. The inscriptions honoring the empress with current titles were likely intended to help maintain relations with the emperor, the locus of power. On the other hand, even the imperial administration sometimes failed to ensure that its own inscriptions included the empress's full titles. In the eyes of the *populus Romanus* and the imperial administration itself, the empress was far less powerful and influential than she has been traditionally depicted in scholarship. I base this interpretation not only on the lack of response to the maternal megalomania that the imperial administration was promoting, but also on the inaccuracy and apparent carelessness with which she and her titles were recorded in official and dedicatory inscriptions. Contrast this to the manner in which Severus, his sons, and their titles are handled. The *populus Romanus* might have appreciated Julia Domna for her sophisticated, elegant manners and lifestyle, but I see no evidence that she was considered to be either powerful herself, or employed as a conduit to the real source of power, the emperor.

CHAPTER 3

Mater Senatus, Mater Patriae

Julia Domna as Senatorial Savior

Despite the community-building experience of his first *adventus*, the pageantry of Pertinax's funeral, and his conciliatory address to the Senate, Severus failed to achieve the consensus he so desired. Cassius Dio records the Senate's critique:

> There were many things that Severus did that were not to our liking and he was blamed for making the city turbulent through the presence of so many troops and for burdening the state by his excessive expenditures of money, and most of all for placing his hope of safety in the strength of his army rather than in the Senate's good will.[1]

By contrast, Pliny's *Panegyricus* provides a tidy summation of how the ideal emperor should prioritize his relationship with these audiences. He should be a competent general who balanced the affection of his soldiers with rigorous discipline; a generous administrator who weighed financial responsibility against the physical, religious, and entertainment needs of the city and empire; an unpretentious statesman who prioritized the advice of the Senate over *familia*, including imperial women, slaves, and freedmen.[2] Modern scholars help to round out the picture. Paterson's analysis of the imperial court gives voice to what is unspoken in the literary sources: a good emperor ought to minimize the differences between himself and his senatorial corulers, specifically by recognizing the structures and organizations by which senators distinguished themselves from other classes and each other by promoting through the senatorial *cursus* in an orderly and predictable manner.[3] The type of respect that an *optimus princeps* displayed for his senatorial colleagues would allow individual senators to act as powerful patrons in their hometowns and provinces by providing services, building projects, and advancement for their talented countrymen.

By this definition, Septimius Severus was no *optimus princeps*.[4] Although every emperor walked a fine line between the demands and expectations of his various subjects, maintaining a balance between the military and Senate was particularly problematic for Severus. After all, he had seized power only because some of the legions had supported his bid. However enlightened he wished to be in treating the Senate as his coruler when he entered Rome in 193, his troops provided a sobering reminder that they, too, must be appeased. As Severus addressed the members of the Senate promising respect and cooperation, his troops surrounded the Curia and threatened their commander until he agreed to pay a donative equal to that Octavian paid his soldiers upon returning from Actium.[5] For senators, such a display proved that Severus was at the mercy of the military and that he would tolerate their bad behavior at the expense of his relationship with the Senate. As the opening passage illustrates, the Senate closely monitored the relationships that the emperor shared with the *populus Romanus* and with the military, and used them as a measure of the quality of their own relationship with Severus. The emperor's perceived inability to control his troops and his lavish expenditures designed to buy the goodwill of the populations of Rome left the Senate out in the cold. In this zero-sum game, any favor that the emperor showed to his troops, the *populus Romanus*, a Praetorian praefect or, most horrifically, imperial women or freedmen, meant that the Senate lost. Their only real revenge was to plot against him—and to their detriment, some did—or to write histories in order to condemn the memory of the tyrant.

Over the course of his reign, Severus offended senatorial sensibilities in other ways, as well. Cassius Dio outlined the ideal relationship between an emperor, the Senate, equestrians, armies, and provincial cities in the speech he placed in the mouth of Maecenas to Octavian. He asserted the importance for maintaining the distinction between the *ordines* through promotion along a predictable and established *cursus*.[6] Severus, on the other hand, did not respect the senatorial *cursus* or the niceties of court by allowing senators to feel that they were corulers rather than subjects. In his court, senators found themselves jockeying for prominent positions with equestrians who served as an alternate source of administrative and military leadership. Even Cassius Dio recognized that there were real benefits to the emperor in employing the equestrians in administrative duties.[7] Severus must have seen the equestrians as more attractive partners in government. They offered expertise similar to senatorial candidates' without the senatorial sense of entitlement. As an outsider, he would have appreciated a less-snobbish attitude concerning his birth, accent, and the like.[8] The downside of preferring equestrians, however, was that their promotion to senatorial positions threatened the *dignitas* of the Senate.[9] The meteoric rise of Severus's friend and Praetorian praefect, C. Fulvius Plautianus, typified Severus's flagrant disrespect for these niceties and threatened the Senate's sense of priority and entitlement.

Severus had awarded him the equestrian consular *ornamenta* earlier, not an uncommon honor, but then degraded the dignity of the consular designation by equating Plautianus's *ornamenta* with the actual completion of the duties of the office.[10] Plautianus made matters worse by mixing honors: "not only did he wear the broad strip on his toga, but he wore a sword at his side and on his one person wore the badge of every rank."[11]

Keenly aware of the tensions between the rivals for his attentions, Severus employed the images of Julia Domna to help him negotiate the individual ideologies he created with these populations. The earliest advertisement of the empress was understated but respectful; these coin types recognized Julia Domna as the consort of Severus but claimed for her no unprecedented domains. Once Severus had defeated Pescennius Niger, however, Julia Domna's advertisement, especially as the Mater Castrorum, became ubiquitous in inscriptions, dedications, sculpture, and numismatic portraits. Like Marcus Aurelius, Severus exploited maternal images in legitimating his nascent dynasty; Faustina the Younger, as detailed in the introduction and chapter 1, was the model upon which he based Julia Domna's advertisement. Yet Antonine maternal propaganda seemed to have succeeded in winning the Senate's support for Commodus's succession, whereas Severan maternal propaganda fell flat with the same audience, perhaps because the Senate had lived through Commodus and now knew to be suspicious of inherited succession.[12] If this were the case, the Severan propaganda that endowed Julia Domna with the similar maternal qualities and associated her with mother goddesses must have been distasteful for the Senate. And it must have been downright offensive to see Severus equate Julia Domna with the Magna Mater (see figure 6). Whereas Antonine familial advertisement seemed to have created a sense of inclusion and importance in the viewer, Severan propaganda was heavier handed. The elevated claims found in Julia Domna's advertisement constituted a sort of maternal megalomania of which Severus's Senate wanted no part. Throughout his reign, the Senate remained mute concerning the empress, refusing to engage in the sort of dynastic ideology that would elevate her stature and thereby endorse the emperor's dynastic plans. When Severus died, however, the Senate could no longer afford to ignore the empress. She alone wielded influence that both young emperors respected. It was only when the Senate had need of Julia Domna as an ally and peacemaker that it responded to the maternal propaganda. Quite abruptly and perhaps unexpectedly, the Senate embraced the empress's maternal imagery, but only on its own terms. It awarded Julia Domna a bevy of extraordinary maternal titles, yet unlike the administration's earlier, extravagant claims that equated the empress with the Magna Mater, these titles were emphatically mortal in their scope and reminded the empress of her duties in maintaining peace and harmony in her household and, by extension, the empire. After Caracalla murdered his brother and thus exposed Julia Domna's inability to control her son's savagery, however, a new ideology had to be negotiated.

Cassius Dio and the Senate readjusted the empress's image to suit these new circumstances. While Caracalla was campaigning (or gallivanting, as Dio would characterize it) in the East, Julia Domna was left in Antioch to assume the duties of the civil half of the empire. She conscientiously answered the emperor's correspondence in Latin and Greek and met with senatorial and provincial delegations. She was the philosopher, much like Marcus Aurelius, who did her duty despite the personal tragedies she suffered. This assessment of the empress was valid for the Senate, however, only so long as she had a contemptible foil in Caracalla. After his murder in 217, Julia Domna's image required radical adjustment; it would no longer do for the Senate to esteem the empress and allow her to maneuver outside the gender restrictions imposed upon other women. At Dio's hand, the philosophical civil servant was transformed overnight into a megalomaniacal Semiramis as Julia Domna plotted to seize the imperial office for herself. In order to fully appreciate how the image of the empress was manipulated in these negotiations, however, one must consider the history between imperial women and the Senate.

Natural Rivals: Imperial Women and the Senate

Certain targets of imperial propaganda, especially the Senate, tended to be more hostile toward imperial women and their presumed influence in state affairs than others. In his examination of the court culture in the early empire, Paterson envisions the proximity that imperial women had to the emperor as a source of tension within the court. Their proximity upset the structure of *cursus honorum*, whereby men of talent or high birth were promoted through a series of offices in an orderly fashion. With each step on the *cursus*, an individual moved closer to the office and to the emperor, thus becoming more powerful and more influential. The rituals created in the court not only honored the emperor but also placed checks upon his autocratic power. They created a sense of order and accountability that the aristocracy craved and helped to stave off the perceived arbitrariness of monarchic rule.[13] Because of their intimate access to the emperor, however, individuals who were normally powerless because of their gender or social status could gain far more influence with the emperor than those climbing the *cursus*. Among these individuals were freedmen, slaves, and of course imperial women.[14]

The undefined and extraconstitutional power of an empress was a special source of anxiety and fascination for her contemporaries. Though her husband, sons, and subjects publicly celebrated an empress for her merciful and pious interventions, competitors for the emperor's ear slandered her for interfering in masculine spheres of governing. Senatorial authors like Pliny and Tacitus drew from their contemporary discourse on gender to disparage the political contributions of imperial women and to paint the emperors who listened to them as weak, ineffectual, and unworthy of his office.[15] The connection between the success of an emperor in the eyes of his senatorial courtiers and his ability to control his women is explicitly stated in Pliny's *Panegyricus.*

> Splendid though it is to keep yourself unspotted by any form of vice, it is even more so to do the same for the members of your family . . . *Many distinguished men have been dishonored by an ill-considered choice of wife or weakness in not getting rid of her; thus their fame abroad was damaged by their loss of reputation at home and their relative failure as husbands denied them complete success as citizens.* But your own wife contributes to your honor and glory as a supreme model of the ancient virtues . . . How modest she is in her attire, how moderate the number of her attendants, how unassuming when she walks abroad! *This is the work of her husband who has fashioned and formed her habits; there is glory enough for a wife in obedience* [emphasis mine].[16]

Pliny encouraged Trajan in his position of *optimus princeps* to maintain right order in his home and the empire by keeping his women under control and away from political matters. Pliny's objective here is laid bare by the fact that, as he praised the emperor's wife and sister for their obedience and modesty, he neglected to mention their names. This omission allowed Pliny to exhort and to praise by example while keeping the imperial women humble and unassuming, out of the public eye to prevent them from doing any real damage. Though his description of the empress is all compliments, Pliny's warning against influential women within the home or administration is a clarion call. History and contemporaries do not judge kindly emperors who fail to keep their women under control (*et ne maximi cives haberentur, hoc efficiebat, quod mariti minores erant*).

Passages of this type clearly reflect the anxiety and rivalry senators felt toward imperial women, and this anxiety grew considerably when the question of succession was raised. The Senate preferred adopted succession because it increased the chances of a truly experienced administrator and military man becoming *princeps*. Even better, adopted succession opened up the choice of successor to a wider field of applicants—that is, the ranks of the Senate. Pliny and Tacitus, for example, were heavily vested in adopted succession, and attempted to educate Trajan on the importance of choosing a successor from the ranks of the Senate. To warn the emperor against falling under his women's sway, the senators employed gender stereotypes and the authority of medical discourse to claim that right order could be maintained only when imperial women were excluded from decisions regarding succession. In doing so, they raised the specter of women's irrationality, bodily pollution, intellectual inferiority, and tendency toward tyranny.[17]

Contemporaries considered Pliny's *Panegyricus* a masterpiece, but until recently modern scholars have dismissed it, not least of all because of obsequiousness Pliny exhibits toward Trajan. A glance at his *Epistulae*, however, shows that Pliny certainly did not conceive of his speech in that fashion:

> I hoped in the first place to encourage our emperor in his virtues by a sincere tribute, and secondly, to show his successors what path to follow to win the same renown, not by offering instruction but by setting his example before them. *To proffer advice on the emperor's duties might be a noble enterprise, but it would be a heavy responsibility verging on insolence, whereas to praise an excellent ruler and thereby shine a beacon on the path posterity should follow would be equally effective without appearing presumptuous* [emphasis mine].[18]

Pliny clearly aimed to praise Trajan, and he insisted both within the *Panegyricus* and here that his praises were sincere (*veris laudibus*). Just as striking, however, is Pliny's admission that he hoped to shape imperial actions by his praise. The passage suggests that this praise was meant for future emperors, but turning to the *Panegyricus* it becomes apparent that Pliny also attempted to shine a beacon on the path that Trajan himself should follow, especially with regard to succession.

Early on in his speech, Pliny praises Trajan's adopted succession: "Oh, novel and unprecedented path to the Principate!"[19] Trajan had no apparent familial connection to his predecessor, Nerva. Such a succession was unprecedented, but circumstances had forced Nerva's hand. With his authority compromised and facing revolts by the Praetorian Guard, Nerva adopted the experienced and respected governor of Upper Germany as his son and heir, hoping the move might buy him the support of the legions stationed on the borders. From the security of hindsight, Pliny expressed his relief and pleasure with Nerva's choice:

> There was no blood relationship between the two of you, no obligation except that you were both the very best of men—one worthy of choosing and the other of being chosen. And thus you were adopted not as any before you, *not to please a wife*. It was not as a stepfather that he adopted you, but as your emperor. The divine Nerva was made your father in the same sense that he was the father of us all. It is not right to accept a son in any other way if he is recognized by the emperor. If you are about to transfer to a successor the Senate and people of Rome, the army, the provinces and allies, would you pluck him *from your wife's lap*? Would you seek the heir of such supreme power from within your household? Wouldn't you cast your eye over the entire state and would you think this one nearest to you was the one you would choose to be most like the gods? *Since your successor is destined to rule over all the people, he must be chosen from among them all.* Indeed, no related heir can satisfy you when you are appointing not a *master* for your household of *little slaves*, but a *princeps* for the *citizens of Rome* [emphasis mine].[20]

Behind Pliny's enthusiasm for Nerva's decision and Trajan's accession lies an explicit criticism of dynasties. The derogatory references to imperial women are perhaps not as evident in English as they are in Latin, but when placed in a cultural context, they exude disgust for the women's bodies as the source of inherited successors. Pliny's rhetoric is fueled by the traditional Roman dichotomy of the house as the realm of the woman and the state as the domain of the man. The association of women with *domus* and men with *res publica* is an old one. Good Roman *matronae*, as Livy's Lucretia reminds us, stayed close to home, caring for their families and children and spinning late into the night.[21] Aside from a handful of public religious festivals and priesthoods, Roman women were assigned the *res privata*. Conversely, Roman men carried responsibility for the *res publica*, voting in assemblies, waging war, and pursuing legal matters. Though there are numerous violations of this simplistic division of male/public and female/private spaces in literature and history, these exceptions prove the rule. The folly of mixing the two realms is nowhere more dangerous than in the imperial household. It was in the best interests of the emperor to maintain the illusion that he did not allow women to influence his actions in the public, masculine-coded spheres.[22] For Pliny, because the future emperor must see to the welfare of the entire state and not just of his household, he must look through the entire state (*totam per civitatem*) to find his successor. Significantly, Pliny distinguished the public as being the realm of senators, soldiers, and provincials and allies (*senatum populumque Romanum, exercitus provincias socios*) as opposed to the private sphere, which were occupied by a *dominus* and *servuli*. The affairs of state were characterized by equality and political participation, while the home was a place of tyranny, occupied only by an overlord and not simply slaves (*servi*), but slavelings (*servuli*). In the opposition of liberty/state and tyranny/home, Pliny implies that imperial women are tyrants in the home, and that their tyranny violates the "natural" order of the sexes in which men dominate women. Should such a situation be limited to the confines of a home, it is perhaps tolerable because it affects relatively few people. Should this tyranny of women be extended to the state, however, citizens would quickly be reduced to little slaves (*servuli*).

Pliny's choice of words suggests that women by their very nature are unsuited to make decisions regarding the *res publica*. His language is replete with images invoking the capriciousness of women and the nasty feminine juices associated with parturition and menstruation. The Julio-Claudians, and specifically Augustus and Claudius, chose stepsons as successors from a wife's lap (*e sinu uxoris*) and in order to please a wife (*in gratiam uxoris*), two phrases that raise the specter of qualities long associated with women in medical treatises. In identifying the source of inherited succession as the *e sinu uxoris,* Pliny yokes dynasty with the pollution inherent in a woman's body. One meaning of the *sinus* of a woman—her lap—is the place for nursing and coddling a child. But in this instance, Pliny uses the word to invoke revulsion for the pollution associated with childbirth and menstruation.[23] Ancient medical writers employed the humoral system and divided cosmic elements (water, earth, air, fire), bodily fluids (blood, phlegm, yellow and black bile), and human characteristics in essentially masculine and feminine terms. Composed of the baser elements, water and earth, women were thus cool and wet, whereas men were hot and dry, being composed of fire and air. This basic division worked in tandem with the mind/body division found in Hippocratic and Greek philosophical writings and allowed medical writers to associate women with the flesh. In short, women were thought to be carnal, lusty, and emotional because they were composed of baser elements. Men, on the other hand, were ethereal; theirs was the realm of the mind. As the medical writers portrayed it, these traits were endowed by nature; they were descriptive of the sexes.[24] Pliny sullies the practice of inherited succession by invoking the revulsion of parturition and the toxicity of menstrual blood. Future emperors who spring *e sinu uxoris* quite literally have the taint of a woman's pollution upon them. By contrast, successors selected from the state/Senate are pure, rational, and cerebral. The state—a rational and pollution-free institution—is the source of an adopted heir and, as such, the adoption is rational, masculine, and destined to be successful.

Pliny denigrated the role of women in succession not just to flatter Trajan about his novel path to the principate. He also hoped to coax the emperor into choosing a successor by adoption, the same way Trajan had been chosen. This shift from narration into persuasion is marked by Pliny's use of second-person singular verbs in the subjunctive—*accipias, quaeras, circumferas tibi, existimes, inveneris.* Pliny assumed an instructor's role in lecturing the emperor about the proper manner of selecting a successor. He employed the third-person verb *debet* and a passive verb, as if to instruct without being too presumptuous by using an imperative: "The future emperor must be chosen by all men from all men" (*imperaturus omnibus eligi debet ex omnibus*).[25]

Pliny's instructions to the emperor and his denigration of imperial women in succession matters were attempts to shore up the dignity and power of the Senate in maintaining its influence with the emperor. He was not alone in this effort. His contemporary and fellow senator Tacitus also contributed to the cause. From the time of Nero's death, the Senate had been responsible for the appointment of only two emperors, Galba and Nerva. Both these emperors had chosen their successors in accordance with Pliny's recommendation as outlined above, looking outside their homes and, not coincidentally, finding their ideal candidates in the Senate. In his *Historiae*, Tacitus relates how Galba came to choose Piso as his successor. Galba's situation was remarkably similar to Nerva's when he adopted Trajan: the Senate promoted him to the principate after the death of Nero, who was an excellent example of the dangers of inherited succession. Like Nerva, Galba also faced military insurrection and had to act quickly to bolster his position. Instead of choosing a proven military man as Nerva did, however, he adopted a man who, outside of an impressive pedigree, had little to recommend him. It is therefore justifiable to hear echoes of Nerva's words in Galba's speech to his successor Piso:

> If the vast body of the empire were able to stand on its own and be free without a master, I would be a worthy man to reinstitute the Republic. But the need for a master has come and my old age is able to confer no more upon the people than a good successor, nor can your youth offer more than a good *princeps.* Under the reigns of Tiberius, Gaius and Claudius, we were the birthright, as it were, of one family. The choice that we now instigate will be our substitute for liberty. The Julio-Claudian dynasty has ended and adoption will discover the worthiest successor. Indeed, to be bred and born to the principate is mere chance and is not considered more than that. But adoption is entirely a faculty

of good judgment. When you wish to choose the successor, unanimous opinion designates the man.[26]

Tacitus's Galba dwells upon male rationality in the selection of a successor; a properly chosen emperor would in some measure mean liberty for the Senate. If rationality were the guiding principle, the consensus of the citizenry must necessarily follow. Like Pliny, Tacitus's Galba uses second-person singular verbs (*velis*) when he instructs Piso in selecting a successor. Adoptive successions are entirely a function of the mind and rationality (*iudicum integrum*) and can allow the Senate a degree of liberty, but inherited succession is the result of nothing but dumb luck (*fortuitum*). Strikingly, this capriciousness of fortune is a result of birth and breeding, by definition, the realm of a woman.

These passages illustrate the type of rhetoric senators used to discredit the influence of imperial women. When women stayed out of the political process, they were praised to the heavens as the unnamed Plotina and Marciana were in the *Panegyricus*. But when women meddled in political affairs, especially matters of succession, they were subject to the greatest censure.[27] Though senatorial frustration might have been vented in the direction of imperial women, the real object of their ire was the emperor, who would allow himself to fall under a woman's influence rather than prefer the guidance of the masculine, rational, and cerebral senators.

Severus's Senate

The Senate that Severus faced in 193 had suffered one humiliation after another under Commodus, and though it had a slight respite under Pertinax, Didius Julianus soon after bullied the Senate, too. Cassius Dio complained that Commodus had relied too heavily upon his Praetorian praefects, who had proved corrupt and ambitious. When such men governed the empire, there was little room for the Senate to act as an advisory committee, as it had under the "good" emperors. About all that was left to the Senate under Commodus was to award the emperor his titles. As Dio bitterly complained, even that right was taken away, because Commodus instructed the Senate as to which titles he wanted.[28]

Despite these humiliations, Severus's Senate was far from moribund, nor were its powers limited to bestowing titles and honors at the behest of the emperor. Severus's Senate offered valuable contributions to ruling the empire. Senators governed most of the provinces, and Severus wooed them to keep them loyal.

Severus's Senate was a diverse group both ethnically and financially. As early as the mid-second century, the Senate's membership began to mirror the ethnic diversity of the empire. By Severus's day, it was composed of about one thousand senators. Roughly 40 percent were Italian, and the remainder came from the East, Africa, Gaul, and Spain.[29] Emperors had systematically supplemented these numbers by promoting talented equestrians from the provinces.[30] Senators had to meet a minimal level of prosperity that was apparently a struggle for some families to maintain generation after generation. Though senators varied significantly with respect to their wealth and economic interests, they nonetheless shared a common education and social perspective. *Paideia* dictated that all civil servants had similar rhetorical training, and each senator was cosmopolitan because his duties required travel throughout the empire to fulfill administrative obligations. Senators maintained close ties to their hometowns and, as Pliny demonstrated, poured money back into the infrastructure and networked tirelessly to promote their own countrymen through the government—activities that helped build the senators' sense of importance and prestige. Like emperors, senators had to walk a tightrope, though of a different sort: they balanced the demands of their relationship with the emperor with those of their clients. Their sense of worth, as Hoffer demonstrated with Pliny the Younger, not only came from the recognition and benefits bestowed by the emperor but from what they themselves could give. Senators competed constantly against one another in wealth, in literary pursuits, in patronage, and for the emperor's ear. They could easily slip into "a vicious circle of envy, detraction and revenge," but if a few banded together, "they eagerly and selflessly help[ed] each other and they incidentally derive[d] benefit for themselves as a side-effect." While this struggle for prominence occurred between senators, each was mindful to strike a balance in his approach to the emperor, to navigate between being a faithful follower and maintaining a sense of autonomy as his colleague.[31]

For Severus, the most meaningful distinction between senators in 193 was which contender for the principate they supported.[32] Some factions were active even before Severus arrived in Rome. Supporters of Niger, for instance, had organized public demonstrations calling upon their champion to rise up and throw out Julianus before Severus had reached Rome.[33] Severus was keenly aware that the supporters of Didius Julianus, Pescennius Niger, and Clodius Albinus had to be wooed, marginalized, or removed. Except in the case of a few close supporters of Julianus who could not be rehabilitated, Severus's default strategy was to woo. He seems to have had some success, too, at least in the beginning.

Cassius Dio was one of these senators and he serves as a fine case study for exploring the shifting nature of senators' opinions of the emperor. Dio's father had a distinguished career in the Senate and brought Dio to Rome in his late teens, in 180. Dio's education was likely initiated in his hometown, Nicaea, perhaps followed by stints with prominent sophists in the great cities of Asia Minor such as Smyrna or Ephesus. Though both Dio and his father maintained close ties to Bithynia and referred to it as their home, they owned land in Capua, as well. Dio's description of the humiliations of the Senate under Commodus are couched in the first-person plural, a point that led Millar to place his adlection to the Senate around 192.[34]

In his judgments of the emperors he served under, Dio was biting toward Commodus, basically respectful concerning Pertinax, and outraged by Julianus. His assessment of Severus is more complicated. He wrote a flattering account of the *omina imperii* that foretold Severus's rise to power, likely completed and sent to Severus by 196 or 197. Though Severus thanked him for the pamphlet, it seems to have done little for fast-tracking Dio's career, which Millar suggests might have motivated the senator to put pen to paper; Dio did not become a suffect consul until 205 or 206.[35] In making Dio wait for this distinction, Severus seemed to be respecting the senatorial *cursus*. Though Dio might not have been thrilled with his regular promotion through the *cursus*, his colleagues would certainly have appreciated Severus's restraint in not promoting a young man simply because he wrote a sycophantic pamphlet.

For some scholars, the positive tone Dio adopts for the earliest years of Severus's reign are snippets from the pamphlet that were recycled for his later, much larger, and more critical history.[36] Despite his occasional criticisms, Dio's assessment of Severus's reign is mostly positive. Whether the optimism he felt for Severus predated the reigns of Caracalla and Elagabalus is uncertain; Severus might have appeared better in comparison with those who succeeded him. Some time around 205, Dio became an *amicus* of Severus and began to attend meetings of the imperial *concilium*, though notably we hear nothing of Dio actively participating in discussion or debate in the Curia.[37] The lack of discussion may be because the few scenes in which Dio places action in the Senate are incredibly tense: surely no one would want to call attention to himself while the witness who ultimately implicated Baebius Marcellinus in the conspiracy of the proconsul of Asia cast an eye over the Senate's members.[38]

It seems that Dio's opinion of the emperor was shaped by how he had been treated.[39] This does not necessarily mean that Dio was only positive when Severus was generous toward him: Millar and Harrington suggested that the *omina* pamphlet was intended to get on the better side of Severus returning from Lugdunum, burning for vengeance.[40] For me, the hope that pervades Dio's description of Severus's first *adventus* at least sounds genuine, though it is difficult to assess whether it really was sincere, or whether Dio was just a very convincing sophist. Surely, Dio's private assessments of Severus were less favorable than his public ones, but that does not mean that either was necessarily negative. Still, it would be satisfying to know answers to certain questions regarding the historian: To what degree was Dio disingenuous in that pamphlet? Did he really believe that Severus was divinely elected to become emperor? Does the occasional criticism of the emperor imply that he had changed his mind about Severus's divine election? These questions are difficult to answer because Dio engaged in the treacherous activity of speaking to a tyrant. Just as treacherous, however, was the ground upon which Severus trod. The senators he faced in 193 were experts on how to speak to the powerful, whereas Severus was powerful for the first time. As a former senator himself, he must have been cognizant that the senators' claims of sincerity, such as those that Pliny constantly touted, should be taken with a grain (or maybe several bags) of salt.[41]

Creating Consensus in the Senate: Wooing, Marginalizing, and Exterminating

Literary sources disagree about Septimius Severus's first encounter with the Senate upon seizing Rome in 193.[42] Cassius Dio's account features a Severus signaling his willingness to cooperate with the Senate and treat it with respect:

> He advanced as far as the gates on horseback, but there he changed to civilian attire and proceeded on foot. The entire army, both infantry and cavalry, accompanied him in full armor ...The soldiers too stood out conspicuous in their armor as they moved about like participants in some holiday procession; and finally, we [senators] were walking in state.[43]

The emperor's self-presentation was a significant visual indicator of his attitude toward the Senate and populace of Rome. When he exchanged his military attire for the toga at the city gate, Severus presented himself as ruler rather than a conquering warrior.[44] He walked among citizens and cast himself in the traditional role of a first among equals, rather than conquering general. According to Dio, the emperor then honored the Senate by proceeding immediately to the Curia. He addressed the senators with respect and was careful to align himself to the good and just emperors of old. Like Marcus Aurelius, he made an oath that no senator should be killed.[45] This oath was an important moment for building ideology: Severus signaled to the Senate by both his dress and his manner the esteem in which he intended to hold it. As a tangible demonstration of the co-operation that Severus wished for in his relationship with the Senate, he invited senators to participate in the spectacle of the procession. Even more attractive to a senatorial audience, Dio's Severus had embraced an adopted succession by appointing Albinus as his Caesar before he arrived in Rome. The Severus that Dio presented in this passage emerged from the Curia that day with the potential to become another *optimus princeps*. What remains unclear is whether Severus's motive for claiming an adopted succession was to woo the Senate, disarm Albinus, or both. The complete absence of Severus's wife and children from the ideology-building spectacles of his entrance into Rome and Pertinax's funeral could mean one of two things: either Dio took Severus at his word regarding adopted succession and, like Pliny, chose to play down the emperor's family in state affairs, or Severus kept his own family away from the action in order to maintain his deception.

Cassius Dio's optimism abruptly changed with his report of a number of telling senatorial criticisms. Significantly, most of the Senate's complaints concerned Severus's management of the army. They faulted him for spending too much money on the troops and allowing soldiers to make the city turbulent, but more seriously, Severus placed "his hope of safety in the strength of his army rather than in the good will of his associates in the government."[46] Even these criticisms seem tame, however, when we realize that Dio passes over a meaningful event in the *adventus*: in that most important first speech before the Senate, Severus's soldiers surrounded the Curia and demanded the same donative that soldiers had received when Octavian returned from Actium.[47]

The *adventus* in the *Historia Augusta* is of quite a different stamp from Dio's. There, Severus marched into Rome and went straight to the palace, apparently in full military regalia while his soldiers seized and occupied temples, porticos, and even houses on the Palatine, perhaps even the homes of senators. Only on the next day did he address the Senate after his soldiers had already looted and threatened the citizens:

> Severus's entry inspired both hate and fear, for the soldiers seized goods they did not pay for and threatened to lay the city waste. On the next day, accompanied not only by armed soldiers but also by a body of armed friends, Severus appeared before the Senate, and there, in the Senate house, he gave his reasons for assuming the imperial power, alleging in defense thereof that men notorious for assassinating generals had been sent by Julianus to murder him. He

> secured also the passage of a senatorial decree to the effect that the emperor should not be permitted to put any senator to death without first consulting the Senate. But while he was still in the Curia, his soldiers, with threats of mutiny, demanded of the Senate ten thousand sesterces each, citing the precedent of those who had conducted Augustus Octavian to Rome and received a similar sum. And although Severus himself desired to repress them, he found himself unable; eventually, however, by giving them a bounty he managed to appease them and then sent them away.[48]

The Severus of the *Historia Augusta* was emphatically defensive and, as if tortured by a guilty conscious, he immediately began justifying his usurpation. One senses rather than actually hears the loathing he feels for the Senate because of its complicity with Didius Julianus and his alleged assassination attempt. Yet the account of the soldiers surrounding the Curia almost immediately undermined the righteous indignation of the new emperor. His own men unraveled Severus's attempts to paint himself as the pious avenger of Pertinax who swept into Rome to bring justice to a corrupt government. This military dictator was as bullied as the Senate; instead of commanding his men, they commanded him.

In the last extant source for Severus's *adventus*, Herodian painted the city's inhabitants as astounded by Severus's incredible daring and good luck (τοῖς οὕτω τετολμημένοις τε καὶ εὐτυχηθεῖσιν ἔργοις).[49] Significantly, there is no mention of the troops surrounding the Curia. After sacrificing at the temple of Jupiter, as was customary for the emperor, Severus proceeded to the palace.

> On the next day, he went down to the Senate house where he made a very moderate and promising speech in the assembly, greeting them collectively and individually. He told them that he had come to avenge the murder of Pertinax and assured them that his reign would mark the reintroduction of senatorial rule. No man would be put to death or have his property confiscated without a trial; he would not tolerate informers; he would bring unlimited prosperity to his subjects; he intended to imitate Marcus's reign in every way; and he would assume not only the name but also the manner and approach of Pertinax.[50]

Herodian's Severus walked the middle ground between Cassius Dio's unpretentious *optimus princeps* and the indignant but morally questionable usurper of the *Historia Augusta*. This Severus emphasized the justice of his motivations to set things aright—to avenge the guilty, yes, but also to reintroduce senatorial rule. Noticeably, he mentioned Marcus, a nod to the respect with which he intended

Figure 1. RIC 4a.175, 114; ANS 1959.228.33. Aureus of Septimius Severus (201). Obverse: SEVERVS PIVS AVG P M TR P VIIII, bust facing right. Reverse: FELICITAS SAECVLI, bust of Julia Domna between those of Caracalla and Geta. Reproduced courtesy of the American Numismatic Society

Figure 2. RIC 4a.886, 211; BM 1992,0401.77 Dupondius of Julia Domna (196–211). Obverse: IVLIA [AVGVSTA], draped bust, facing right. Reverse: [PIETATI] AVGVSTAE SC, Julia Domna facing center between two male figures, Caracalla in military attire and Geta in a toga. She rests a hand on the shoulders of each. Together the men hold a globe. NB: The RIC identifies the male figures as Severus and Caracalla. © The Trustees of the British Museum

Figure 3. *RIC* 4a.844, 207; BM 1844,1015.35. Dupondius of Julia Domna (196–211). Reverse: FECVNDITAS SC, Julia Domna seated on throne right. She suckles one child in her arms while another child places his hand on her knee.

Figure 4. *RIC* 3.1711, 350. Sesterius of the divine Faustina the Younger (post-175). Obverse: DIVAE FAVSTINA PIAE. Bust facing right, veiled. Reverse: MATRI CASTRORVM S C, Faustina enthroned, facing left and holding a phoenix in her right hand. Before her are three military standards. Reproduced with permission of Classical Numismatic Group, Triton VIII, Lot 1030

Figure 5. *RIC* 4a.540, 166. Aureus of Julia Domna (196–211). Obverse: IVLIA AVGVSTA, bust facing right. Reverse: AETERNIT(AS) IMPERI, Caracalla laureate facing right, Geta with bare head facing left. Reproduced with permission of Numismatica Ars Classica NAC AG, Auction 24, 137

Figure 6. *RIC* 4a.562, 168. Aureus of Julia Domna (196–211). Obverse: IVLIA AVGVSTA, bust facing right. Reverse: MATER AVGG(VSTORUM), Julia Domna facing left in the guise of the Magna Mater seated upon a lion quadriga, holding a branch in the right hand. The nominative case of MATER suggests an equation of the Mater Augustorum with the Magna Mater. Reproduced with permission of Classical Numismatic Group, Triton VI, Lot 978

Figure 7. *RIC* 4a.381, 273. Aureus of Julia Domna (212–217). Obverse: IVLIA PIA FELIX AVG, bust facing right. Reverse: MAT(ER) AVGG(VSTORVM) MAT(ER) SEN(ATVS), M(ATER) PATRIAE, Julia facing left and enthroned, left hand holding a branch and scepter. Reproduced with permission of the Classical Numismatic Group, Triton VIII, Lot 1160

Figure 8. *RIC* 3.434, 81. Aureus of Marcus Aurelius (145–147). Obverse: AVRELIVS CAESAR AVG PII F COS II, Marcus Aurelius, head bare. Reverse: VOTA PVBLICA, Faustina the Younger and Marcus clasping right hands as Concordia the Elder looks on. NB: RIC identifies the center figure as Concordia. Reproduced courtesy of Numismatica Ars Classica

Figure 9. *RIC* 3.507a, 94; ANS 1944.100.49221. Denarius of Faustina the Younger (struck under Antoninus Pius). Obverse: FAVSTINAE AVG PII AVG FIL, diademed and draped bust, facing right. Reverse: PVDICITIA, S-C. Pudicitia standing left, holding out cloak in right hand. Reproduced courtesy of the American Numismatic Society

Figure 10. *RIC* 3.676, 268; ANS 1941.131.844. Denarius of Faustina the Younger (struck under Marcus Aurelius). Reverse: [FE]CVND(ITAS) AVGVSTAE, Faustina stands holding two infants in her arms while another two children reach up to her on either side. Reproduced courtesy of the American Numismatic Society

Figure 11. *RIC* 4a.574, 170. ANS 1957.172.1782. Denarius of Julia Domna (196–211). Reverse: PIETAS PVBLICA, Julia Domna standing left, raising hands before an altar. Reproduced courtesy of the American Numismatic Society

Figure 12. *RIC* 3.381b, 72; ANS 1944.100.48331. Denarius of the Divine Faustina I (post-140). Reverse: CONCORDIAE, Antoninus Pius togate on left, holding a scroll, Faustina holds a scepter on right. Reproduced courtesy of the American Numismatic Society

Figure 13. *RIC* 4a.577, 170; ANS 1944.100.51309. Denarius of Julia Domna (197–211). Reverse: SAECVLI FELICITAS, Isis, wearing polos on head, standing right, left foot on prow, suckling Horus; behind, a rudder rests against altar. Reproduced courtesy of the American Numismatic Society

Figure 14. *RIC* 4a.575, 170; ANS 1948.19.1515. Denarius of Julia Domna (197–211). Reverse: PVDICITIA, Julia Domna facing forward, seated on an elaborate throne, holding a scepter in her left hand while her right hand rests upon her breast. Reproduced courtesy of the American Numismatic Society

Figure 15. East panel of the Porta Argentarii. Severus sacrifices as Julia Domna stands by; an image of Geta originally occupied the empty space. Reproduced with permission from Art Resources

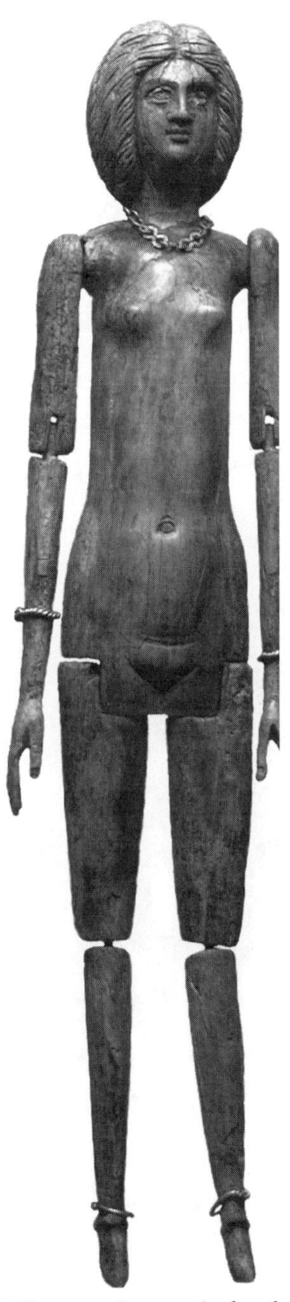

Figure 16. Ivory articulated doll found in the Tomb of the Vestal Virgin Cossinia. Photograph courtesy of the VRoma Project (www.vroma.org) with permission from the Ministero per i Beni e la Attività Culturali–Sporintendenza Speciale per i Beni Archeologici

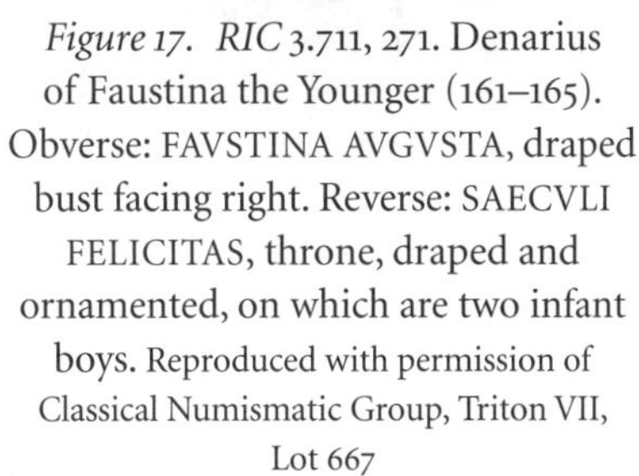

Figure 17. *RIC* 3.711, 271. Denarius of Faustina the Younger (161–165). Obverse: FAVSTINA AVGVSTA, draped bust facing right. Reverse: SAECVLI FELICITAS, throne, draped and ornamented, on which are two infant boys. Reproduced with permission of Classical Numismatic Group, Triton VII, Lot 667

Figure 18. With a direct glaze that recalls the Julia Domna featured on Roman coinage, this iconic American image exhorted civilians to enlist in the military. Poster by James Montgomery Flagg. "I Want You," 1917. Library of Congress Prints and Photographs Division, Washington, DC

Figure 19. Painted wooden tondo dated 199; Geta's image has been rubbed out. Staatliche Museen, Preussischer Kulturbesitz, Berlin, Germany. Reproduced with permission from Art Resources

Figure 20. ANS 1967.152.461; SNG von Aulock 2679, struck in Stratonicea. Obverse: Caracalla and Geta vis-à-vis, but later Geta was rubbed out, countermarked. Reverse: Zeus Panamaros on horseback. Reproduced courtesy of the American Numismatic Society

to treat the Senate. In his unwillingness to tolerate informers, the scourge of senators, this Severus presented himself as unpretentious and approachable as Pertinax had been. According to Herodian, the speech put most senatorial minds at rest, but some smelled a rat, especially the senior senators (πρεσβυτέρων) more familiar with Severus. He was, in their opinion, "a crafty man and a master of the art of contrivances" particularly adept at pretending whatever was necessary to get what he wanted in the end.[51]

Divergent reports of Severus's entrance into Rome might represent various senatorial interpretations of the events of 193. The *Historia Augusta* emphasized skeptical senatorial responses, while Cassius Dio's were more optimistic, at least at first, and Herodian's Senate was largely convinced except for the few older senators who had reservations. Still, it was probably clear to all senators that as the self-proclaimed avenger of Pertinax, Severus had some mopping up to do from the short time that Julianus was in office. In this arena, Severus departed from his wooing strategy and, as a good avenger should, executed the former supporters of Didius Julianus. This round of executions, however, seems not to have struck the Senate as particularly odious.[52] What seems to have been more troubling for Severus and the senators was his troops surrounding the Curia; it severely damaged the emperor's *auctoritas*, thus rendering problematic the ideology of cooperation that Severus had set out to create. He had one other chance at consensus before he marched east to face Niger, and he would make the most of it.

Severus was in Rome for less than thirty days, but the new emperor managed his time admirably, laying the foundation for a new ideology in which the Senate would play an important role in government and he would in turn offer respect for its contributions.[53] The funeral for Pertinax provided an excellent opportunity for the emperor to build ideology with several audiences by a show of universal consensus for his rule. He was keen to attach himself to the memory of Pertinax—a senatorial champion—in order to obtain a degree of legitimacy.[54] The spectacle of a grand imperial funeral allowed Severus to accomplish both goals at once. Represented at the funeral was every conceivable population: senatorial, equestrian, plebeian, male and female, young and old, living and dead, Roman, provincial and barbarian, human, divine, and animal. Particularly noteworthy, however, is the inclusion of the entire *ordo senatorius* as witnesses and participants in this transfer of power and prestige from Pertinax to Severus. In his description of the events leading to this marvelous display, Cassius Dio writes of Pertinax's wax effigy that was laid before the palace, kept cool by a comely youth with a peacock feather fan, and checked periodically by a physician. The senators, their wives, and Severus dressed in mourning garments, approached the effigy, and chanted together praises for the former emperor.[55]

Dio's inclusion of senatorial women taking part in the spectacle along with choruses of children is striking considering that we hear nothing of Severus's family in this most important ideology-building spectacle. They were surely on the minds of Severus and the Senate, however. Julia Domna was awarded the title Augusta at this time and began to appear, along with Clodius Albinus, on coinage minted at Rome. By advertising both, Severus promoted the impression that he was devoted to adopted succession. Still, for those who were paying attention, the choices for Julia Domna's reverses must have suggested dynasty building.[56]

Severus kept his promise to treat the Senate as corulers, at least initially, by communicating his activities in the East via written correspondence. Though his letters perhaps gave a sense of transparency, they did not foster senatorial independence or honest exchange, perhaps owing to the medium more than to intentions.[57] But it was surely with great interest that the Senate learned of Severus's treatment of those senators who had supported Niger's cause. According to Cassius Dio, the emperor did not execute these senators, but chose instead to seize their property in order to fill his empty coffers.[58] It is curious that Dio focused on the monetary advantage to the emperor but failed to mention that Severus neutralized these senators by depriving them of their property and thus disqualifying them for senatorial seats. Were Severus's confiscations more like punitive fines, rather than disqualifying conditions for a Senate post? One senator, Cassius Clemens, complained of these punishments to Severus, explaining that he was only concerned with getting rid of Julius Didianus and, in doing so, found himself in the faction of Niger, whom he continued to support after Didianus was killed. He reasoned that Severus would have been outraged had his men deserted him and so he should not be faulted for his continued support of Niger. Severus admired the man's frankness, Dio tells us, and he allowed him to retain half his property.[59] This anecdote suggests that Severus cleaned out the holdings of Niger's senatorial supporters, but it is not clear whether taking half of Clemens's estate allowed the senator to retain his position. Nonetheless, it demonstrates that Severus preferred marginalization of Niger's senatorial supporters to extermination. Severus's clemency, or at least his unwillingness to punish the innocent, was also apparent in his treatment of Niger's family. Severus kept Niger's children with him throughout the campaign, apparently treating them the same way he treated his own children. Upon Niger's defeat, Severus sent them into exile with their mother. Ultimately, however, he ordered both mother and children executed.[60] Again, Severus likely acted this way for political expediency and, considering the circumstances, it seems that Severus was as merciful as he could be without endangering his position.

Severus's attention next turned to punishing those buffer states that had supported Pescennius Niger, likely in an attempt to put a pretty face on the ugliness of civil war. Though the campaign accomplished little, Severus allowed his troops four different acclamations in 195, each surely accompanied by a donative. It was also in 195 that Severus began advertising his adoption into the Antonine clan, awarded Julia Domna the Mater Castrorum title, and promoted Caracalla to the position of Caesar while changing his name to reflect the new Antonine heritage. Severus sent home reports of his victories, which spurred the Senate to vote him both a triumph and a triumphal arch upon his return.[61] The news that reached Rome was strategically selective: though Severus did not assume victorious cognomina in Rome before the Senate had voted for them, inscriptions from several provinces already hailed Severus as Arabicus Adiabenicus or Parthicus Arabicus Parthicus Adiabenicus, at least a year before he returned to Rome.[62] Severus turned down the triumph offered to him by the Senate, worrying that it might be interpreted as a triumph over Niger rather than the Osrhoeni or the Adiabeni. Instead, he accepted the Arch of Septimius Severus.

The arch is a powerful expression of the shifting nature of the relationship between Severus and his Senate. Scholars examining it have typically viewed the arch either as an expression of Severan propaganda or as senatorial attempts to rein in the emperor's dominance.[63] If we take the *Tabula Siarensis* (in which the Senate voted to erect a triumphal arch to Germanicus) as our template, however, the *senatus consultum* that declared the Senate's wish to build an arch to Severus was probably quite specific about the content of the inscription; it would have listed the titles it had just awarded to the emperor for having reconquered lost territory, along with a recognition that he had brought peace to the state after a period of civil war.[64] Because the Senate that voted for the arch still had a significant contingent of Albinus supporters, the Senate's initial version might have celebrated Severus and Albinus in the same manner in which arches and titles were shared by Marcus and Lucius Verus.[65] The *senatus consultum* of 195, like that of 19 AD, most likely indicated that the arch should be decorated with ornaments of his victory, though these would not have been specified with much precision, and that a statue of the emperor in a triumphal chariot should be placed atop the attic. Furthermore, if the *senatus consultum* of 19 AD is any indication, the Senate likely designated the arch's location, material, and financing at public expense. Finally, and most importantly, the *senatus consultum* of 195 probably contained a similar phrase to that in the *senatus consultum* of 19 AD, inviting the emperor to accept that which was pleasing to him and allowing him to modify the gift as he desired. The arch's inscription today bears the scars of the ideological mauling that the relationship between the emperor and Senate suffered during the civil wars:

> The Senate and the People of Rome [dedicate this arch] to *the Best and Bravest Princes*, Imperator Caesar L. Septimius Severus Pertinax Augustus, son of Marcus, Father of his Country, Conqueror of the Arabians and Adiabeni, Pontifex Maximus, in the eleventh year of his tribunician power, hailed Imperator eleven times, thrice consul with proconsular power, and to the Imperator Caesar Marcus Aurelius Antoninus Augustus *Pius Felix*, son of Lucius, consul, proconsul, Father of his Country, in the sixth year of his tribunician power, for restoring the state and increasing the empire with evidence of their virtues at home and abroad [emphasis mine].[66]

There are several obvious differences between what the Senate would have proposed and what greets today's visitor to the forum. The expansive titles of Caracalla (Pius, Felix) and Severus (Optimi Fortissimique Principes) fill the gaps left from Geta's *damnatio memoriae* in 212. One can eliminate them from a reconstruction of the original inscription that was originally proposed by the Senate. Caracalla's Pater Patriae title is not otherwise testified before 199, while Severus's Parthicus Maximus title, also awarded in 199, is missing. The remaining inscription is a mishmash of titles that belong to both 195 and 203. Severus's titles Parthicus Arabicus and Parthicus Adiabenicus were those officially awarded by the Senate in August 195; noticeably absent, however, is Severus Caesar Clodius Albinus, whom the Senate likely intended to honor beside Severus. The reason for his absence is perhaps understandable, as there would have been a lag time between when the arch was proposed and completed. During that interval, Albinus would have lost his life at Lugdunum on February 19, 197. If the Senate approved honors for Albinus beside Severus on the arch in August 195, they may have done so unaware that Severus had promoted Caracalla to Caesar, probably in mid–195. By December of that year, however, it would have been hard to ignore, because medallions minted at Rome advertised Caracalla's new name and title. Scholars studying the inscriptions have interpreted the *tribunicia potestas* dates as an indication of the arch's completion and dedication in 203. According to Dio, Severus did not announce his adoption into Marcus's family until after he had eliminated Clodius Albinus in 197, though coinage minted in Rome in 195 names the emperor "Son of the Divine Marcus Pius."[67]

I believe the inscription's inconsistencies are the result of imperial-senatorial negotiations and of the selective nature of Severus's reports to the Senate. The war with Albinus, of course, made apparent Severus's plans for establishing his own dynasty, and so the inscription proposed by the Senate in 195 would have to be modified to take this into account as well. Severus kept his announcement of Caracalla's promotion to Caesar away from the ears of the Senate while he actively advertised it before the military and in provincial cities.[68] The adoption of Severus into Marcus's family, his promotion of Caracalla to Caesar, and calling him by Marcus's name must have raised red flags for an impending bid for dynasty. These political maneuvers undermine the adopted succession ideology that Severus had built with the Senate and threatened to reveal prematurely the emperor's plan to remove Albinus and establish his own dynasty. Rubin suggested that Albinus's supporters in the Senate, who fully recognized the dangers in the family propaganda that Severus selectively advertised, might have been behind the rather anemic M(ARCI). FIL(IO)ILIVS, instead of Severus's more robust DIVI M[ARCI] PII F[ilius] apparent on coinage.[69] The inscription that finally appeared on the arch reflected and distorted the original senatorial dedication: it paid slight homage to Severus's self-adoption, but because there was no original inclusion of Caracalla or Geta, their titles and *tribunicia potestas* dates reflected the date of the arch's completion. Significantly, there was still no mention of Julia Domna or her Mater Castrorum title, despite her military-sounding title or the precedence for women appearing on arches.[70] The Senate, after all, had limits on what it would endorse, and Julia Domna—and the family's close relationship with the military that she represented—was where the Senate drew the line.

The cracks in the imperial-senatorial ideology evident in the inscription of the arch were not based solely upon the question of succession. Another complicating factor was Severus's choice to appoint equestrian commanders for his three newly raised legions. To add insult to injury, Severus appointed an equestrian to govern the newly created province Syria-Coele.

It is not clear, however, that Severus really intended to oppress the Senate, for he needed the administrative support that senators provided.[71] It might be more accurate to say that the feelings of the Senate, at least during this period, were not particularly germane to Severus's agenda. As Southern puts it, "Severus did not set out to damage the Senate, though he curbed it by making it clear that he would have what he wanted with or without its co-operation . . . Severus did not rely on the Senate, but tolerated it; he did not pander to the senators' collective sense of importance."[72]

Severus's attitude in dealing with the senatorial supporters of Clodius Albinus was hardly surprising. On the eve of the emperor's showdown with his Caesar, some senators continued to communicate with Albinus and to keep his friends happy with appointments. Severus declared that anyone who communicated with Albinus would be considered a public enemy.[73] Even in the midst of the war, the Senate published praises for Clodius Celsinus, a native of Albinus's hometown and his kinsman, an act that angered Severus because he interpreted it as a show of support for Albinus. Fighting fire with fire, Severus demanded deification of his new brother, Commodus, a clear case of dueling ideologies.[74]

As Dio describes him, the Severus who returned to Rome after the defeat of Albinus had little in common with the Severus who courted the Senate in 193:

> While reading to the Senate a speech, in which he praised the severity and cruelty of Sulla, Marius and Augustus as a safer course and deprecated the mildness of Pompey and Caesar as having proved the ruin of those very men, he introduced a sort of defense of Commodus and inveighed against the Senate for dishonoring that emperor unjustly in view of the fact that the majority of its members lived worse lives . . . After reading this address, he released thirty-five prisoners who were charged with having sided with Albinus and behaved toward them as if they had not incurred any charge at all (they were among the foremost members of the Senate), but condemned to death twenty-nine other men.[75]

Severus's executions had effectively removed his rivals, but winning a military victory did not equate to winning the hearts and minds of civilians. Dio's distressed account depicts a Senate weakened and humiliated after the purge, yet Severus needed the Senate's support both in ruling and in securing the future of his dynasty. He faced a difficult task—to sell dynasty to a Senate that had long preferred adopted successors like Trajan, Antoninus Pius, and Marcus Aurelius to inherited successors such as Caligula, Nero, Domitian, and Commodus. He would turn to Antonine family propaganda in the hopes of rebuilding his relationship with the Senate.

Negotiating Dynasty: Maternal Megalomania and Senatorial Subversions

When Severus and his family returned to Rome in 201, he came ready to mend fences with the Senate. A coin type he issued during this time—only in gold—reflected his willingness to make peace. The reverse shows the emperor on horseback with a spear; the legend reads SPQR OPTIMO PRINC.[76] It seems doubtful that Severus ever intended to be the kind of emperor that Pliny describes in the *Panegyricus*. Instead, his objective was to appease the members of his ruling class in order to sell them on the idea of dynasty. Though his strategies paralleled those of Antoninus Pius and Marcus Aurelius—namely, using family connections to claim legitimacy for his heirs—Severus faced a much tougher audience than the Antonines had. The reign of Commodus reminded the Senate, if it needed any reminding, that inherited succession was disastrous for the state. If the son of someone so temperate and wise as Marcus Aurelius could turn out to be the megalomaniac of Dio's history, what would the sons of Severus be like once their father died?[77] Furthermore, Antonine imagery spoke to the senators of the day in a way that Severan imagery did not. The viewer of Faustina's coinage was treated to an intimate moment in the imperial family and could thus consider himself an honorary member of the *familia*. The primary difference was that Antoninus Pius and Marcus Aurelius already enjoyed the good will of the Senate, especially concerning the question of succession, because they themselves had been adopted into the family and the position. Faustina the Younger was the link that bound together these three generations of emperors.

Severus's Senate was not quite so gullible. Few senators were likely to trust an emperor who had claimed to prefer adopted succession only to fight devastating civil wars in order to establish a dynasty. Even worse, rumors swirled through Rome concerning the jealousies and discord in Severus's family. The more insistent Severus's Antonine family propaganda in promoting virtues such as FELICITAS SAECULI, CONCORDIA, and AETERNITAS IMPERII became, the greater the sense of senatorial foreboding.

The combined celebrations of the emperor's decennalia, triumph over the Parthians, the Ludi Saeculares, and the marriage of Caracalla to Plautilla meant that advertisement of the imperial family reached a fevered pitch between 202 and 204.[78] The empress was especially prominent in family propaganda because she served as a legitimizing link between the emperor and his sons, evidenced by the AETERNIT IMPERI types distributed at Severus's decennalia. Julia Domna appears on the obverse of these coins with two different reverse types. In the first, the laureate busts of Severus and Caracalla are vis-à-vis (*RIC* 4a.539, 166); in the second, the laureate bust of Caracalla faces the bare-headed Geta (see figure 5). The second of these reverses also appears on Severus's coinage (cf. *RIC* 4a.155a-c, 111).[79] Julia's function on the obverse of the coins was to link the two generations of emperors on the first, and to bestow legitimacy on her sons in the second.

Julia Domna also became the imperial administration's representative of family and Roman tradition. The empress appeared in the Ludi Saeculares, leading a procession of 109 noble women (mostly senatorial with eighteen equestrian women).[80] The role that Julia Domna played in this ritual likely echoed that of Livia, the other Julia Augusta, and stretched back to the days of Augustus.[81] Participating in this solemn occasion accomplished several things at once: in the stately procession of *matronae*, the empress projected herself as a Roman matron, pious, chaste, and princeps-like. Her participation in the procession of senatorial women echoed the fictional equality that Severus exhibited with the senators during his first *adventus* to Rome. By walking beside these women, the empress showed herself, if not exactly the first among equals, as one who mingled with senatorial wives in the same way Severus had with senators.[82]

Julia Domna's coinage also boasted the qualities most desired in a Roman matrona: *pudicitia* and *pietas*. They guaranteed the integrity of a family both by the matrona's chastity as well as by her prioritization of family, the state, and the gods over her individual wants. On dupondi minted in Rome (see figure 2), Julia Domna stands between her sons, gazing out at the viewer. She rests a hand on her son's shoulders as they clasp hands, projecting a spirit of unity and harmony between each other and within the family as a whole. The legend, PIETATI AVGVSTAE S C, stresses pious devotion and a sense of duty the empress encourages in her family.

Recurring themes concerning Julia Domna were the harmony and divine approbation of the family. On a reverse type of Severus dated between 200 and 201, Julia Domna gazes directly at the viewer, flanked by Caracalla and Geta, who look placidly upon their mother (see figure 1).[83] This frontal depiction of Julia Domna breaks the expectations of the viewer accustomed to the usual profile busts. The startling yet steady gaze of the empress inverts the relationship between the viewer and the viewed, demanding the attention of its audience in a way that ordinary busts simply do not.[84] It is not unlike the startled feeling one has reading Victorian literature, when the narrator suddenly addresses the "dear reader." The reader, who up to that point thought she was an undetected voyeur, suddenly feels the gaze of the author and characters upon her. Likewise, the gaze of the empress demands the personal attention of the viewer and guarantees the promise of FELICITAS SAECVLI, the blessedness of and for a generation. An unmistakably dynastic message, the legend FELICITAS SAECVLI had earlier advertised Faustina's twin boys playing on the throne in 161 (see figure 17). Yet Julia Domna's type lacks the charm of Faustina's. It is not an intimate family moment like the one conveyed by Faustina's children; the Severan portraits are stiff and formal busts, unapologetically official. Still, the frontal depictions suggest that the type intended to personalize its message to each viewer of the coin. The second-person address created by the *en face* depiction is thus parallel to the individualized messages of James Montgomery Flagg's 1917 Uncle Sam poster (figure 18). When faced with a stern gaze, pointed finger, and the message "I WANT YOU," the viewer has no choice but to recognize himself as the addressee of the message. Unlike Faustina's reverse type, which might evoke a viewer's fondness for the infant boys who held so much promise, Julia Domna's reverse dictates the official version of reality to its viewer. The direct gaze of the empress feels more imperial—more formal—than the affectionate rendering of the boys playing on the throne. Faustina's FELICITAS SAECVLI was a descriptive statement; Julia Domna's is imperative, much like the Uncle Sam poster. It tells the viewer how to interpret the princes that Julia Domna has produced: the blessing of and for YOUR generation.

Imperial advertisement of Julia Domna and her association and assimilation with maternal goddesses betray the same heavy-handedness displayed in the FELICITAS SAECVLI type. During this period, Julia Domna was associated with maternal goddesses, especially Cybele, Isis, Diana Lucifera, Ceres, and Vesta Mater.[85] Except for Isis, Faustina had been likewise associated with these goddesses. Julia Domna's types are more insistent than Faustina's, as is especially evident in a comparison of the two empresses' Magna Mater types. Faustina's types feature the goddess seated on a throne with a lion, a tympanum, and occasionally a branch (e.g., *RIC* 3.706, 270). The branch is unusual for Magna Mater imagery and, as suggested earlier, I believe that in this context, it is probably a dynastic symbol: Faustina, as mother of the twin heirs to the principate, is the source of the dynasty. Julia Domna had been associated with the Magna Mater in the early phase of her coinage in this same way. But from 209, the association became more insistent and extravagant, as discussed in chapter 2. It was in this year that Geta was promoted from Caesar to Augustus, earning Julia Domna a unique title, Mater Augustorum (usually abbreviated as MATER AVGG in coinage and inscriptions). Accompanying this legend are types of the Magna Mater enthroned upon a lion-drawn carriage, resting her left arm on a tympanum and extending a branch in her right hand (see figure 6).[86] As the nominative case of the legend indicates, it is assimilation and equation: Julia Domna *is* the Magna Mater. No longer content to advertise Julia Domna as the Mater Castrorum or Mater Augustorum, with this type, the imperial administration expanded Julia's maternal purview to embrace all living things.

Julia Domna in Cassius Dio

Despite the official claims of Julia Domna's Roman and maternal qualities, Cassius Dio subverted images of the empress to explore the tensions in the relationships between Severus and Plautianus and Caracalla and Geta. The rivalry between Julia Domna and Plautianus had several components; they each competed for Severus's attention, but if Herodian can be believed, the rivalry was as much sexual as political.[87] Both Julia Domna and Plautianus were likely before the walls of Hatra, and the treasonous words uttered by the Praetorian Julius Crispus might be a reflection of Plautianus's hostility for the empress's influence.[88] Plautianus and Julia Domna had their own visions of how the succession would play out: the empress wanted her sons to be recognized, thus allowing them to secure the principate; Plautianus's celebration as the fourth Caesar and his betrothal of Plautilla to Caracalla destabilized Geta's position. Though Cassius Dio reported that Severus sought out Plautilla for Caracalla, the marriage was an incredible coup for Plautianus. With Plautilla's betrothal, Plautianus became an official member of the imperial family. Dio reports that Plautianus had become so powerful that he surpassed even the emperor in influence and respect.

> Thus, on one occasion, Severus went to visit him when he had fallen ill at Tyana. Plautianus would not permit the emperor's escort to enter with him. And again, when the man who arranged the cases that were to be pleaded before Severus was once ordered by the emperor in a moment of leisure to bring forward some case or other, he refused saying, "I cannot do so, unless Plautianus bids me."[89]

Plautianus, as a member of the imperial family, received statues and honors in the provinces and at Rome, where monuments and inscriptions like the Porta Argentarii included his name and image. Dio made clear where his sympathies lay. At the culmination of a tirade against Plautianus and his tyrannical behavior even in dealing with Severus, Dio added one last, damning charge:

> So greatly did Plautianus have mastery in every way over the emperor that he often treated even Julia Augusta in an outrageous manner; for he cordially detested her and was always abusing her violently to Severus. He used to conduct investigations into her conduct as well as gather evidence against her by torturing women of the nobility. For this reason she began to study philosophy and passed her days in the company of sophists. As for Plautianus, he would gorge himself at banquets and vomit as he ate, as the mass of food and wine

> that he swallowed made it impossible for him to digest anything. And though he made use of lads and girls in notorious fashion, yet he would not permit his wife to see anybody or to be seen by any person whomsoever, not even by Severus or Julia, to say nothing of others.[90]

By using Julia Domna as a foil for Plautianus, Dio depicts the empress as an innocent victim, much like the noble ladies who were interrogated and tortured for information incriminating Julia Domna. Though Dio did not make explicit the nature of these investigations, it seems likely that Plautianus accused the empress of adultery, the one charge that would allow him to get rid of her handily and cast doubt on the Geta's legitimacy. Dio clearly favored Julia Domna in this battle because he has her taking the high road, retreating from court to study philosophy. In his portrayal, she follows in the footsteps of such esteemed figures as M. Tullius Cicero, who found solace during the collapse of the Republic and his waning political influence in the bosom of Lady Philosophy. The empress's self-control, rationality, and intellect mark her as masculine, while Plautianus receives effeminate traits, especially those associated with capricious tyrants. For instance, one of the marks of a tyrant is to see without being seen.[91] Dio's depiction of Plautianus embodies this characteristic: the praefect maliciously investigated the life and sexual habits of the empress, but prevented even the emperor and Julia Domna from seeing his wife. Cloistering his wife and forbidding the emperor entrance into his tent in Tyana suggests that Plautianus was unwilling to have his own life to be examined by others, another mark of a tyrant. His effeminacy is also made apparent by his inability to control his excessive desires for food or sex. Just as damning, however, is Dio's depiction of Severus: he was easily controlled by the man whom he ought to control.[92]

Dio's sympathetic portrayal of the empress here stemmed not from affection or empathy for Julia Domna herself. She is the masculine foil that allows Dio to accuse the men around her of effeminacy. In the contest between the Praetorian praefect and the empress, Julia Domna was clearly the lesser of two evils. Senators may even have recognized in the empress their own strategies for living under an alpha male.[93] In the seemingly too-close relationship between Severus and Plautianus—as much a threat to the Senate as to the empress—Julia Domna seems not unlike a senator faced with a tyrant who must be managed rather than controlled. In contrast with Plautianus, the empress is presumably reasonable: her philosophical leanings and interests in the sophists make her preferable to Plautianus, sex fiend and glutton.

Though suffering under the shadow of Plautianus was clearly uncomfortable for the Senate and the empress, his downfall was imminent. Cassius Dio reported that as the emperor's brother, Severus Geta, lay on his deathbed, he accused Plautianus of conspiring against Severus and his sons.[94] This revelation would precipitate a summons in 205 to the palace where the Praetorian praefect was executed. The details differ in the ancient sources; Dio reported that Caracalla framed Plautianus and killed his father-in-law by his own hand.[95] In Herodian, Plautianus was actually plotting to murder Severus and Caracalla and was betrayed by his agent Saturninus.[96] Dio's hatred for Caracalla perhaps led him to accept the more damning version of the story, but there is not sufficient evidence to decide which rendition is likelier.[97] In either case, the children of Plautianus were undone by the death of their father. Julia Domna was with Plautilla when a centurion presented the empress and her daughter-in-law with a handful of hairs saying, "'Behold your Plautianus,' thus giving grief to one and joy to the other."[98] Plautilla and her brother were quickly removed from the seat of power and sent into exile. Plautianus underwent a *damnatio memoriae* as the Porta Argentarii bears witness, but Dio reports that when the emperor appeared before the Senate to report his former friend's demise, he did not speak a word against him.

Once the praefect had been removed, the boys' behavior spiraled out of control and their enmity became apparent to those outside the imperial palace.[99] As the relationship worsened, the boys developed circles of friends who were just as hostile toward the other party. Herodian reports that as early as 200, the relationship between the boys was contentious, and Severus used every opportunity to plead with them to be harmonious.[100] In 208, the emperor decided to undertake a campaign in Britain against the Caledonians. His motivations, Dio explained, were twofold—to gain the glory of conquering all of Caledonia, but also to remove his sons from the factions in Rome in the hope of creating peace in his family.[101]

> Severus, seeing that his sons were changing their mode of life and that the legions were becoming enervated by idleness, made a campaign against Britain, though he knew that he should not return.[102]

Once he arrived in Caledonia, however, he left Julia Domna and Geta in the province while he and Caracalla set out to complete the conquest. The separation between the boys seemed not to have done much good in improving their relationship. According to Dio, Caracalla became even bolder in Britain and, being eager to seize sole power, made an attempt on Severus's life before the army.[103] Severus died shortly thereafter, on February 4, 211. For Dio, the emperor's last words were portentous. "Be harmonious, enrich the soldiers and ignore all others."[104] In such a formulation, there was no room for the Senate or, for that matter, Julia Domna.

Moderating Maternal Megalomania

Upon hearing news of Severus's death and the family's intention to return to Rome, the Senate voted that sacrifices should be made to Concordia and other gods. For although "the two [brothers] pretended to love and commend each other, in all that they did they were diametrically opposed. Nor was it unpredictable that something awful would happen between them."[105] Omens warned that the Senate's solution would not be sufficient to avert impending crisis; the priest performing the sacrifice and the sacrificial attendants were unable to locate one another. Even more worrisome, two wolves were spotted stalking about the Capitoline, fighting in a fearsome manner. The worst fears were confirmed when one of them was found dead the next day.[106]

Fears that the brothers would either kill one another or tear the empire apart in civil war caused the Senate to cast about for a champion. Severus had filled Rome with propaganda featuring Severus and Julia Domna as the guarantors of family harmony. But Severus was dead, and only Julia Domna seemed to carry any influence with both young emperors. I imagine that some senators swallowed a bitter pill as they realized that Julia Domna was their savior—the only person capable of preventing the empire from being torn apart in a vicious civil war.[107]

The aureus advertising Julia Domna as Mater Senatus, Mater Patriae (figure 7) is evidence of the new ideology that the Senate negotiated with the imperial administration. On the obverse, Julia Domna appears with a new coiffure and titles unprecedented for a woman, PIA and FELIX. The reverse depicts the empress enthroned, holding a scepter in her left hand and a branch in her right, iconographic shorthand for her role as *genetrix* of the dynasty. The legend surrounding her provides evidence of the Senate's official recognition of the breadth of her purview: MAT(ER) AVGG(VSTORUM) MAT(ER) SEN(ATVS) M(ATER) PATR(IAE), Mother of the Emperors, Mother of the Senate, Mother of the Empire. Unlike the uncertain motivations or agency in awarding the Mater Castrorum title, there can be little doubt that the Senate granted Julia Domna these unprecedented titles. Cassius Dio complains loudly when this right of the Senate is usurped; notably, we hear nothing of what would be the supreme humiliation were Caracalla to bully the Senate into calling his mother "Mater Senatus."[108]

It was probably with great trepidation that the Senate turned to Julia Domna as its savior. But desperate times call for desperate measures, and the Senate realized that it could both flatter its champion and at once remind her of what duties this honor entailed. Inherent in these titles is the Senate's acceptance of Julia Domna's patronage and the role that her maternity had played in dynastic propaganda. Yet the Senate did not wholly embrace the maternal megalomania so apparent in Magna Mater types (see figure 6). The Senate's recognition of the empress's maternal domain was more modest, but it nonetheless constitutes senatorial capitulation to the influence of imperial women—or at least this imperial woman. But such honors come at a price. The Senate sought a favor in exchange for its recognition of the empress's influence within the palace. Now, the Senate seems to implore, was the time to show herself as PIA in maintaining harmony in her family, in the Senate, and throughout the empire; all the charisma and favor of the gods implied in FELIX must be harnessed to this end. Still, the Senate was able to retain a little pride despite what must have felt like groveling toward a woman. At least MATER CASTRORVM does not appear beside MATER SENATVS. If senators felt emasculated because they had to appeal to an imperial woman as their savior, at least the Senate could take comfort in eclipsing the military in her affections.

It is impossible to tell whether the historical Julia Domna recognized the Senate's remarkable capitulation to her maternal images. As a well-read woman who spent time with sophists and philosophers, my guess is that she did. But I wonder if she was personally invested enough in politics to consider it a victory. Did she ever recognize herself in all those good, Roman matrona images? Or did some part of her still yearn for the exotic East, where women like Nitocris and Semiramis commanded armies and ruled their kingdoms without the aid of male relatives?[109]

Conclusion

The Senate designed Julia Domna's new titles—Pia, Felix, Mater Senatus, Mater Patriae—to remind the empress of the heavy burden that it placed upon her shoulders. With all of Rome dividing its loyalties between her two sons, only she held the respect of both boys.

Only she could avoid the impending clash and ultimate conflict between the new emperors that omens had so vividly foretold. Still, propaganda could not acknowledge the tensions that prompted the empress's honors. Though the imperial administration was quick to adopt Julia Domna's new titles on coins and inscriptions, it refused to acknowledge publicly the tensions between the young emperors. Instead, the imperial administration leapt at the opportunity afforded by the *adventus* of the imperial family to create an ideology with Rome's various populations:

> On their arrival at Rome, the people welcomed them [the new emperors] waving branches of laurels and the senate joined in presenting an address of greeting. The two brothers headed the procession wearing the imperial purple, followed by the consuls who were then in office, carrying the urn containing the remains of Severus. Those who were there to salute the new emperors also went forward to bow before the urn. Then a procession went ahead escorting the urn and laid it in the temple where the sacred memorials of Marcus and his imperial predecessors were displayed. After completing the rites prescribed for the entry of emperors into the city, the young men returned to the palace. There they lived separate lives; the buildings were partitioned off, all the private connecting passages were bricked up and only the outer, public entrances were left in use. Both established their own private guard and were never seen together except occasionally for brief appearances at public functions. The first thing they did was to carry out the funeral of their father.[1]

The funeral was a particularly important time for the young emperors to demonstrate their legitimacy by honoring their father and predecessor. But it also allowed the populations of Rome to display their consensus for the young men's rule. In Herodian's description, all the ranks of the inhabitants of Rome are represented, even the honored dead. Beside them, the provinces, *municipia*, and *colonia* clamor to lend their support to the new emperor.[2]

This was the last time, Herodian tells us, that the young emperors worked together. Immediately after the funeral, the tension between the brothers that had barely been disguised in public now became well known. In typical rhetorical fashion, Herodian casts the boys in diametrically opposing roles, apparently to heighten the drama of the impending clash. Geta is intellectual while Caracalla prefers the physical life; Caracalla courts the military while Geta finds his support in the Senate. Alarmingly, the populations of Rome chose sides, lining up behind their favorite:

> The opinion of everyone in Rome who held rank and honor was also divided. Each of the brothers sent out confidential and secret letters trying to win favor and drawing support for themselves by making extravagant promises.[3]

In Herodian's account, the young men wrangled for sole rule, attempting to claim everyone and everything for themselves. They even divided the palace in two by bricking up the passageways that had previously connected their halves into the whole. Julia Domna, it seems, was the only person or institution who remained undivided. "In this bitter antagonism between the brothers over every single thing they did, right down to trivial matters, their mother made an attempt to effect a reconciliation."[4] Julia Domna, or more specifically, Julia's body, was the one element that prevented the dissolution of the entire empire. In the anecdote we first encountered in the introduction, Caracalla and Geta have all but finalized their agreement to divide the empire in two, when Julia Domna offered them her body as well:

> "You have discovered a way to divide the earth and sea, my sons, and to cleave in two the continents at the Pontic Sea. But your mother, how do you propose to divide her? And how am I, wretched woman, to rend myself in two and distribute myself between you? So kill me! Then each of you, after you have carried me off, bury your part near you. And in this way, I should be split along with the earth and sea." Then amid tears and lamentations, Julia stretched out her hands and clasping both her sons in her arms, tried to draw them together

> to her. And with everyone pitying her, the meeting adjourned and the project was abandoned. Each youth returned to his half of the imperial palace.[5]

The effect of this dramatic offer called attention to the violence the emperors intended to enact upon the body of the empire. It would be no less shocking and violent to do the same to the body of their mother.

Cassius Dio also envisioned Julia Domna's body as a metaphor for the empire. In his account of Geta's assassination, Caracalla plotted to kill his brother in his mother's chambers. Because Geta was afraid for his life, he went nowhere without bodyguards. Nonetheless, Caracalla pried his brother from their watchful eye by convincing his mother to attempt a private reconciliation between the two in her apartments. As Geta entered the room, the centurions posted there by Caracalla attacked the young prince.

> Thus Geta was persuaded, and went in with him [Caracalla]; but when they were inside, some centurions, previously instructed by Antoninus [Caracalla], rushed in a body and struck him down. At the sight of them, Geta ran to his mother, hung about her neck and clung to her bosom and breasts, lamenting and crying, "Mother, you who bore me, Mother, you who bore me, help! I am being murdered!" And so tricked in this way, she saw her son perishing in her arms in a most impious fashion. She received him at his death into the very womb, as it were, whence he had been born. For she was all covered with his blood so that she took no notice of the wound she had sustained on her hand. But she was not permitted to weep or mourn for her son, though he had met so miserable an end before his time (for he was only 22 years and nine months old), but on the contrary, she was forced to rejoice and laugh, as though at some great good fortune, so closely were all her words, gestures and changes of color observed. Thus, she alone, the Augusta, wife of the emperor and mother of the emperors, was not permitted to shed tears even in private over so great a sorrow.[6]

Though the murder of an emperor must have been a disquieting event under any circumstances, the dramatic infantilization of Emperor Geta makes this version particularly shocking. In one sentence, Geta sheds his imperial purple and becomes a child crying out for his mother, clinging to her neck and breasts, and finally dying in the very place he had been born. At Dio's hand, murder is sensationally upgraded to savage infanticide.

If we take earlier palace propaganda of Julia Domna as the universal mother *ad absurdum*, the empress was the source of all living things and her maternal purview required the protection of them, just like the Magna Mater or Vesta Mater. The womb and the breasts that received the infantile Geta, then, were the origins not just of Julia Domna's sons but of the entire empire. The wound that the empress sustains invites further parallels between her sufferings and the empire's. She fails to notice the injury done to her body at first because of the horror that surrounds her. When she does, she is not permitted to mourn her loss. This is in essence the same restriction that Caracalla placed upon the empire with the *damnatio memoriae* of Geta, but with one very important distinction: everyone but Julia Domna was allowed to shed tears in private. Under Caracalla's constant surveillance, even the empress's private domain was public as she was scrutinized for any sign of grief rather than joy.

Ideological Crisis

Herodian reports that when Caracalla burst into the Praetorian camp on the evening of December 26, 211, he dramatically threw himself to the ground before "the temple where the standards and images of the soldiers were worshipped."[7] After arising, he offered thanks and made a sacrifice for his safety, thankful for the safety that providence provided him. The guard quickly assembled, and Caracalla bawled out his incredible news:

> He had escaped from a dangerous plot of a man—he was referring to his brother—who was a public and private enemy and whom he had just managed to defeat after a desperate fight. Although both had been in great danger, one of them at any rate had been preserved by fortune to be emperor.[8]

Dio's Caracalla was less dramatic but far cagier. He made his announcement with the intention to win over his audience from the start, saying, "Rejoice, fellow soldiers, for now I am in a position to do you favors!"[9] Though Dio's Caracalla did not reveal to the soldiers the manner of Geta's death, he identified himself as their comrade-in-arms and promised them the contents of the treasuries for their support.

Both historians have Caracalla visiting the Senate the next morning. Dio records nothing of his main speech, only that as he left the Curia he tossed off one last fiat: "In order that the whole world may rejoice, let all the exiles who have been condemned, on whatever charge or in whatever manner be restored."[10] The command was apparently designed to please the Senate, though it did little to endear him to Dio. For though he had emptied the islands of exiles, Dio snidely reports, he had them filled again in no time and, what is worse, ordered some twenty thousand of Geta's supporters slaughtered. Despite Dio's criticism, it seems that Caracalla was attempting to make nice with the Senate. He even honored the assembly in coin types, as in *RIC* 4a.234, 245, whose reverse legend reads GENIO SENATVS.[11] The story that Herodian has Caracalla reporting to the Praetorians was the official version of events that took place in the palace that night. Whispers about the unofficial narrative of Geta's death and its clash with Caracalla's official "truth" would have been enough to bring about an ideological crisis. But the shock waves created by rumors that the emperor had murdered his brother rendered Caracalla's position especially precarious. In desperation, Caracalla acted like a usurper as he sought out supporting populations rather than wait for the legitimizing acclamation of the legions and guard or the delegation from the Senate.[12] He offered his version of the conspiracy of Geta along with incentives for those who would support him; in return, he sought evidence from those populations of their loyalty. From the military, he wanted vows; from the Senate, Geta's *damnatio memoriae*; from his mother, silence.

Dio lingers over the horrors of the *damnatio memoriae*, attributing the erasure of Geta's memory to an expression of the emperor's anger and hatred for his brother. He reports that not even this vengeance could sate Caracalla's wrath, and he resorted to performing unholy rites to Geta's *manes*.[13]

Yet to minimize the ideology inherent in *damnatio memoriae* is to also underestimate its impact. The imperial administration immediately began a propaganda campaign to support the official version of Geta's death. It had two goals: to celebrate the safety of the emperor and to condemn the memory of his attempted assassin. On a denarius struck in 213, Caracalla is shown under the protection of Salus (*RIC* 4a.196, 240). One easily identifies the virtue by the cistophoric basket to which she offers a libation. On her right arm she carries a cornucopia, perhaps suggesting that the empire will experience abundance because of the emperor's deliverance.

The systematic erasure of Geta began on the monuments that the imperial administration had sponsored, but the creation of ideology demanded that other populations participate in the *damnatio*, ushering in a massive response to Caracalla's attempts to renegotiate ideology. Inhabitants of Rome such as the *argentarii* and the *boarii* dutifully excised Geta's name from the inscription of the Porta, and his image from the interior panel (see figure 15). Military men at home and abroad chiseled Geta's name from inscriptions and in some cases, such as in *CIL* 06 00354 erected by the *princeps castrorum peregrinorum*, filled the gaping holes resulting from the erasure with the victorious cognomina of Caracalla.

Legionaries in Dura-Europos scrambled to do the same in an inscription that was months old at most (*AE* 1984 00921). Private art was not spared; the famous painted Berlin tondo from Egypt (see figure 19) bears the scars of Geta's brutal erasure. Individual cities in Asia Minor, like Stratonicea in Caria, recalled their bronze coins that originally featured Caracalla and Geta vis-à-vis (see figure 20). The mint workers mutilated Geta's image one at a time by hand, only then counterstamping and reissuing the coins. Simply recalling old coins and issuing new ones free of the scars where Geta's image had been would deprive the city of an opportunity to show its support for Caracalla.

Despite the visual outpouring of official support evident in the *damnatio memoriae*, the unofficial version of Geta's assassination quickly seized the minds of contemporaries, who responded to the rumors in various fashions. Dio's description of the murder is evidence of the horror and disgust that he felt toward Caracalla. Surely he was not alone in this assessment, but if there were others who felt the same, they were wise not to display it, as Caracalla went on a rampage, slaughtering twenty thousand of Geta's friends and sympathizers. Evidence for resistance to the official narrative comes in the form of jokes and rumors concerning the event. As Geta's name and titles were erased and overwritten with Caracalla's imperial cognomina, Helvius Pertinax quipped that Geticus Maximus should be added to the emperor's titles.[14] Caracalla had no sense of humor about his brother; Pertinax paid for that quip with his life. Likewise, the Alexandrians suffered a horrific massacre at Caracalla's hands, probably because they had labeled the empress "Jocasta" and, by extension, the emperor as Oedipus. The rumor that suggested Julia Domna seduced Caracalla to maintain her position might have sprung from this joke.[15]

Thus began the crisis in which the negotiation of ideology and consensus was undermined by rumors that called into question the credibility of propaganda. The far-fetched official narratives and unofficial responses to rumors seemed to confirm suspicions on both sides, which only confused further the ideological negotiations between the emperor and his target audiences. Loyal populations hurried to supply the emperor with evidence that they accepted his official narrative, while the unofficial response not only whispered about Caracalla's savagery but also demonized Julia Domna. How could a mother be so ambitious that she would resort to incest in order to maintain her position?[16] Some even speculated that the empress had a hand in Geta's murder. The propagandistic "truths" were so incredible and the rumors so salacious that the artificiality of ideology and its negotiation became uncomfortably visible. Once this happened, the imperial administration was forced to either abandon the official report or to shore it up with additional claims. This is especially apparent in the claims and counterclaims regarding Julia Domna's body in the relationship between the Senate and the emperor. Caracalla wanted her to laugh and be joyful; the Senate (or at least Dio) wanted to see and participate in her grief. Both sides wanted to claim her and her body in order to support the veracity of their truths.

In such an environment, Dio once again employed images of the empress to cast Caracalla in the worst possible light. Twisting the rhetoric developed by Pliny and Tacitus that paints imperial women as irrational, capricious, and self-serving, Dio applied these characteristics to Caracalla while Julia Domna became the rational, pious, stoic—and indeed masculine—element in the palace. Dio described the empress managing the administration of the empire in Antioch while her son campaigned in an unnecessary and self-glorifying war against the Parthians.[17] While the empress held audiences with prominent men and became increasingly philosophical, the emperor donned effeminate trousers and a wig, played soldier with his troops, and refused to meet with the Senate either socially or for business.[18] As Julia gave sane and rational advice to curb military expenditures, Caracalla pointed to his sword and exhorted her not to worry; all the money they would ever need would come from this.[19]

> Neither in these matters nor in any others did he heed his mother, who gave him much excellent advice. And yet he had appointed her to receive petitions and to have charge of his correspondence in both languages, except in very important cases, and used to include her name, in terms of high praise, together with his own and that of the legions, in his letters to the Senate, stating that she was well. Need I add that she held public receptions for all the most prominent men, precisely as did the emperor? But, while she devoted herself more and more to the study of philosophy with these men, he kept declaring that he needed nothing beyond the necessaries of life and plumed himself over his pretended ability to live on the cheapest kind of fare; yet there was nothing on land or sea or in the air that we did not regularly supply to him both by private gifts and by public grants.[20]

As Dio depicts Julia Domna, she bears a great deal of resemblance to the beloved Marcus Aurelius. She honored and respected senators by receiving their delegations, she turned to philosophy to guide her in troubled times, and she preached wisdom to her son, exhorting him toward a life of temperance and restraint.[21] In Dio's depiction, she had truly grown into the Mater Senatus and Mater Patriae titles by piously looking after the interests of the state in the best manner she could. While the empress might have failed in keeping peace and harmony between her sons, she nonetheless recognized far more than Caracalla the wisdom inherent in keeping the military under control, respecting the Senate, and maintaining a sense of balance through her study of philosophy.

Depicting Julia Domna in a rational and measured way might lead the unsuspecting reader to assume genuine esteem in the titles that the Senate lavished upon the empress. Her exemplary behavior in doing her duty the best she could while living under a tyrant, her association with good men who were busy trying to do the same, and her retreat to the bosom of Lady Philosophy to find comfort in the midst of chaos, all point toward a reading of Dio's Julia Domna that bespeaks the Senate's respect, empathy, and affection. In fact, the empress's behavior sounds much like Tacitus's exhortation to those who would criticize senators serving under a bad emperor:

> Let it be clear to those who insist on admiring disobedience that even under bad emperors men can be great and that a decent regard for authority, if backed by industry and energy can reach that peak of distinction which most men attain only by following a perilous course, winning fame without benefiting their country by an ostentatious self-martyrdom.[22]

On the Dangers of Taking Ideology Too Seriously

One needs only to turn to the accounts of Julia Domna's behavior after the death of Caracalla in order to realize that the pious, self-sacrificing image of the empress, like so many others we have examined, was merely rhetorical, used solely for the sake of making Caracalla look bad. Upon hearing of Caracalla's murder, Dio's Julia Domna lost her philosophical perspective and began to show her effeminate, capricious side by mourning for a worthless son:

> Now Julia, the mother of Tarautas [Caracalla], happened to be in Antioch, and at the first information of her son's death, she was so affected that she dealt herself a violent blow and tried to starve herself to death. Thus she mourned now that he was dead, the very man whom she had hated while he lived. Yet it was not because she wished that he were alive, but because she was vexed at having to return to private live . . . for she hoped to make herself the equal of Semiramis and Nitocris, inasmuch as she came in a sense from the same parts as they.[23]

Cassius Dio signals the empress's demotion in his esteem by referring to her not as Julia Augusta or Julia, wife of Severus, or Julia, mother of the Antoninus, as he had in describing her trials at the hands of Plautianus or in the moments following Geta's death. She is now simply the mother of the hated tyrant Tarautas, the name of a gladiator that Dio uses to mock Caracalla.[24] Even the empress's willingness to submit to a noble death is compromised—she desires it not to end her suffering, as a good Stoic would, but because she did not want to relinquish her position as empress. Doing away with the noble characteristics he had earlier ascribed to Julia Domna, Dio now found her ambitious, conniving, and perhaps even self-delusional in believing that she could rule alone in the manner of women who had come from the East.

Dio reports that the empress schemed with the soldiers assigned to her detail, and seemed intent on a coup until she heard that Rome was rejoicing at the news of her son's death. Demoralized by this news and Macrinus's order to leave Antioch, Julia Domna committed suicide, either by starving herself or as a result of beating her breasts in grief, thus rupturing the tumor lying dormant there. The emphasis on the empress's body, especially her breasts, reminds us that, despite earlier depictions in which she exhibited piety, rationality, and manly self-control, Julia Domna was a woman.

As I see it, there are two possible ways to explain this radical shift in Dio's depictions of the empress. He might have been painting the portrait of a woman who had trusted too much in the transformative power of images. Fooled into trusting the obsequious attentions of the senatorial delegations, the protection of the Praetorian Guard who surrounded her, and the petitions from around the empire that addressed her in such flattering terms, Dio's Julia Domna came to believe that she could rule alone. She would have been bitterly disappointed to learn that without Caracalla as her foil, she was stripped of all those qualities that she might have imagined qualified her to rule. She was a woman—an extraordinary one no doubt—but still a woman. No amount of clever propaganda or ideology could transform her into a viable candidate for the principate.

But I believe a less dramatic explanation is the more likely one. As I have repeatedly suggested in the course of this book, the images of Julia Domna were not descriptions of the historical figure so much as rhetorical tools by which to praise or blame the men in her life. They were lenses through which her husband and sons promoted themselves and invited their subjects to participate in negotiating ideology. In the hands of the enemies and critics of her male relatives, her images were manipulated to highlight the cruelty, shamelessness, and general incompetence of her men. In a twist on the usual senatorial rhetoric concerning imperial women, Dio painted Julia Domna in the most masculine and pious of terms in order to highlight the effeminate and impious behavior of the men in the imperial family. Once those men were dead and gone, however, Dio had no further need of the empress. He then reverted to the stereotypes with which senators had painted imperial women since the inception of the principate. Julia Domna was finally revealed to be conniving and amibitious, capricious and emotional. As a final blow, Dio stripped from Julia Domna even of the FELIX title that the Senate had endowed her. He demonstrated that her life indeed lacked any good fortune (εὐτυχία) the gods may have once seemed to afford her.

> And so this woman, sprung from the people and raised to high station, who had lived during her husband's reign in great unhappiness because of Plautianus, who had beheld her younger son slain in her own bosom and had always from first to last born ill will toward her elder son while he lived, and finally had received tidings of his assassination, fell from power during her lifetime and thereupon she destroyed herself. Hence no one could, in the light of her career, regard as happy each and all who attain great power (ἐν ταῖς μεγάλαις ἐξουσίαις), unless some genuine and unalloyed pleasure in life and unmixed and lasting good fortune (εὐτυχία) is theirs. This then, was the fate of Julia. Her body was brought to Rome and placed in the tomb of Gaius and Lucius. Later, however, both her bones and those of Geta were transferred by her sister Maesa to the precinct of Antoninus.[25]

Julia Domna was divinized, probably by Elagabalus, as part of an effort to legitimate his reign. Coins advertised her apotheosis, celebrating her no longer as the mother of the Augusti of the camp, of the Senate, or the fatherland. She was simply DIVA IVLIA AVGVSTA.[26] Even in death, Julia Domna's images proved useful to her male relatives. This time, it was her great-nephews who would use her to connect them to Severus and by extension, the Antonines.

My approach of exploring the use of Julia Domna's images in negotiating imperial ideology stands in stark contrast to recent scholarly work on the empress. I have made no attempts to reconstruct her life, thoughts, or ambitions. I have not attempted to better understand Julia Domna at all, except perhaps to recognize that her power might not have been so great as scholars have traditionally understood it. Instead of exploring the empress's power and influence over her contemporaries—which she could have wielded, however difficult it is for us to quantify or qualify that power—I have chosen instead to consider the power of her images in the ideological negotiations between the imperial administration and important populations in the empire.

Over the course of her lifetime, Julia Domna was the subject of all kinds of talk. The imperial administration carefully cultivated an image of the empress who played down her exotic qualities and origins in favor of a good Roman *matrona* and mother. Her images were cleverly deployed to give Severus the roots he lacked in Roman history, topography, and ethnicity. Her motherhood was employed to legitimize her sons, thus preparing the empire for a new dynasty, but it was also used to claim for Severus the unwavering allegiance of the military. Her maternal purview in official propaganda took on megalomaniacal proportions as she came to be associated and eventually equated with the Great Mother goddess, Cybele.

The imperial administration was only one entity that spoke of Julia Domna. As the administration targeted their messages to different populations, each responded to official images of the empress in ways that promoted their own best interests. Sometimes her images were echoed back to the administration, sometimes they were augmented, and sometimes they were simply ignored. Occasionally, the empress was the object of admiration and emulation, but more often the critics of her husband and sons used her talents and faults to embarrass her men. No image of the empress was innocent, none were simply descriptive, all were ideologically loaded.

APPENDIX A

Hoard Details of the Severan Hoard Analysis Database by Clare Rowan

Hoard	Date	Source	Further information
		Zone A: Britain	
Brickendonbury	250	Evans, J. 1896. "Roman Coins Found at Brickendonbury, Hertford." *Numismatic Chronicle* 16: 191–208.	Earliest coins are from the reign of Commodus. Hoard might have originally contained more than that recorded.
Bristol	208	Mattingly, H., and B. W. Pearce. 1938. "The Bristol Hoard of Denarii, 1937." *Numismatic Chronicle* 18: 85–98.	Hoard possesses coins dating back to Marc Antony and Nero. Hoard contained 1,478 pieces of silver and two pieces of copper. Hoard found at Rochester Rd., St. Anne's, Bristol.
Caister by Yarmouth	260–270	Jenkins, G. K. 1947. "The Caister by Yarmouth Hoard." *Numismatic Chronicle* 7: 175–179.	The hoard may have originally been larger.
Cambridge	248	Boyd, W. C. 1897. "A Find of Roman Denarii Near Cambridge." *Numismatic Chronicle* 17: 119–126.	Earliest coins are from the reign of Commodus.
Darfield	250	Walker, J. 1946. "The Darfield Hoard of Roman Denarii." *Numismatic Chronicle* 6: 147–150.	Hoard possesses coins dating from Marc Antony and Nero. The latest coins date from the reign of Maximinus.
Darfield II	215	Corder, P. 1948. "A Second Hoard of Roman Denarii from Darfield." *Numismatic Chronicle* 8: 78–80.	The uncirculated condition of the coins of Caracalla and Septimius Severus seems to indicate the hoard was made up at this date. Hoard was found in an earthenware pot.
Denbighshire	226	Mattingly, H. 1923. "Find of Roman Denarii in Denbighshire." *Numismatic Chronicle* 3: 152–155.	There were originally 551 coins in the hoard, but only 507 have been published.
East England	230	Evans, J. 1898. "A Hoard of Roman Coins." *Numismatic Chronicle* 18: 126–184.	Hoard has coins dating back to the reign of Nero.
Edston, Peebles-Shire	222	Holmes, N., and F. Hunter. 1997. "Edston, Peebles-Shire." *Coin Hoards from Roman Britain* 10: 149–168.	

continued

Hoard	Date	Source	Further information
Falkirk	230	MacDonald, G. 1934. "A Hoard of Roman Denarii from Scotland." *Numismatic Chronicle* 14: 1–30.	The latest coin dates from 230, but the hoard might have been buried in 240–250, given the wear of some of the coins.
Muswell Hill	210	Mattingly, H. 1929. "Muswell Hill." *Numismatic Chronicle* 9: 315–319.	Hoard possesses coins dating to Marc Antony and Nero, 653 denarii and one drachm of Caesarea Cappadocia in all. The hoard also contained a silver spoon and a broken bronze ring.
Shapwick Villa	224	Abdy, R., and S. Minnitt. 2002. "Shapwick Villa." *Coin Hoards of Roman Britain* 11: 169–233.	Earliest coins are from Marc Antony, then Vespasian. Hoard also contained one silver drachm of Domna from Caesarea and twenty-five plated/barbarous imitations.
St Mary Cray	228	Robertson, A. S. 1935. "The St. Mary Cray Hoard." *Numismatic Chronicle* 15: 62–66.	Hoard found in an earthenware jar, and possessed coins dating from Marc Antony.
Stevenage	263	Bland, R. 1988. "Stevenage, Hertfordshire." In *The Normanby Hoard and Other Roman Coin Hoards*, edited by R. Bland and A. Burnett, 43–71. London: British Museum.	Earliest coinage dates from Septimius Severus. The hoard contains 387 denarii and 2,192 radiates.
		Zone B: Western continent	
Aïn	215	Salama, P. 2001/2002. "Le trésor de deniers d'Aïn Témouchent et ses 'satellites' dans l'Afrique romaine." *Trésors Monétaires* 20: 185–222.	
Baden-Baden	228	Christ, K. 1964. *Die Fundmünzen der römischen Zeit in Deutschland* 2.2, no. 2196: 182–191.	
Clavier III	255	Lallemand, J. 1969. "Le trésor de Clavier III: Deniers et antoniniens de Commode à Valérien-Gallien." *Revue Belge de Numismatique* 115: 263–331.	
Eauze	261	Schaad, D., P. Agrinier et al. 1992. *Le Trésor d'Eauze*. Toulouse: Association pour la promotion du Patrimoine Archéologique et Historique en Midi-Pyrénées.	Earliest coinage is from the reign of Commodus.
Eining	235	Kellner, H.-J. 1970. *Die Fundmünzen der römischen Zeit in Deutschland* 1.2, no. 2034: 98–102.	
Elliginies Saint Anne	240	Lallemand, J. 1968. "Le trésor d'Elliginies-Sainte-Anne: Deniers de Marc-Auréle à Gordien III." *Revue Belge de Numismatique* 114: 138–168.	Earliest coinage is from Marcus Aurelius. The hoard also contains a fragmentary piece with the legend ANTONINVS.
Kempten Lindenberg III	235	Alföldi, R.-M. 1962. *Die Fundmünzen der römischen Zeit in Deutschland* 1.7, no. 7186: 287–304.	

Hoard	Date	Source	Further information
Kirchmatting	235	Kellner, H.-J. 1970. *Die Fundmünzen der römischen Zeit in Deutschland* 1.2, no. 2116: 173–200.	
Köln	238	Nuber, E. 1984. *Die Fundmünzen der römischen Zeit in Deutschland* 6.1.1, no. 1004/3a–b: 254–355.	Hoard has been reassembled by a modern author.
Mainz	228	Wigg-Wolf, D. 2005. *Die Fundmünzen der römischen Zeit in Deutschland* 4.1, no. 1153: 249–259.	
Nanterre	254	Gentilhomme, P. L. 1947. "La Trouvaille de Nanterre." *Revue Numismatique* 9: 15–114.	Earliest coinage is from the reign of Septimius. Hoard has a mixture of denarii and antoniniani.
Niederaschau	238	Kellner, H.-J. 1970. *Die Fundmünzen der römischen Zeit in Deutschland* 1.1, no. 1229: 202–216.	
Pfünz	235	Kellner, H.-J. *Die Fundmünzen der römischen Zeit in Deutschland* 1.5, no. 5042: 71–74.	
Viuz-Faverges	252	Pflaum, H. G. 1981. "Le Trésor de Viuz-Faverges." *Trésors Monétaires* 3: 33–76.	
Welzheim	225	Christ, K. 1964. *Die Fundmünzen der römischen Zeit in Deutschland* 2.4, no. 4596: 354–373.	
Wiesbach	254	Keinast, D. 1964. *Die Fundmünzen der römischen Zeit in Deutschland* 3, no. 1082: 124–133.	
Wiggensbac	235	Alföldi, R.-M. 1962. *Die Fundmünzen der römischen Zeit in Deutschland* 1.7, no. 7199: 312–322.	
		Zone C: Italy	
Via Tritone	244	Cesano, L. 1925. "Nuovi ripostigli di denari di argento dell'impero romano." *Atti e memoriae dell'Istituto Italiano di Numismatica* 5: 57–72.	
Vicenza	235	Bernardelli, A., ed. 1995. *Ritrovamenti Monetali di Età Romana nel Veneto* IV/1 45/3, no. 1: 369–374.	Earliest coinage dates from the reign of Vespasian. The hoard was given to the Museo Civico di Vicenza sometime after 1908, and though it is likely from this region, there is no precise indication of provenance.
		Zone D: Danubian regions	
Barza	235	Depeyrot, G., and D. Moisil. 2008. *Les Trésors de Deniers de Trajan à Balbin en Roumanie*, vol. 174. Wetteren: Moneta.	
Börgöndi	235	Aladár, R. 1936. "A börgöndi éremlelet." *Numizmatikai közlöny* 34/35: 24–27.	

continued

Hoard	Date	Source	Further information
Ercsi	228	Soprini, S. 1964. "Az ercsi éremlelet." *Numizmatikai közlöny* 62–66: 9–17.	
Frânceşti	235	Depeyrot, G., and D. Moisil. 2004. *The Trésor Frânceşti*. Wetteren: Roumanie.	
Ghirişa	198	Depeyrot, G., and D. Moisil. 2008. *Les Trésors de Deniers de Trajan à Balbin en Roumanie*, vol. 141. Wetteren: Moneta.	
Gračič	253	Kos, P., and A. Semrov. 1995. *Die Fundmünzen der römischen Zeit in Slowenien* 3, no. 176: 374–400.	
Gunzenhausen	244	Kellner, H.-J. 1965. *Die Fundmünzen der römischen Zeit in Deutschland* 1.5, no. 5057: 84–91.	
Köngen	249	Christ, K. 1964. *Die Fundmünzen der römischen Zeit in Deutschland* 2.4, no. 4135/1: 90*ff.*	
Leskovec	236	Kos, P. 1988. *Die Fundmünzen der römischen Zeit in Slowenien* 2, no. 408: 143–148.	
Linsberg	238	Dembski, G. 2007. "Ein römischer Münzschatzfund aus Linsberg, Gem. Erlach, BH wieder Neustadt." *Numismatische Zeitschrift* 115: 33–55.	Earliest coinage dates from Marc Antony, then Nero.
Munteneşti	228	Depeyrot, G., and D. Moisil. 2008. *Les Trésors de Deniers de Trajan à Balbin en Roumanie*, vol. 183. Wetteren: Moneta.	
Nicolaévo	249	Seure, G. 1923. "Trésors de Monnaies Antiques en Bulgarie III: Le Trésor de Nicolaévo." *Revue Numismatique* 26: 111–153.	Hoard also contained jewelry.
Plevna	259	Mattingly, H., and F. S. Salisbury. 1924. "A Find of Roman Coins from Plevna in Bulgaria." *Numismatic Chronicle* 4: 210–238.	Total number of coins in the hoard was 4,033, but only 3,296 were examined and recorded. The authors state that those not included in the list were antoniniani of later emperors (Gordian III-Trajan Decius).
Postojna	238	Koss, P. 1998. *Die Fundmünzen der römischen Zeit in Slowenien* 1, no. 91/2: 108–118.	
Reka Devnia	251	Depeyrot, G. 2004. *La Propagande Monétaire (64–235) et le trésor de Marcianopolis (251)*. Wetteren: Moneta. Mouchmov, N. A. 1934. *Le Trésor Numismatique de Réka-Devnia (Marcianopolis)*. Sofia: Editions du Musée National Bulgare.	
Rustschuk	249	Muschmow, N. A. 1918. "Münzfunde aus Bulgarien." *Numismatische Zeitschrift* 11: 43–51.	

Hoard	Date	Source	Further information
Singidunum	254	Kondic, V. 1969. *The Singidunum Hoard of Denarii and Antoniniani.* Belgrade: Belgrade Museum.	
Ţaga	239	Protase, D., and I. H. Crişan. 1968. "Tezaurul de Monede Imperiale Romane de la Ţaga." *Studii şi Cercetări de Numismatică* 4: 139–173.	
Uskub	249	Kubitschek, W. 1908. "Ein Denarfund aus der Gegend von Usküb." *Numismatische Zeitschrift* 41: 37–47.	
		Zone E: The East	
Dura Hoards 3 and 4	218	Bellinger, A. R. 1949. *The Excavations at Dura Europos.* Vol. 6, *The Coins.* New Haven, CT: Yale University Press.	Found in a priest's house. Hoard also contained some tetradrachms.
Haydere	264	Ashton, R. 1991. "The Haydere Hoard and Other Hoards of the Mid-Third Century from Turkey." In *Recent Turkish Coin Hoards and Numismatic Studies*, edited by C. S. Lightfoot, 91–180. Oxford: Oxbow.	Hoard contained an estimated total of 5,578 coins but only 2,330 are recorded. This probably represents two hoards, one terminating under Elagabalus and another terminating in 264.
Kecel	215	Katalin, B. S. 1986. "A Keceli Éremlelet." *Cumania* 9: 27–74.	Earliest coinage is from the reign of Nero. Hoard also contained 46 forgeries.
South East Turkey	251	Bendall, S. 1966. "An Eastern Hoard of Roman Imperial Silver." *Numismatic Chronicle* 6: 165–170.	A hoard that passed through the Spink auction house. Some 800 further denarii appeared after publication.
Syria	212	Cesano, L. 1925. "Nuovi Ripostigli di Denari di Argento dell'Impero Romano." *Atti e Memorie dell'Istituto Italiano di Numismatica* 5: 57–72.	

APPENDIX B

Frequency of Julia Domna Coin Types in Hoards around the Mediterranean

In calculating the ratios, I included only Julia Domna coins minted during Severus's reign (193–211). I did so in order to make the comparison between Severus's and Julia Domna's coinages as meaningful as possible, hopefully reflecting ancient ratios. The first column displays coin type, the second its legend, with the third and fourth columns giving the total number and percentage, respectively.

Zone A: Britain

Roman Mint under Severus: IVLIA DOMNA AVG

RIC 4a.536	VENERI VICTR	52	66%
RIC 4a.538	VESTA	23	29%
RIC 4a.534	FECVNDITAS	2	2.5%
RIC 4a.535	VENER VICTOR	1	1.3%

Roman Mint under Severus: IVLIA AVG

RIC 4a.580	VENVS FELIX	165	11.7%
RIC 4a.574	PIETAS PVBLICA	161	11.4%
RIC 4a.587	VESTAE SANCTAE	116	8.2%
RIC 4a.577	SAECVLI FELICITAS	100	7.1%
RIC 4a.572	PIETAS AVGG	93	6.6%
RIC 4a.564	MATER DEVM	89	6.3%
RIC 4a.548	DIANA LVCIFERA	87	6.2%
RIC 4a.560	IVNO REGINA	86	6.1%
RIC 4a.551	FELICITAS	71	5.3%
RIC 4a.556	HILARITAS	55	3.9%

Roman Mint under Caracalla: IVLIA PIA FELIX AVG

RIC 4a.373A	DIANA LVCIFERA	53	34%
RIC 4a.391	VESTA	24	15.3%
RIC 4a.388	VENVS GENETRIX	20	12.8%
RIC 4a.390	VESTA	19	12.1%
RIC 4a.382	MATRI DEVM	17	10.8%

Eastern Mints (Alexandria, Emesa?, Laodicaea ad Mare, Pannonia?)

RIC 4a.644	PVDICITIA	43	26.7%
RIC 4a.637	CONCORDIA	34	21.1%
RIC 4a.641	LAETITIA	21	13.0%
RIC 4a.639	HILARITAS	13	8.0%
RIC 4a.648	VESTAE SANCTAE	11	6.8%

Total number of coins in Zone A	22,671
Julia Domna's coins (193–211) from Roman Mint	1,642
Severus's coins from Roman Mint	3,917
Proportion of Severus's to Julia Domna's coins	1:2.39

Zone B: Western continent

Roman Mint under Severus: IVLIA DOMNA AVG

RIC 4a.536	VENERI VICTR	9	53%
RIC 4a.538	VESTA	6	35%
RIC 4a.534	FECVNDITAS	1	0.58%
RIC 4a.535	VENER VICTOR	1	0.58%

Roman Mint under Severus: IVLIA AVG

RIC 4a.574	PIETAS PVBLICA	58	10.4%
RIC 4a.572	PIETAS AVGG	46	8.3%
RIC 4a.559	IVNO	44	7.9%
RIC 4a.577	SAECVLI FELICITAS	40	7.2%
RIC 4a.564	MATER DEVM	36	6.5%
RIC 4a.580	VENVS FELIX	34	6.1%
RIC 4a.557	HILARITAS	32	5.7%
RIC 4a.551	FELICITAS	29	5.2%
RIC 4a.560	IVNO REGINA	26	4.7%
RIC 4a.552	FORTVNAE FELICI	21	3.8%

Roman Mint under Caracalla: IVLIA PIA FELIX AVG

RIC 4a.373A	DIANA LVCIFERA	52	26.7%
RIC 4a.388	VENVS GENETRIX	34	17.4%
RIC 4a.390	VESTA	26	13.3%
RIC 4a.391	VESTA	25	12.8%
RIC 4a.389	VENVS GENETRIX	22	11.2%
RIC 4a.382	MATRI DEVM	14	7.1%
RIC 4a.380	MAT AVGG MAT SEN M PAT	7	3.5%
RIC 4a.381	MAT AVGG MAT SEN M PAT	4	2.0%

Eastern Mints

RIC 4a.637	CONCORDIA	10	22.7%
RIC 4a.644	PVDICITIA	7	15.9%
RIC 4a.636	CERERI FRVGIF	6	13.6%
RIC 4a.632	VENERI VICTR	4	0.9%
RIC 4a.646	VENVS FELIX	4	0.9%

Total number of coins in Zone B	43,991
Julia Domna's (193–211) coins from Roman Mint	765
Severus's coins from Roman Mint	1,446
Proportion of Severus's to Julia Domna's coins	1:1.89

Zone C: Italy

Roman Mint under Severus: IVLIA DOMNA AVG

RIC 4a.536	VENERI VICTR	6	66.7%
RIC 4a.538	VESTA	3	33.3%

Roman Mint under Severus: IVLIA AVG

RIC 4a.574	PIETAS PVBLICA	10	13.8%
RIC 4a.551	FELICITAS	8	11.1%

RIC 4a.556	HILARITAS	5	6.9%
RIC 4a.587	VESTAE SANCTAE	5	6.9%
RIC 4a.575	PVDICITIA	4	5.5%
RIC 4a.576	PVDICITIA	4	5.5%
RIC 4a.580	VENVS FELIX	4	5.5%
RIC 4a.581	VENVS VICTRIX	4	5.5%
RIC 4a.546	CERERI FRVGIF	3	4.1%
RIC 4a.554	FORTVNAE FELICI	3	4.1%
RIC 4a.572	PIETAS AVG	3	4.1%

Roman Mint under Caracalla (only one hoard, Via Tritone): IVLIA PIA FELIX AVG

RIC 4a.382	MATRI DEVM	5	27.7%
RIC 4a.373A	DIANA LVCIFERA	4	22.2%
RIC 4a.391	VESTA	3	16.6%
RIC 4a.390	VESTA	2	11.1%
RIC 4a.388	VENVS GENETRIX	2	11.1%
RIC 4a.389	VENVS GENETRIX	1	0.56%

Nothing from the Eastern Mints

Total number of coins in Zone C	938
Julia Domna's (193–211) coins from Roman Mint	87
Severus's coins from Roman Mint	212
Proportion of Severus's to Julia Domna's coins	1:2.43
Total coins for Severus from Via Tritone	214
from eastern mints	8
Total coins for Julia Domna from Via Tritone	75
from eastern mints	0
Proportion of Severus's to Julia Domna's coins	1:2.5
Total coins for Severus from Vicenza	9
from eastern mints	0
Total coins for Julia Domna from Vicenza	6
from eastern mints	0
Proportion of Severus's to Julia Domna's coins	1:1.5

Zone D: Danubian regions

Roman Mint under Severus: IVLIA DOMNA AVG

RIC 4a.538	VESTA	41	67.2%
RIC 4a.536	VENERI VICTR	17	27.8%
RIC 4a.534	FECVNDITAS	3	4.9%

Roman Mint under Severus: IVLIA AVG

RIC 4a.574	PIETAS PVBLICA	356	11.7%
RIC 4a.564	MATER DEVM	234	7.76%
RIC 4a.577	SAECVLI FELICITAS	234	7.76%
RIC 4a.572	PIETAS AVGG	229	7.6%
RIC 4a.580	VENVS FELIX	228	7.5%
RIC 4a.576	PVDICITIA	193	6.4%
RIC 4a.551	FELICITAS	186	6.2%
RIC 4a.587	VESTAE SANCTAE	177	5.9%
RIC 4a.559	IVNO	156	5.2%
RIC 4a.557	HILARITAS	151	5.0%
RIC 4a.560	IVNO REGINA	145	4.8%
RIC 4a.548	DIANA LVCIFERA	121	4.0%
RIC 4a.546	CERERI FRVGIF	107	3.5%

Roman Mint under Caracalla: IVLIA PIA FELIX AVG

RIC 4a.373A	DIANA LVCIFERA	234	32.3%
RIC 4a.388	VENVS GENETRIX	123	17.0%

RIC 4a.390	VESTA	111	15.3%
RIC 4a.391	VESTA	105	14.5%
RIC 4a.382	MATER DEVM	44	6.0%
RIC 4a.389	VENVS GENETRIX	43	5.9%
RIC 4a.381	MAT AVGG MAT SEN M PATR	18	2.5%
RIC 4a.380	MAT AVGG MAT SEN M PATR	17	2.4%

Eastern Mints

RIC 4a.632	VENERI VICTR	77	43%
RIC 4a.637	CONCORDIA	56	31.3%
RIC 4a.644	PVDICITIA	5	2.8%
RIC 4a.616A	CERER FRVG	3	1.7%
RIC 4a.627	LIBERAL AVG	3	1.7%

Total number of coins in Zone D	1,608,080
Julia Domna's (193–211) coins from Roman Mint	3,078
Severus's coins from Roman Mint	7,771
Proportion of Severus's to Julia Domna's coins	1:2.52

Zone E: The East

Roman Mint under Severus: IVLIA DOMNA AVG

RIC 4a.536	VENERI VICTR	5	62.5%
RIC 4a.538	VESTA	3	37.5%

Roman Mint under Severus: IVLIA AVG

RIC 4a.574	PIETAS PVBLICA	33	16%
RIC 4a.577	SAECVLI FELICITIAS	25	12.1%
RIC 4a.564	MATER DEVM	21	10.1%
RIC 4a.572	PIETAS AVGG	19	9.2%
RIC 4a.551	FELICITAS	15	7.3%
RIC 4a.559	IVNO	14	6.8%
RIC 4a.557	HILARITAS	11	5.3%
RIC 4a.576	PVDICITIA	9	4.4%
RIC 4a.553	FORTVNAE FELICI	8	3.9%
RIC 4a.556	HILARITAS	8	3.9%
RIC 4a.587	VESTAE SANCTAE	8	3.9%

Roman Mints under Caracalla

RIC 4a.373A	DIANA LVCIFERA	10	48%
RIC 4a.391	VESTA	5	23.8%
RIC 4a.382	MATRI DEVM	4	19%
RIC 4a.381	MAT AVGG MAT SEN M PAT	1	4.8%
RIC 4a.388	VENVS GENETRIX	1	4.8%

Eastern Mints

RIC 4a.648	VESTAE SANCTAE	5	23.8%
RIC 4a.637	CONCORDIA	3	14.3%
RIC 4a.631	VENERI VICT	2	9.5%
RIC 4a.639	HILARITAS	2	9.5%
RIC 4a.641	LAETITIA	2	9.5%

Total number of coins in Zone E	7,454
Julia Domna's (193–211) coins from Roman Mint	235
Severus's coins from Roman Mint	498
Proportion of Severus's to Julia Domna's coins	1:2.12

APPENDIX C

Dating the Mater Senatus, Mater Patriae Titles

In chapter 3, I claimed that shortly after the death of Severus the Senate awarded Julia Domna a series of extraordinary titles (Pia, Felix, and Mater Senatus, Mater Patriae) to solicit the empress's help in creating harmony between her sons. There is significant scholarly debate about the precise date for awarding these titles, and my thesis requires an explanation of how I dated the titles and why I believe that the Senate—and not the imperial administration—gave them to her.

Coinage minted in Rome advertised Julia Domna's Mater Senatus, Mater Patriae titles.[1] The prominence of these titles and their connection with the Senate suggest that they were awarded at the hands of the Senate. Senators guarded carefully their right to confer titles, especially ones that made reference to the Senate. Cassius Dio complained whenever any emperor usurped titles without waiting for the Senate to confer them.[2] Dio's silence concerning Julia Domna's titles, combined with his complimentary treatment of the empress up to Caracalla's death, suggests that the titles were awarded at the hands of the Senate.

The question of when the titles were conferred, however, is more complex. The Mater Senatus, Mater Patriae titles never appear on Julia Domna's coinage without the Pia and Felix titles. This fact leads numismatists to date both sets of titles to the same historical moment. From their introduction, the Pia and Felix titles become standard in obverse legends of the empress's coinage.[3] Seeing a model in Livia for granting titles to the emperor's widow, most numismatists accept the appearance of PIA FELIX as occurring shortly after the death of Severus.[4] The combination of the PIA FELIX obverse legend with the MAT(ER) AVGG(ustorum) MAT(ER) SEN(ATVS) M(ATER) PATR(IAE) titles gives boundaries to the time frame between 209 and December 26, 211. Julia Domna received the MAT AVGG title upon Geta's accession to Augustus. After Geta's death and *damnatio memoriae*, inscriptions no longer referred to Julia Domna as Mater Augustorum, but as Mater Augustri Nostri (M AVG N), a title not found on imperial coinage. For Instinsky, the titles fall between Severus's death in February 211, with the incidence of the Pia and Felix titles, and the death of Geta in December 211.[5]

The question for epigraphers is far more tortured, and the inscription on the Porta Argentarii in the Forum Boarium illustrates the reason. Dedicated in 204, the panels and inscriptions celebrated the entire imperial *domus*: Severus, Caracalla, Geta, and Julia Domna along with Caracalla's new wife, Plautilla, as well as her father and Severus's Praetorian praefect, Plautianus. In 205, the execution of Plautianus shattered the harmony of the imperial *domus*, and his memory was condemned and his children sent into exile. Geta's memory was likewise condemned after his murder in 212. The big sticking point is in determining when Plautilla's titles were replaced by Julia Domna's Mater Senatus, Mater Patriae titles. Were they erased with her father's in 205, or were they removed with Geta's in 212?

As they appear on the Porta inscription, Julia Domna's and Caracalla's titles are at their fullest:

> IMP(ERATORI) CAES(ARI) L(VCIO) SEPTIMIO SEVERO PIO PERTINACI AVG(VSTO) ARABIC(O) ADIABENIC(O) PARTH(ICO) MAX(IMO) FORTISSIMO FELICISSIMO / PONTIF(ICI) MAX(IMO) TRIB(VNICIA) POTEST(ATE) XII IMP(ERATORI) XI CO(N)S(VLI) III PATRI PATRIAE ET / IMP(ERATORI) CAES(ARI) M(ARCO) AVRELIO ANTONINO PIO FELICI AVG(VSTO) TRIB(VNICIA) POTEST(ATE) VII CO(N)S(VLI) I<<II P(ATRI) P(ATRIAE) PROCO(N)S(VLI) FORTISSIMO FELICISSIMOQVE PRINCIPI>> ET / IVLIAE AVG(VSTAE) MATRI AVG(VSTI) <<N(OSTRI)>> ET CASTRORVM ET <<SENATVS ET PATRIAE ET>> IMP(ERATORIS) CAES(ARIS) M(ARCI) AVRELI ANTONINI PII FELICIS AVG(VSTI) / <<PARTHICI MAXIMI BRITTANNICI MAXIMI>> / ARGENTARI(I) ET NEGOTIANTES BOARI(I) HVIVS LOCI QVI / INVEHENT / DEVOTI NVMINI EORVM.[6]

Noticeably, the empress is not the MATER AVGG who appears on the coinage of 211; she has been reduced to MATER AVG N, a clear indication that this title was altered post-212. Caracalla's titles, too, were altered because we see both the Pius and the Felix titles that do not appear together until 213 on his coinage. His victorious cognomina also reflect campaigns well after the erection of the original inscription.

For Benario, the Porta Argentarii inscription is not sufficient evidence to determine when Julia Domna received her Mater Senatus, Mater Patriae titles, and he turns to another inscription, *CIL* 6 03401 = *CIL* 14 02255, for clarification. He reports that Pallottino had seen no trace of erasures on the stone:[7]

> [PRO SALVTE?] / IMP(ERATORIS) CAES(ARIS) L(VCI) SEPT(IMI) SEVER(I) PII PERT(INACIS) AVG(VSTI) ET IMP(ERATORIS) CAES(ARIS) / M(ARCI) AVREL(I) ANT(ONINI) PII FELIC(IS) AVG(VSTI) PARTH(ICI) MAX(IMI) BRITANN(ICI) / MAX(IMI) P(ATRIS) P(ATRIAE) ET IVLIAE AVG(VSTAE) MATR(IS) AVG(VSTI) N(OSTRIS) ET SENAT(VS) ET PA/TRIAE ET CASTR(ORVM) MINERV(AE) AVG (VSTAE) SACR(AE) DASIMIVS / FIRMIN(VS) CORN(ICVLARIVS) LEG(IONIS) ET AVREL(IVS) VICTORIN(VS) ACTAR(IVS) / CVM IMM(VNIBVS) LIBR(ARIIS) ET EXACTIS VOT(VM) M(ERITO) F(ECERVNT)[8]

Benario notes that there are irregularities with this inscription: it cannot be securely dated owing to the absence of a *tribunicia potestas* or consular date, the jumbled order of Julia Domna's titles, and the award of Caracalla's victorious cognomina anachronistically listed before Severus's death. The omission of Plautilla or Geta gives Benario little pause. What is more troubling to me, however, is that this inscription was apparently erected for the health (or some such thing as PRO SALVTE) of Severus *after his death*.[9] In the end, Benario accomplished what he set out to do—that is, not to prove conclusively that the empress's titles were awarded before 211, but simply to muddy the waters. His final words: "We do not claim to have done anything more than marshal some support for the view that the empress did not have to wait for the death of her husband to be so honored."[10] Muddy the waters he did.

Kettenhofen was thoroughly convinced by Benario's arguments and only expresses surprise that Benario did not also cite *CIL* 06 00419 = *CIL* 06 30763.[11] To Kettenhofen, this inscription seems more certain proof of an earlier award of Julia's titles:

> I(OVI) O(PTIMO) M(AXIMO) D(OLICHENO) D(IGNO) / PRO SALVTE IMP(ERATORUM) / L(VCI) SEPTIMII SEVERI / AVG(VSTI) ET M(ARCI) AVRELII / ANTONINI AVG(VSTI) / [[[ET GETAE CAES(ARIS)]]] <<PII FELICIS>> ET / IVLIAE AVG(VSTAE) MAT(RI) / AVG(VSTORVM) ET [[[PLAVTILLAE AVG(VSTAE) TOTIVSQ(VE) DOMVS DIVINAE]]] <<CASTRO/RVM SENATVS ET / POPULI ROMANI>> / SACERDOTES / POSVERVNT

The inscription shows clear signs of erasure, however, and even before the erasures, the titles were clearly not in accordance with imperial usage. Julia Domna's title in the original inscription was not at its fullest because the Mater Castrorum title was not included. The dedicators also slipped up on Julia Domna's Mater Patriae title, calling her instead Mater Populi Romani. These gaffes suggest that the priests were not careful about official titulature when they erected the inscription. Notoriously creative, some titulature found in inscriptions is better discarded when attempting to date the titles.

Kuhoff addresses the question of Julia Domna's Mater Senatus, Mater Patriae titles by revisiting the Porta Argentarii. For him, Julia Domna's mother titles replaced Plautilla's titles in 205, at the same time as her father's *damnatio memoriae*. He apparently believes that such an important inscription on such an important monument must not have been left blank, and thus Julia Domna's mother titles date to 205, not 211, as numismatic evidence suggests. There are several problems with these assertions. Clearly, the *collegia* that erected the Porta Argentarii were okay with blank spaces on the monument, or else the spaces where Geta, Plautilla, and Plautianus stood on the panel reliefs would have been filled with something else. Clay points to another very good reason to rely more heavily on numismatic evidence. Very long honorary titles usually appeared on coinage almost immediately upon being decreed and are generally dropped soon thereafter. For instance, Clay notes that Severus's Parthicus Maximus title appeared for only a short time on coins from the Roman mint (198–201). The same is true with coins celebrating Caracalla's various victories; his victorious cognomen Brittanicus appears only between 210 and 213, until replaced by his newly won title of Germanicus.[12]

Finally, to return to Instinsky's point, there was precedent for the Senate awarding a living empress new titles upon the death of her husband.[13] In 14 AD, Livia was adopted and given a new name, Julia Augusta (coincidentally the same name as Julia Domna was known on coinage during Severus's lifetime). The Senate also wanted to dub her either Parens or Mater Patriae, an honor which Tiberius famously refused on her behalf.[14]

As I see it, the two pieces of epigraphic evidence do not undermine Instinsky's original assessment. I therefore date the award of these titles between February and December 211.

NOTES

Introduction

1. Herodian 4.3.8–9. ἡ δὲ Ἰουλία "γῆν μέν" ἔφη "καὶ θάλασσαν, ὦ τέκνα, εὑρίσκετε ὅπως νείμησθε, καὶ τὰς ἠπείρους, ὥς φατε, τὸ Πόντιον ῥεῖθρον διαιρεῖ· τὴν δὲ μητέρα πῶς ἂν διέλοισθε, καὶ πῶς ἡ ἀθλία ἐγὼ ἐς ἑκάτερον ὑμῶν νεμηθείην ἢ τμηθείην; πρῶτον δὴ ἐμὲ φονεύσατε, καὶ διελόντες ἑκάτερος παρ᾽ ἑαυτῷ τὸ μέρος θαπτέτω· οὕτω γὰρ ἂν μετὰ γῆς καὶ θαλάττης ἐς ὑμᾶς μερισθείην." ταῦτα δὲ λέγουσα μετὰ δακρύων καὶ οἰμωγῆς, ἀμφοτέροις τε τὰς χεῖρας περιβάλλουσα καὶ ὑπὸ τὰς ἀγκάλας λαβοῦσα, συνάγειν ἐπειρᾶτο. πάντας δὲ οἴκτου καταλαβόντος διελύθη τὸ συνέδριον, ἥ τε σκέψις ἀπεδοκιμάσθη, ἑκάτερός τε ἐς τὰ ἑαυτοῦ βασίλεια ἀνεχώρησε. All translations of Herodian are based upon those of Whittaker 1969.

2. Cass. Dio 78.2.3–6. ἐπεὶ δὲ εἴσω ἐγένοντο, ἑκατόνταρχοί τινες ἐσεπήδησαν ἀθρόοι, παρὰ τοῦ Ἀντωνίνου προπαρεσκευασμένοι, καὶ αὐτὸν πρός τε τὴν μητέρα, ὡς εἶδέ σφας, προκαταφυγόντα καὶ ἀπό τε τοῦ αὐχένος αὐτῆς ἐξαρτηθέντα καὶ τοῖς στήθεσι τοῖς τε μαστοῖς προσφύντα κατέκοψαν ὀλοφυρόμενον καὶ βοῶντα· "μῆτερ μῆτερ, τεκοῦσα τεκοῦσα, βοήθει, σφάζομαι." καὶ ἡ μὲν οὕτως ἀπατηθεῖσα τόν τε υἱὸν ἐν τοῖς ἑαυτῆς κόλποις ἀνοσιώτατα ἀπολλύμενον ἐπεῖδε, καὶ τὸν θάνατον αὐτοῦ ἐς αὐτὰ τὰ σπλάγχνα τρόπον τινά, ἐξ ὧν ἐγεγέννητο, ἐσεδέξατο· καὶ γὰρ τοῦ αἵματος πᾶσα ἐπλήσθη, ὡς ἐν μηδενὶ λόγῳ τὸ τῆς χειρὸς τραῦμα ὃ ἐτρώθη ποιήσασθαι. οὔτε δὲ πενθῆσαι οὔτε θρηνῆσαι τὸν υἱόν, καίπερ πρόωρον οὕτως οἰκτρῶς ἀπολωλότα, ὑπῆρξεν αὐτῇ (δύο γὰρ καὶ εἴκοσι ἔτη καὶ μῆνας ἐννέα ἐβίω), ἀλλ᾽ ἠναγκάζετο ὡς καὶ ἐν μεγάλῃ τινὶ εὐτυχίᾳ οὖσα χαίρειν καὶ γελᾶν· οὕτω που πάντα ἀκριβῶς καὶ τὰ ῥήματα αὐτῆς καὶ τὰ νεύματα τά τε χρώματα ἐτηρεῖτο· καὶ μόνῃ ἐκείνῃ, τῇ Αὐγούστῃ, τῇ τοῦ αὐτοκράτορος γυναικί, τῇ τῶν αὐτοκρατόρων μητρί, οὐδ᾽ ἰδίᾳ που ἐπὶ τηλικούτῳ παθήματι δακρῦσαι ἐξῆν. All translations of Cassius Dio are based upon those of Cary 2001.

3. Gerding 2002; Ginsburg 2006; Hälikkä 2002; Hillard 1989; Flory 1996; Flower 2002; Joshel 1997; Keltanen 2002; Leppin 2002; Matheson 1996; Patterson 2007; Staples 1998. For many years, the study of imperial women labored under the assumption that one could actually find or rehabilitate the "real" Livia, Julia, or Agrippina. I confess that I am skeptical of ever finding the "real" anyone in antiquity, regardless of the amount of information that survives, whether a person's writings are extant or even if one examines all available evidence in coinage, art, inscriptions, and literature. I am therefore very much in agreement with scholars who read the surviving images of imperial women as rhetorical tools.

4. Perhaps the most obvious ancient instance of this is Plin. *Paneg.* 83–84, in which Pliny attributes to the emperor the positive qualities of Trajan's wife and sister. Plotina learns her good qualities from Trajan, especially the value of obedience and modesty: *Mariti hoc opus, qui ita imbuit, ita instituit: nam uxori sufficit obsequi gloria.* Marciana learns her *simplicitas* and *veritas* from her brother. The two are such fine reflections of Trajan that it would be hard to decide which is more efficacious for an upright life: *Soror autem tua, ut se sororem esse meminit! Ut in illa tua simplicitas, tua veritas, tuus candor agnoscitur! Ut, si quis eam uxori tuae conferat, dubitare cogatur, utrum sit efficacius ad recte vivendum, bene institui, aut feliciter nasci.* I discuss this phenomenon in more detail in chapter 3. For a similar interpretation of this passage, cf. Keltanen 2002, 144–145.

5. Anderson calls the scene in Herodian "a recourse to the world of declamation" (1993, 107). Both vignettes are problematic. No other source besides Herodian mentions so momentous a decision as dividing the empire between Geta and Caracalla. Anderson doubts the scene ever occurred. Dio's scene is equally problematic. Official propaganda depicted Geta as conspiring to murder Caracalla. The reliability of Dio's report is little better than palace whispers, but the high drama and symmetry of the scene suggest that it also was a "recourse to the world of declamation."

6. This is not a new approach to women and antiquity, but it has not been applied to Julia Domna. For republican women, cf. Hillard 1989. For imperial women, cf. Ginsburg 2006; Temporini 1978, 2002.

7. Milnor calls attention to the political advantages inherent in exposing the domestic sphere to public consumption: "The domestic sphere offered an uncontroversial place to focus public attention—a place where tradition, virtue and the nostalgic comforts of home might be invoked as the basis of a renewed sense of national purpose" (2005, 27). Whereas Augustus used this domestic sphere to promote himself and to legitimate his social legislation, Herodian and Cassius Dio instead highlighted the intrusion of the imperial domestic sphere into politics, and then used this intrusion as a means to criticize the young emperors. Just as untenable, however, is the imperial administration's portrayal of Julia Domna as disinterested in politics except to preserve the empire. Dio undermines this image when he claims that Julia Domna sought to rule the empire after Caracalla's death (79.23.2–4).

8. A small sampling of scholars who assign Julia Domna power well beyond that of her predecessors includes Babelon and von Domaszewski 1957; Baharal 1992; Boatwright 1991; Ghedini 1984; Gorrie 2004; Hemelrijk 1999; Leppin 2002; Levick 2007; Ricciardi 2007; Ryberg 1955; Turton 1962; Saavedra Guerrero 1994.

9. Milnor recognizes the increased visibility of the domestic sphere during the age of Augustus as being politically motivated and rhetorically expressed. She sees that ancient sources often neglect large sections of society and that those underrepresented peoples, especially women, "are so clearly figments of an elite male author's imagination" (2005, 41). For this reason, evidence culled from rhetorically motivated authors that highlights the visibility of imperial women ought to be considered with caution.

10. I agree with Levick when she says "there is no evidence . . . that any effective right to strike coins rested after Augustus on anyone but the emperor" (2007, 67). With regard to the extent to which other imperial women controlled their own images, cf. Boatwright 1991; Keltanen 2002; Staples 1998; Wood 1999.

11. Langford 2008, 135. Any qualities particular to Julia Domna—such as her exotic origins, her interests in philosophy, or her influence with her husband—were glossed over or ignored in official propaganda.

12. For this approach to imperial women in general, cf. Boatwright 1991, 1992, 2003; Corbier 1995; Flory 1996; Leppin 2002, 486. Lusnia postulated that Julia Domna's extraordinary titles and the output of her types in the imperial mint are best explained as props meant to support her husband's legitimacy and the foundation of his dynasty (1995, 138–139).

13. Exploring relationships between the emperor and a population on the basis of favors and honors is not a new approach, although scholars over time have come to recognize that the givers of favors had as much to gain as the receivers (cf. Ando 2000; Millar 1977; Price 1984; Rose 1997).

14. On Julia Domna's background, cf. Levick 2007, 6–22.

15. HA *Sev.* 3.9. *Cum amissa uxore aliam vellet ducere, genituras sponsarum requirebat, ipse quoque matheseos peritissimus, et cum audisset esse in Syria quandam quae id geniturae haberet ut regi iungeretur, eandem uxorem petiit, Iuliam scilicet, et accepit interventu amicorum. Ex qua statim pater factus est.*

16. Agrippina's proximity to several emperors, living and dead, made her a favorite target of senatorial authors. Her character, heritage, and behavior made her especially useful in praising or blaming her powerful male relations (Ginsburg 2006).

17. HA *Cl. Alb.* 3.4–6. *Nec negari potest, quod etiam Marius Maximus dicit, hunc animum Severo primum fuisse, ut, si quid ei contingeret, Pescennium Nigrum et Clodium Albinum sibi substitueret. Sed postea et filiis iam maiusculis studens et Albini amori invidens sententiam mutasse atque illorum utrumque bello opressisse, maxime precibus uxoris adductus.*

18. Cass. Dio 77.15.2. ὁμονοεῖτε, τοὺς στρατιώτας πλουτίζετε, τῶν ἄλλων πάντων καταφρονεῖτε.

19. HA *M. Ant.* 10.

20. Cass. Dio 79.4. Other scholars have seen this passage as a sort of encomium for the empress (e.g., Taylor 1945), but I suspect that Dio meant to indict Caracalla's shirking of his civil duties by leaving them to a woman.

21. Cass. Dio 79.23.3. [fragmentary] μνημονεύοντας, ὅπως αὐταρχήσῃ τῇ τε Σεμιράμιδι καὶ τῇ Νιτώκριδι, ἅτε καὶ ἐκ τῶν αὐτῶν πρόπον τινὰ χωρίων αὐταῖς οὖσα, παρισουμένη.

22. Cass. Dio 79.23.6. καὶ τὰ ἐν τῇ Ῥώμῃ περὶ τοῦ υἱέος αὐτῆς λεχθέντα ἤκουσεν, οὐκέτ' ἐφιλοψύχησεν, ἀλλ' ἤδη τρόπον τινὰ καὶ ὑπὸ τοῦ καρκίνου, ὃν ἐν τῷ μαστῷ ἐκ πάνυ πολλοῦ χρόνου ἡσυχάζοντά πως ἔχουσα τότε ἠρέθισεν ἐκ τῆς πληγῆς ἣν ἐπὶ τῷ τοῦ παιδὸς θανάτῳ κοψαμένη κατὰ τῶν στέρνων ἐπέπληκτο, συναιρουμένη προσδιέφθειρεν ἑαυτὴν ἀποκαρτερήσασα.

23. Other works helping to inform my ideas of how the imperial center communicated with populations in the periphery are Burrell 2004, Howgego et al. 2005, and Rose 1997. An earlier generation of scholars also explored these communications (e.g., Millar 1977).

24. Ando notes that individuals can accept several conflicting interpretations of reality at once with little trace of discomfort. In some cases, the propaganda produced by the imperial administration represented clear untruths. For example, L. Septimius

Severus claimed that he was the adopted son of Marcus Aurelius. Marcus did not adopt Severus; rather, Severus adopted himself into the family long after Marcus's death (2000, 21–27).

25. Though Ando mostly limits his observations to communications between the provinces and the imperial center, he briefly explores the variety of Severus's propaganda to the military, the Senate, and provincial cities during the early years of his reign (2000, 182–190).

26. Jones 1956.

27. These questions were largely in response to Jones's criticisms. Several prominent numismatists have weighed in on this issue, including Alföldi 1956; Burnett 1987; Buttrey 1972; Crawford 1983; Ehrhardt 1984; Hekster 2003; Levick 1982, 1999; Metcalf 1999; Noreña 2001, 2007; Sutherland 1959; Wallace-Hadrill 1981. For some of the most recent work on propaganda on republican coinage, see Farney 2007; Kondratieff 2004; Meadows and Williams 2001. Duncan-Jones explored the coinage of Trajan and concluded that only a small portion of coins were "news" coins. For him, this "makes it difficult to argue that propaganda was an important purpose behind coinage" (2005, 485).

28. More recently, some numismatists have suggested that the variation in types and legends between metals and denominations may indicate that the imperial administration used coinage to target audiences of different economic strata. See Ehrhardt 1984, 44; Hekster 2003, 25–29; Legutko 2000, 25–29; Metcalf 1993.

29. Mattingly et al. 1923–1994.

30. Before Noreña 2001, numismatists chiefly looked to hoards to determine the mobility of coinage and to speculate the total number of coins produced or in circulation; see Duncan-Jones 1994, 1996, 2001, 2003; Howgego 1992, 1995b. Other numismatists used hoards to determine die production (e.g., Christiansen 1988), though there are serious methodological flaws with this approach (Howgego and Christiansen 1990). Rowan provides an excellent overview of the historiography as well as the general issues involved in a quantitative study of coin hoards in "A Quantitative Perspective on Roman Coinage" (2009, 33–44). Duncan-Jones 1994, 134n28; Metcalf 1999, 3; Noreña 2001, 148.

31. Noreña 2001, 149.

32. Kemmers 2005, 2006. Hekster and Manders take a slightly different approach: they combine the method of Noreña 2001 with an analysis of the variety of issues to develop an overall image of an emperor's propaganda (2006, 135–144). Manders 2008 uses this methodology to examine trends in the coinage of the third-century emperors as well as case studies of three emperors.

33. Rowan 2009.

34. Rowan's Severan Coin Hoards database is now available online as part of the Severan Database Project at http://web3.cas.usf.edu/main/other/severan. The complete bibliography of the coin hoards appearing in her database is in Appendix A. There are only two hoards published in Rome and Italy, and they are too small to be reliable representatives of what was circulating in Rome. Rowan also notes that it would be more useful if the hoards could be divided by other classifications, such as by military or civilian context, rather than by geographical zones (2009, 39).

35. Clay 1972 goes only as far as 198 and, as he notes in personal correspondence,

Domna's coinage still requires scholarly attention up to and beyond her death in 217 in order to include the diva issues. Fittschen 1982 offers an excellent example of how much can be accomplished with this method and through the comparison to sculptural portraits. Hill offers a far less satisfying effort, with little explanation of his methodology. His study is problematic because he based his interpretations strictly upon stylistic criteria (1964b, 8). Demonstrating the limitations of stylistic criteria in their chemical analyses of coinage are Butcher 1996; Butcher and Ponting 2005; Gitler and Ponting 2003, 2007.

36. Scholars have largely accepted Mattingly and Sydenham's standard divisions for analyzing Julia Domna's coinage produced by the mint at Rome: 193–196, in which she is referred to as IVLIA DOMNA AVG; 196–211, as IVLIA AVG; and 211–217, as IVLIA PIA FELIX AVG (1936, 73–74, 89).

37. My approach is not without its critics. Responding to an explanation of my methodology, Potter wrote, "coins, titles and monuments all reflect facets of the discourse between these different groups. They cannot be seen really as shaping the discussion except in so far as they are memorials of messages that were sent in different forms" (personal correspondence, January 11, 2011). The evidence examined here—coins, titles, and monuments—are evidence of the negotiations and as such not only are they memorials of messages sent between populations, but it seems to me that they also constitute attempts to shape the discourse. Through them, the imperial administration demonstrated its vision of the dynasty and the "truths" of the imperial family's connections to the Antonines. Different populations responded to these claims, also through coins, titles, and monuments, often with variations of what the imperial administration originally said. To me, the response (whatever its medium) is an attempt make a population's voice heard in the process of creating ideology.

38. See http://web3.cas.usf.edu/main/other/severan/jdi/.

39. Dixon claims for imperial women a power that cannot be quantified or qualified: "If the term 'politics' is synonymous with suffrage, the magistracies and membership of the Senate, these were purely male preserves. If 'politics' is, rather, to be taken in the sense of the pursuit and exercise of *real power* [emphasis mine], it alters the question of female involvement" (1988, 91).

40. Alexandridis 2004 represents an important exception to this approach. Though she recognizes that the primary function of women in official representations was to promote and stabilize the dynasty, she also believes, like Wood 1999, that representations of imperial women were meant to be exempla to other nonimperial women.

41. Dating Julia Domna's coins is more complicated than her male relatives'. Some scholars have attempted to assign dates to Julia Domna's coinage on the basis of stylistic criteria, a problematic methodology (Hill 1964b, 8; Lusnia 1995). Nonetheless, the similarity of themes that are securely dated to the period for the male members of the family are echoed in those of Julia Domna's coinage, making it likely that the types were distributed at the same time, between 202 and 204.

42. Cass. Dio 76.15.6. καὶ οὕτω καὶ ἐς τὰ ἄλλα πάντα ὁ Πλαυτιανὸς αὐτοῦ κατεκράτει ὥστε καὶ τὴν Ἰουλίαν τὴν Αὔγουσταν πολλὰ καὶ δεινὰ ἐργάσασθαι· πάνυ γὰρ αὐτῇ ἤχθετο, καὶ σφόδρα αὐτὴν πρὸς τὸν Σεουῆρον ἀεὶ διέβαλλέν, ἐξετάσεις τε κατ᾽ αὐτῆς καὶ βασάνους κατ᾽ εὐγενῶν γυναικῶν ποιούμενος. Though it is difficult to

assign an exact date to the waning of Julia Domna's influence in court, it must occur before Plautianus's death in 205. The apex of his power was most secure once he had arranged for his daughter to marry Caracalla, around 203.

43. It is by no means clear that Julia Domna was powerful in the same concrete terms as those used by Boatwright; some imperial women had abundant resources of their own and were able to do as they wished (1991, 515–525). It is not clear, however, that Julia Domna had the same resources at her disposal. Zwalve 2001 discusses a disputed will in which Julia Domna might have been an heir; the judgment was not in her favor. Levick, however, assumes that Julia Domna must have been wealthy: "Domna carried what must have been a handsome dowry with her, not only the property that under Roman law and custom was due to her husband, but also her beauty and accomplishments and the high descent she claimed; she can have lacked no adornment to enhance her attractions" (2007, 18–19). Levick can provide no evidence, however, that the empress had her own resources at hand, as Trajan's women did.

44. "From the time of Livia onward, the ability of women to intercede with their husbands in matters of official policy was a matter of public knowledge, and apparently of widespread public approval" (Wood 1999, 316).

45. Syme 1960, 322. The quote is in reference to the perception of Augustus's power: for his friends, the princeps wielded *auctoritas*, but for his enemies, it was *potentia*.

46. Boatwright 1991, 515.

47. The greatest contribution of Kokkinos 1992 is to gather the various pieces of evidence concerning Antonia, but he never addresses effectively how to define or quantify power. Instead, he compares Antonia to Livia and finds that the only reason Livia gets more attention is because of her connection to Augustus. In the second edition, Kokkinos 2002 again skirts the issue. Barrett provides concrete moments in which Livia was able to intervene on behalf of others (2002, 186–214). Levick also successfully uses this approach (2007, 69–73).

48. Hillard 1989, 176.

49. Ginsburg 2006.

50. Boatwright 1991, 533. "[Slanderous rumors] reveal the fear and envy that the concept of an influential empress aroused at this time" (530). By the same token, we ought to be just as wary of literary sources that praise imperial women as those that malign them. Women could also serve as vehicles for praising their men. For instance, Gerding 2002 came to the conclusion that the chief motivation behind the enormous tomb erected for Caecilia Metella on the Via Appia was to enhance not her own reputation, but that of her male relatives.

51. Flower 2002, 160.

52. Temporini asserts that imperial women appear in state art only when they were useful to their husbands or sons (2002, 17).

53. Corbier 1995. Dixon took this statement a step further, saying "the chief celebration of motherhood—or of mothers—as such was primarily dynastic" (1988, 91).

54. Wood 1999, 22.

55. Keltanen 2002, 140–146; Leppin 2002, 486; Temporini 2002, 192.

56. Leppin 2002, 485–486.

57. The practice of awarding imperial women the title Augusta immediately upon an emperor's accession became common after Antoninus Pius. Under Trajan, Plotina

and Marciana had to wait seven years to receive the title, while Faustina the Elder held the title from Pius's accession and well beyond her death and divination. Faustina the Younger was advertised as Augusta only after the birth of her first child, despite being the daughter of Antoninus Pius and wife of Marcus Aurelius. This suggests that her real propagandistic importance to the dynasty was as the producer of successors to the imperial throne. Cf. Plin. *Paneg.* 83–85. For Keinast, Plotina and Marciana were not awarded the title Augusta until 105, though apparently the Senate offered them the title upon Trajan's succession (1996, 125–126). Pertinax stands in stark contrast to this trend of offering the Augusta title to imperial women immediately after their husbands' accession. His rejection of the Augustus and Augusta titles for his son and wife was exceptional; see Cass. Dio 74.7. Didius Julianus returned to the Antonine precedents by accepting the Augusta title for his wife and daughter immediately, as evident in *RIC* 4a.7–10, 16; *RIC* 4a.18–21, 18.

58. Coins minted after 195 advertise the empress as IVLIA AVGVSTA. Clay has shown convincingly that between June 193 and mid–195, the mint was concurrently striking a total of five issues: three for Severus, one for Albinus, and one for Julia Domna. When tensions arose, apparently in mid–194, Albinus's issue was dropped in favor of a fourth issue for Severus. This remained the case until December 195, when the mint stopped production of Severus's fourth issue in order to produce an issue for Caracalla (1972, 123–132).

59. Cass. Dio 74.15.1.

60. Plin. *Paneg.* 7. For a further discussion of the Senate's preference for adopted succession, see chapter 3.

61. Cass. Dio 74.15.1.

62. As Corbier 1995 has shown with the Julio-Claudians, imperial women in official media served as legitimizing links between emperors. When a new dynasty came to power, women tended to be ignored if they could not provide any legitimatization between earlier emperors and the current one. Boatwright notes that the female relatives of Trajan and Hadrian who could not provide the emperors with any additional legitimacy kept low profiles (1991, 540). Even Empresses Plotina and Sabina are only slightly represented in the numismatic record in comparison to empresses who could contribute to legitimizing their men, such as Faustina the Elder or Faustina the Younger. Occasionally, female relatives of the emperor were overlooked because the new emperors wished to call attention to how different they were from their predecessors. This was likely the case with Nerva's female relatives, as no trace of them remains in official media. Alexandridis and I (independently) examined how, when, and which imperial women were advertised and the importance of dynasty from Livia to Julia Domna (2004, abhang 3; Langford-Johnson 2005, 14–103). Wood 1999 explores the Julio-Claudian women. For a list of the titles and honors without comment, cf. Keinast 1996.

63. Herodian 2.15.4.

64. Cass. Dio 74.13.

65. Cass. Dio 75.4.3–6.

66. Herodian 3.2.3–5. In the struggle for empire, wives and children became political tools in the hands of rivals. Commodus had made a practice of holding hostage the children (and presumably the wives) of provincial governors while they served their terms in order to ensure loyalty. The *HA* reported that Severus seized Niger's wife and

children, and though he initially treated them in the same fashion he treated his own children, he then exiled and finally killed them (*Sev.* 8.11, *Niger* 6.1). The *HA* suggests that he did so because of the upcoming conflict with Albinus (*Sev.* 10.1). The wife and children of Albinus, according to the *HA*, fared no better. Severus ordered their bodies dumped in the Rhone while the body of Albinus was mangled, decapitated, and displayed for a time outside of his family residence in Rome, presumably as an object lesson for any of his more intransigent supporters (*Sev.* 11.9, *Albinus* 9.6–7; Herodian 3.8.1; Cass. Dio 76.7.3).

67. Appendix B lists the most prolific types according to zones and time periods.

68. Lusnia 1995, 121–123. Lusnia writes that these "themes were all used since the time of Julius Caesar" (122n9). Nonetheless, these themes were revolutionary in that they did not appear on women's coinage until the second century.

69. These images are characterized by the lack of "two curls of natural hair that escape coquettishly from beneath her wig." Nodelman reports that these images are "rather mechanical, mediocre representations of a provincial character, certainly not original works of art." Because these are replicas, however, he posits that there must have been much finer originals in antiquity. Nodelman dated these portraits by comparing them to the coinage dated from this period (1965, 117).

70. Scholars offering this interpretation include, among others, Baharal 1992, Clay 1972, and Fejfer 1985.

71. Lusnia 1995, 121–123.

72. From 195, the obverse legends of Julia Domna's coinage named her simply as IVLIA AVGVSTA, a name and title that Livia received after the death of Augustus. In the East, the majority of inscriptions maintain the DOMNA in Julia's titles, regardless of whether the inscriptions or coins were in Greek or Latin.

73. Clay uses medallions minted and distributed in Rome to date the announcement of Caracalla's position as Caesar to the last few days of 195 (1972, 133–152).

74. Cass. Dio 76.4.1. Τῷ δὲ Σεουήρῳ πόλεμος αὖθις, μήπω ἐκ τῶν βαρβαρικῶν ἀναπνεύσαντι, ἐμφύλιος πρὸς τὸν Ἀλβῖνον τὸν Καίσαρα συνηνέχθη. ὁ μὲν γὰρ οὐδὲ τὴν τοῦ Καίσαρος αὐτῷ ἔτι ἐδίδου τιμήν, ἐπειδὴ τὸν Νίγρον ἐκποδὼν ἐποιήσατο, τά τε ἄλλα τὰ ἐνταῦθα ὡς ἐβούλετο κατεστήσατο· ὁ δὲ καὶ τὴν τοῦ αὐτοκράτορος ἐζήτει ὑπεροχήν.

75. Sources for the purge following Albinus's defeat include Herodian 3.8.6–7; HA *Sev.* 11.3–6, *Niger* 6.3; Cassius Dio 76.7.7–8.5.

76. Cass. Dio 76.8.1–5. Clearly, these events did not occur at the same time. Severus's adoption into the Antonine house occurred before the war against Albinus in 196/197 (it is advertised on coins dating from 195 to 196; cf. *RIC* 4a.65–66, 99; *RIC* 4a.686, 185; *RIC* 4a.700–702A, 187). The *HA* dates Commodus's deification to the campaigns against Albinus (*Sev.* 11.3), while Dio seems only to have heard of it when Severus returned to Rome after the war. It is significant, however, that Dio links them together, for they were all steps in legitimizing Severus's reign and founding his dynasty. Dio might have been reporting the information in the fashion he obtained it. It might be that Severus chose to keep this detail from the Senate but broadcasted it among his troops as a way of currying favor. Among the senators that Severus purged was Sulpicianus, the father-in-law of Pertinax. Dio gives no further details on this execution, but one supposes that this action represents the rupture of the final link between Severus and Pertinax.

77. Cass. Dio 76.7.4 on Severus's capriciousness: τῷ τε Κομμόδῳ, ὅν πρῴην ὕβριζεν, ἡρωικὰς ἐδίδου τιμάς. For the apology, 76.8.1: ἀπολογίαν τινὰ ὑπὲρ τοῦ Κομμόδου ἐπήγαγε, καθαπτόμενος τῆς βουλῆς ὡς οὐ δικαίως ἐκεῖνον ἀτιμαζούσης, εἴγε καὶ αὐτῆς οἱ πλείους αἴσχιον βιοτεύουσιν.

78. There are coins celebrating the deification of Commodus, but these are struck only until the reign of Trajan Decius (*RIC* 4c.93, 132).

79. Though I posit that family propaganda is used to legitimate Severus and his nascent dynasty, another aspect of family propaganda must be considered. As Bryant 1996 has shown, an important by-product of presenting the emperor and empress as the mother and father of the empire was to discourage political dissent. In the family-as-state metaphor that the Antonines had promoted and Severus adopted and adapted, the emperor is always the father, and his subjects—no matter their age, status, or experience—are always his children. Those who disagreed with the emperor or his policies could be painted as impious children who rebelled against their father, the state, and the gods (the emperor was the chief representative of the gods). If the disagreement should escalate to rebellion, the imperial administration could easily depict its opponents as patricides, thus maintaining the ideological high ground. In other words, family as metaphor discouraged not simply dissent but political activity as a whole.

80. Cf. Lusnia (forthcoming) for the historiography on the Temple of Fortuna Muliebris and on the role of Julia Domna in the refurbishment of the *Aedes Vestae* and the supposed *senaculum matronis*. Ancient sources for the *senaculum matronis* include HA *Heliogab.* 4.4, *Aurel.* 49.6. Modern explorations are Hemelrijk 1999, 12–16; Paschoud 1996, 221n6.4.3; Purcell 1986; Straub 1966.

81. Almost from the moment Severus became emperor, he engaged in a project to gloss over his African origins in favor of constructed (i.e., fictional) Roman ones (Langford 2008). Lusnia 1995, among others, shows that state art ignored Julia Domna's foreign origins in favor of traditional Roman feminine qualities and deities.

82. With Caracalla, *RIC* 4a.542–545, 166; with Geta, *RIC* 4a.571, 169.

83. Cass. Dio 76.15.6.

84. On the personification of virtues and their worship in Rome, cf. Fears 1981a. The same charges of infidelity were leveled against Faustina, presumably by Commodus's detractors, who claimed that his birth was the result of his mother's tryst with a gladiator. HA *Marc.* 19.1–7. *Aiunt quidam, quod et veri simile videtur, Commodum Antoninum, successorem illius ac filium, non esse de eo natum sed de adulterio, ac talem fabellam vulgari sermone contexunt: Faustinam quondam, Pii filiam, Marci uxorem, cum gladiatores transire vidisset, unius ex his amore succensam, cum longa aegritudine laboraret, viro de amore confessam. Quod cum ad Chaldaeos Marcus rettulisset, illorum fuisse consilium, ut occiso gladiatore sanguine illius sese Faustina sublavaret atque ita cum viro concumberet. Quod cum esset factum, solutum quidem amorem, natum vero Commodum gladiatorem esse, non principem, qui mille prope pugnas publice populo inspectante gladiatorias imperator exhibuit, ut in vita eius docebitur. Quod quidem veri simile ex eo habetur quod tam sancti principis filius iis moribus fuit quibus nullus lanista, nullus scaenicus, nullus arenarius, nullus postremo ex omnium dedecorum ac scelerum conluvione concretus. Multi autem ferunt Commodum omnino ex adulterio natum, si quidem Faustinam satis constet apud Caietam condiciones sibi et nauticas et gladiatorias elegisse.*

85. Herodian 3.13.2; Cass. Dio 77.11.

86. Cass. Dio 78.1.4.

87. Cass. Dio 78.1.5.

88. Instinsky 1942, 211. Benario 1958a sees no reason not to allow for an earlier assignment of the titles to Julia Domna. Most careful scholarship now agrees with Instinsky's dating (e.g., Kettenhofen 1979, 79–81), though Keinast apparently has not accepted Kettenhofen's dating (1996, 167). Julia Domna was the first empress to receive the PIA FELIX title combination. The last person to hold both titles prior to Julia Domna was Commodus, who received PIVS around 182/183 and FELIX after 185. Caracalla received PIVS around 198. Opinions differ as to when he received the FELIX. The FELIX title does not appear on Caracalla's coinage until 213 (Sutherland et al. 1984; *RIC* 4a.498e, 294), but Keinast, who seems to work from epigraphical evidence, dates the FELIX title to before 200 (1996, 164). For a fuller discussion on dating these titles, see Appendix C.

89. Cass. Dio 78.18.2-3.

Chapter One · *Not Your Momma*

1. *ILD* 764. IVLIAE AVGVS/TAE MATRI SAN/CTISSIMI PIISSI/MIQ[V]E ANTONINI AVGVSTI/ET CASTRORUM/SENATVSQV[E]| AC PATRIAE COH(ORS) I BRITTA/N(N)ICA (MILLIARIA) ANT/ONIANA. Cf. http://www.manfredclauss.de/gb/index.html for epigraphic conventions and abbreviations.

2. Levick finds that "the specific meaning of the title is obvious: the troops were under the protection of the empress, and she could expect their protection in return; more generally, it expressed the symbiotic relationship between dynasty and army" (2007, 43). Ricciardi goes on to say that "the extension of the presumably steady, maternal hand of the empress to the army not only created a more personal bond between the imperial family and the military, but also helped secure the often tenuous relationship between the emperor and his protectors and chief supporters [i.e., the military]" (2007, 62).

3. These inscriptions are collected in the Inscriptions of Julia Domna database and can be accessed at http://web3.cas.usf.edu/main/other/severan/ as part of the Severan Database Project.

4. Julia Domna is often honored in inscriptions erected by the military during Severus's lifetime, but only once is the sole recipient of honors (*CIL* 02 02529). When she is mentioned, she is the last listed family member, behind male members and even behind Plautianus when he is mentioned. Her name is often followed by *totiusq[ue] domus divinae*. Six inscriptions in which Julia Domna may be the sole dedicatee date from Caracalla's reign: *CIL* 08 18068, *AE* 1914 00038, *AE* 1980 00603, *ILD* 764, *CIL* 13 06671, *RIB* 00976.

5. Though numismatists often speculate that the primary use of the eastern traveling mints was to pay the troops, I have not yet found any scholarly literature proving the assumption. Duncan-Jones comes closest, positing that the state produced coinage to meet public expenses, the foremost of projects (1994, 106). Ziegler 1996 works off the premise that troops stationed in the East were paid in imperial silver and gold. The cities with an army presence thus ramped up the production of bronze denominations in order to handle the influx of imperial silver and gold.

6. Raepsaet-Charlier 1982. Pflaum finds far fewer indications that the wives of imperial procurators accompanied their husbands to the provinces. He finds only thirty-three examples, the majority of which can be dated between 150 and 300 (1950, 297*ff.*).

7. Allason-Jones 1999. Allison 2006 provides a more general overview of how archaeologists address gender in their research.

8. This discussion owes much to Phang 2001, 344–385.

9. Dench 1998, 137–146; McDonnell 2006, 159–165; Phang 2001, 345, 381; Williams 1999, 132–142.

10. Phang 2001, 352.

11. Dench 1998, 137–146; Phang 2001, 345, 381; Williams 1999, 134–142.

12. Phang 2001, 363.

13. Phang 2001, 380–382.

14. Phang cites several examples of republican commanders struggling against the negative influences of lower-class women and camp followers: Liv. *AUC* 23.45.1–5 (Hannibal's army at Cumae); [Frontinus] *Strat.* 4.1.1; Liv. *Per.* 57; Val. Max. 2.7.1; App. *Iber.* 85; Polyaen. 8.16.2 (Scipio Aemilianus before the walls of Numanita) (2001, 355).

15. Phang 2001, 368. Phang cites Fulvia and Cleopatra as being monstrous and associated with civil war, Plancina with sedition, and Agrippina the Younger with tyranny.

16. Hillard 1989.

17. Plut. *Ant.* 10.5. οὐ ταλασίαν οὐδ᾽ οἰκουρίαν φρονοῦν γύναιον οὐδ᾽ ἀνδρὸς ἰδιώτου κρατεῖν ἀξιοῦν, ἀλλ᾽ ἄρχοντος ἄρχειν καὶ στρατηγοῦντος στρατηγεῖν βουλόμενον, ὥστε Κλεοπάτραν διδασκάλια Φουλβίᾳ τῆς Ἀντωνίου γυναικοκρασίας ὀφείλειν, πάνυ χειροήθη καὶ πεπαιδαγωγημένον ἀπ᾽ ἀρχῆς ἀκροᾶσθαι γυναικῶν παραλαβοῦσαν αὐτόν. Translation is Perrin 1920.

18. Cass. Dio 48.10.4.

19. Plut. *Ant.* 58.5–6.

20. Plut. *Ant.* 62, 63.5.

21. Suet. *Tib.* 50.2-3. *Matrem Liviam grauatus velut partes sibi aequas potentiae vindicantem, et congressum eius assiduum vitavit et longiores secretioresque sermones, ne consiliis, quibus tamen interdum et egere et uti solebat, regi videretur. Tulit etiam perindigne actum in senatu, ut titulis suis quasi Augusti, ita et "Lifiae filius" adiceretur. Quare non "parentem patriae" appellari, non ullum insignem honorem recipere publice passus est; sed et frequenter admonuit, maioribus nec feminae convenientibus negotiis abstineret, praecipue ut animadvertit incendio iuxta aedem Vestae et ipsam intervenisse populumque et milites, quo enixius opem ferrent, adhortatam, sicut sub marito solita esset.*

22. Tac. *Ann.* 1.69.1–3. *Pervaserat interim circumventi exercitus fama et infesto Germanorum agmine Gallias peti, ac ni Agrippina inpositum Rheno pontem solvi prohibuisset, erant qui id lagitium formidine auderent. Sed femina ingens animi munia ducis per eos dies induit, militibusque, ut quis inops aut saucius, vestem et fomenta dilargita est. Tradit C. Plinius Germanicorum bellorum scriptor, stetisse apud principium ponti laudes et grates reversis legionibus habentem.*

23. Cass. Dio 48.10.3; Plut. *Ant.* 30.1.

24. Tac. *Ann.* 1.69. *Id Tiberii animum altius penetravit: non enim simplicis eas curas, nec adversus externos [studia] militum quaeri. Nihil relictum imperatoribus, ubi femina manipulos intervisat, signa adeat, largitionem temptet, tamquam parum ambitiose filium ducis gregali habitu circumferat Caesaremque Caligulam appellari velit. Potiorem iam apud exercitus Agrippinam quam legatos, quam duces; conpressam a muliere seditionem, cui nomen principis obsistere non qui verit. Accendebat haec onerabatque Seianus, peritia morum Tiberii odia in longum iaciens, quae reconderet auctaque promeret.*

25. Tac. *Ann.* 2.55. *Et postquam Syriam ac legiones attigit, largitione, ambitu, infimos manipularium iuvando, cum veteres centuriones, severos tribunos demoveret locaque eorum clientibus suis vel deterrimo cuique attribueret, desidiam in castris, licentiam in urbibus, vagum ac lascivientem per agros militem sineret, eo usque corruptionis provectus est ut sermone vulgi parens legionum haberetur. Nec Plancina se intra decora feminis tenebat, sed exercitio equitum, decursibus cohortium interesse, in Agrippinam, in Germanicum contumelias iacere, quibusdam etiam bonorum militum ad mala obsequia promptis, quod haud invito imperatore ea fieri occultus rumor incedebat.*

26. Tac. *Ann.* 3.33. *Inter quae Severus Caecina censuit ne quem magistratum cui provincia obvenisset uxor comitaretur, multum ante repetito concordem sibi coniugem et sex partus enixam, seque quae in publicum statueret domi servavisse, cohibita intra Italiam, quamquam ipse pluris per provincias quadraginta stipendia explevisset. Haud enim frustra placitum olim ne feminae in socios aut gentis externas traherentur: inesse mulierum comitatui quae pacem luxu, bellum formidine morentur et Romanum agmen ad similitudinem barbari incessus convertant. Non imbecillum tantum et imparem laboribus sexum sed, si licentia adsit, saevum, ambitiosum, potestatis avidum; incedere inter milites, habere ad manum centuriones; praesedisse nuper feminam exercitio cohortium, decursu legionum. Cogitarent ipsi quotiens repetundarum aliqui arguerentur plura uxoribus obiectari: his statim adhaerescere deterrimum quemque provincialium, ab his negotia suscipi, transigi; duorum egressus coli, duo esse praetoria, pervicacibus magis et impotentibus mulierum iussis quae Oppiis quondam aliisque legius constrictae nunc vinclis exolutis domos, fora, iam et exercitus regerent.* Scholars disagree about how to interpret this passage. Marshall views it as an expression of genuine distaste for women in the field (1975, 110). Barrett 2005, however, believes that Caecina designed the speech so as to regain Tiberius's good opinion, which he had lost in a failed campaign several years earlier. Caecina played up to Tiberius's unreasonable and old-fashioned distrust of women in a military setting. Barrett concludes that Tiberius's disapproval of women among the troops was a minority opinion.

27. Tac. *Ann.* 3.34.3. *Frustra nostram ignaviam alia ad vocabula transferri: nam viri in eo culpam si femina modum excedat.*

28. Tac. *Ann.* 3.34.5. *Quoties divum Augustum in Occidentem atque Orientem meavisse comite Livia!* It is far from clear whether Augustus brought Livia with him on campaign.

29. "We have thus gone from a situation where female association with the armies was anathema, to one where the emperor's wife could be honored as the 'Mother of the Armies' and a man could publicly thank a woman for interfering in the military domain in his behalf. This apparent change in thinking has eluded explanation and should consequently prompt us to question the basic premise, and to ask if it was in reality the case that the close association of women and the army was *as a general and consistent principle* particularly abominated by the Romans" (Barrett 2005, 304–305). Barrett denies that there was a general anxiety in allowing women to mingle with soldiers. He views the entire Caecina debate in 21 AD as an attempt on the part of the senator to win his way back into Tiberius's good graces. While I find his explanation of Caecina's motivations compelling, his assertion that there was never a "general and consistent principle" of keeping women and the military separate is wrong. The evidence Barrett provides to prove his point is problematic, because he cites one highly restored inscription (*CIL*

14 00040) and imperial coins as proof that "the honour was not an isolated and eccentric one" (2005, 305n18). I will show why this evidence does not support Barrett's claims.

30. Cass. Dio 72.10.5. παρὰ δὲ τῶν στρατιωτῶν τὸ ἕβδομον αὐτοκράτωρ προσηγορεύθη. καίπερ δὲ οὐκ εἰωθώς, πρὶν τὴν βουλὴν ψηφίσασθαι, τοιοῦτόν τι προσίεσθαι, ὅμως ἐδέξατό τε αὐτὸ ὡς καὶ παρὰ θεοῦ λαμβάνων, καὶ τῇ γερουσίᾳ ἐπέστειλεν. ἡ μέντοι Φαυστῖνα μήτερ τῶν στρατοπέδων ἐπεκλήθη.

31. Campbell emphasizes that the acclamations were the right of the troops, that they ideally occurred on the battlefield with the emperor present, and that as the prerogative of the emperor they could be used to mark out a successor to the principate. "Increasingly these salutations had less and less to do with military accomplishments and were granted to intended heirs purely as an honor for political reasons" (1984, 126n27).

32. Isrealowich 2008.

33. There are several troubling issues with this passage. The Christian commentator Xiphilinus was particularly invested in this passage, as is evident from the commentary that precedes it. Regarding the rain miracle, Xiphilinus says, "this is what Dio says about the matter, but he is apparently in error, whether intentionally or otherwise, and yet I am inclined to believe his error was chiefly intentional." How much of this passage has been excerpted or manipulated for Xiphilinus's Christian agenda is uncertain. Another problem is the claim that Marcus usually accepted imperial acclamations only after the Senate had approved them. It is unclear why the Senate would have the right to vote on an honor bestowed by the military. Talbert, equally puzzled by the idea, suggested that this instance reflected Marcus's sensitivity toward the senatorial *dignitas* (1984, 364). I find this explanation unconvincing. Would the emperor really turn down the honor bestowed on him by the military in order to wait for the Senate to approve a military honor? Such an action would send a message to the troops that their acclamation was somehow a lesser honor than that conferred by the Senate. Surely Marcus would not wish to endorse such a message.

34. HA *Marc.* 26.4–9. *Faustinam suam in radicibus montis Tauri in vico Halalae exanimatam vi subiti morbi amisit. Petiit a senatu ut honores Faustinae aedemque decernerent, laudata eadem cum impudicitiae fama graviter laborasset. Quae Antoninus vel nesciit vel dissimulavit. Novas puellas Faustinianas instituit in honorem uxoris mortuae. Divam etiam Faustinam a senatu appellatam gratulatus est. Quam secum et in aestivis habuerat, ut matrem castrorum appellaret. Fecit et coloniam vicum in quo obiit Faustina et aedem illi exstruxit.*

35. *RIC* 3.1659–62, 346.

36. Among these are Barrett 2005; Birley 1971; Clay 1972, 42; Instinsky 1942; Kettenhofen 1979; Levick 2007, 43.

37. Marshall 1975, 112.

38. Boatwright 2003.

39. Keinast 1996, 141.

40. "Faustina had always played so central a role in that dynasty that her most private moments, the births of her children, had been made public. In the increasingly difficult later years of second-century Rome, the imperial family's desire to perpetuate itself and the empire's need for stability became more crucial than the age-old segrega-

tion of women from the military. Thus the 'private' Faustina was elevated to the public role of *Mater Castrorum*, the Mother of the Camps" (Boatwright 2003, 266).

41. *RIC* 3.1641, 345. The empress nursing her child is a remarkable depiction on coinage not only for the intimacy it conveys but because breast-feeding seems to have been frowned upon for elite women. Cf. Quint. *Inst.* 1.1.4–5. There is such an abundance of coins depicting Faustina with different hairstyles and with a varying number of children that art historian Klaus Fittschen was able to date them plausibly, a rare phenomenon in imperial women's coinage (1982). See also Donarini 1974 for Fecunditas (156–157) and Mater Castrorum (159). This iconography was also used for Julia Domna; cf. figure 2.

42. Cass. Dio 72.31.1.

43. The only arguable exception to this statement is to claim that the Pater Patriae title, which Marcus did not assume until 176, was somehow directed at the military. I find this claim unlikely, because the Senate typically awarded the title. It is striking, however, that Marcus chose to accept the title just prior to the advancement of Commodus to the consulship.

44. Herodian 1.5.3–4. ἐκεῖνος γὰρ πάντας ἡμᾶς ὡς ἕνα ἠγάπα. ἔχαιρε γοῦν μᾶλλον συστρατιώτην με ἢ υἱὸν καλῶν. τὴν μὲν γὰρ προσηγορίαν ἡγεῖτο φύσεως, τὴν δ᾽ἀρετῆς κοινωνίαν. φέρων τέ με πολλάκις ἔτι νήπιον ὄντα ταῖς ὑμετέραις ἐνεχείρισε πίστεσι. διόπερ καὶ ῥᾷστα πάσης εὐνοίας μεθέξειν πρὸς ὑμῶν ἤλπικα, τῶν μὲν πρεσβυτέρων τροφεῖά μοι ταῦτα ὀφειλόντων, τοὺς δ᾽ἡλικιώτας εἰκότως ἂν καὶ συμφοιτητὰς τῶν ἐν ὅπλοις ἔργων ἀποκαλοίην. πάντας γὰρ ἡμᾶς ὡς ἕνα ὁ πατὴρ ἐφίλει τε καὶ πᾶσαν ἀρετὴν ἐπαίδευεν.

45. Herodian 1.5.5–6. ἔδωκε δὲ μετ᾽ἐκεῖνον ἐμὲ βασιλέα ἡ τύχη, οὐκ ἐπείσακτον, ὥσπερ οἱ πρὸ ἐμοῦ προσκτήτῳ σεμνυνόμενοι ἀρχῇ, ἀλλὰ μόνος τε ὑμῖν ἐγὼ ἐν τοῖς βασιλείοις ἀπεκυήθην . . . εἰκότως δ᾽ἂν ταῦτα λογιζόμενοι στέργοιτε οὐ δοθέντα ὑμῖν ἀλλὰ γεννηθέντα αὐτοκράτορα.

46. Notably, bronze denominations advertised Faustina as the Mater Castrorum during her lifetime, but not in gold or silver. Silver denarii were the denomination most often paid to soldiers. Bronze coins minted in Rome circulated throughout the western half of the empire, but I suspect that these were initially distributed in Rome.

47. Neither the Packard Humanities Institute Searchable Greek Inscriptions (www.epigraphy.packhum.org/inscriptions) nor Epidgraphische Datenbank Clauss-Slaby (www.manfredclauss.de/gb/index.html) returns any citations that celebrate Faustina as Mater Castrorum. Barrett cites *CIL* 14 00040 but notes that the inscription is heavily reconstructed. The inscription was revisited again in *CIL* 14 04301 and *AE* 1920 00092, both of which reject the Mater Castrorum reading (2005, 305). Boatwright also rejects this reading and calls into doubt one possible inscription from Pannonia (2003, 247n45).

48. Herodian 1.5.8. τοσαῦτα ὁ Κόμοδος εἰπὼν καὶ μεγαλοφρόνως δωρεαῖς χρημάτων οἰκειωσάμενος τὸ στρατιωτικόν, ἐς τὴν βασίλειον ἐπανῆλθεν αὐλήν.

49. Rubin 1975, 419n1.

50. I limit the range of these seseterii to Rome and the West because civic mints supplied bronze coinage in the East.

51. Ando 2000, 183n44. The Senate jealously guarded its right to confer titles, as Dio's gripes concerning Macrinus make clear. Cass. Dio 79.16.2; 80.8.2–3.

52. Ando lists the inscriptions from "Africa, southern Italy, Rome, Cisalpine Gaul,

Gallia Narbonensis the Danubian provinces and throughout the East" that feature these cognomina before they were officially granted to Severus by the Senate in Rome in 196 (2000, 183–184n45).

53. Ando 2000, 185–186.

54. Ando 2000, 182–190.

55. Scholars date the title to April 14, 195. They ascertain the month and day from temple records in Arsinoe (*BGU* II 362.13) and the year from an inscription dated to the third year of Severus's *tribunicia potestas* (*CIL* 08.26498). Cf. also *PIR*[2] "Julia Domna" and Taylor 1945, 16. The possible occasion for awarding the title is something of a puzzle; one wonders whether there was some familial significance to April 14, or whether it commemorated a battle now unknown to us. Clay would feel more comfortable in assigning the date with an imperial acclamation of Severus, but sees no possible acclamations in 195 (and he excludes as a possibility the fall of Byzantium in mid–195) or in 196. He wonders whether the year 196 would coincide with one of Severus's imperial acclamations of that year, though not perfectly (1972, 42–43). Julia Domna's birthday can be rejected as a possible date for the conferral of the title because her birthday is thought to be either January 1 or September 25. On the basis of an inscription from Athens ordering sacrifice in her honor, Oliver suggests January 1 as her birthday. See *IG* II[2], 1076 and Oliver 1940, 521–530. Fink, Hoey, and Snyder 1940 propose September 25 on the basis of their reconstruction of the *Feriale Duranum*. Oliver proposes, on the basis of the Athenian inscription and the missing entry for January 1 in the *Feriale Duranum*, that the date should be understood as a festival dedicated to Julia Domna as the Mater Castrorum, "the patron deity of the Roman army." Fink convincingly shows Oliver's reading to be without basis and instead proposes October 22, VII Kalens (1971, 314).

56. Calabria 1989 is a notable exception to this trend. She asserts that Julia Domna's award was analogous to Faustina's because both can be linked to concrete historical moments: for Faustina, it occurred at the same time as the founding of Regia Castra in Upper Pannonia; for Julia Domna, it was influenced by the reinforcement of the *canabae*, a settlement of veterans from Legio VII Claudia stationed at Viminacium. Yet there are at least two problems with Calabria's assessment regarding Julia Domna's title. First, the reinforcement of the *canabae* occurred some seven years after the awarding of the title and second, unlike Faustina, Julia Domna was in Syria with Severus, nowhere near Viminacium, when she received the award in 195.

57. Hasebroek 1921, 92. Kettenhofen rejects Hasebroek's interpretation of Julia Domna's "Herrschaftsgelüste" but does not seem to reject the connection between the Antonines and the Mater Castrorum title (1979, 81–82). Birley allows for the connection between the events without attributing it to any particular lust for power on Julia Domna's part. He links the titles with the promotion of Caracalla to Caesar (1999, 117).

58. Imperial coinage between 195 and 211 advertised the title. Without a die study, it is impossible to date these coins more accurately. The dates rely upon titles that Julia Domna received at important moments in her husband's and sons' careers. See the introduction for a discussion on dating imperial women's coinage.

59. Mater Castrorum coins minted in Rome: *RIC* 4a.563a–b, 168; *RIC* 4a.567–569, 169; *RIC* 4a.860, 209. For the lack of any mention of the Mater Castrorum in eastern mints, cf. *RIC* 4a.

60. The only criticism of this observation that I have encountered comes from private correspondence with Clay (April 20, 2005), who suggests that there would not have been time enough to mint the coins before Severus marched to Lugdunum to confront Albinus. Unlike most scholars, Clay dates the Battle of Lugdunum to 196, and he believes that Severus marched against Albinus in 196. Even according to Curtis's schema, however, there would have been plenty of time to mint and distribute coins to the troops between the awarding of the title in April 195 and 196 before they moved out to confront Albinus. The troops in Syria would have received two or three payments in 195. On the logistics of military pay, see Southern 2007, 109–110.

61. Rowan 2009 gathered these hoards into a database and published it online with the Severan Database Project (http://web3.cas.usf.edu/main/other/severan/). The *RIC* lists nearly all of these Mater Castrorum coins as being rare or scarce. The Mater Castrorum coinage does not appear in the two hoards from Italy either, but it must be remembered that the sample hoards from Italy are far smaller and fewer in number (two) than those on the frontiers: Britain (fourteen), the western continent (seventeen), the Danubian region (nineteen, including the massive Deva Rekia hoard), and the East (five). Because of this, the Italian hoards are far less representative than those found in Britain, the Danubian region, and to a lesser extent the East. From conversations I have had with Fleur Kemmers, it is apparent that coins featuring Severan imperial women account for only the tiniest percentage of those distributed to the troops in Nijmegen. A survey of coin hoards containing imperial coinage from the third century supports these findings. The most common types found for Julia Domna on the periphery of the empire—and therefore likely targeted to the military—have maternal themes, but are notably not Mater Castrorum coins. See Appendix B for further details.

62. This analysis is based upon the Inscriptions of Julia Domna database published with the Severan Database Project (http://web3.cas.usf.edu/main/other/severan/). I have found forty-two instances of military inscriptions erected by individual officers, units, or *collegia* with the title Mater Castrorum. Fifty percent of these were erected while Severus was still living, and sixteen emanate from Numidia and five from Africa Proconsularis, apparent bastions of support for Severus (Fejfer 1985). Due to the low number of dedications, the fact that the empress was mentioned in concert with her male relatives, and the inconsistent inclusion of Mater Castrorum title, I interpret military inscriptions erected under Severus's reign that mention Julia Domna as echoing imperial propaganda rather than as embracing Julia Domna. I have counted inscriptions erected by veterans (ten in all, nine of which use the Mater Castrorum title) and by the Vigiles (four inscriptions, all of which employ the Mater Castrorum title) separately from active military. This is because the Vigiles, stationed in Rome and operating under the command of the *praefectus urbanus*, would have received the same propagandistic messages as the *populus Romanus*. Likewise, veterans who settled among native populations and acted more as prominent citizens and *decuriones* than as active military received messages targeted for provincial civilian audiences.

63. The sole exception to this rule is *CIL* 02 02529, which is problematic not least of all because it was erected to Mars on behalf of Julia Domna's safety (MARTI/ [P]RO SALVT[E] / IVLIAE AVG[G](VSTAE) / MATRI / [C]ASTROR(VM) / [E]T AVG[G](VSTORVM). The second G in AVGG indicates that this was erected between Geta's elevation to Augustus in 209 and his death at the end of 211.

64. Kettenhofen 1979, 79–80.

65. Cass. Dio 76.4.4. Rubin argued that the demonstration and omens originally appeared in Dio's first historical tract that recorded the signs and omens foretelling Severus's rise to the principate. It was only after Dio felt disillusioned that both the demonstration and the omens appeared in their extant form as signs of unrest rather than support for Severus (1980, 78–82). For Rubin, they do not actually represent criticism of Severus so much as discontent with civil war in general. For Potter, they represent discontent with the performances (1996).

66. Cass. Dio 76.4.2–6. Rubin asked: "A white drizzle descending on the Forum Augusti—can there be a clearer reference to the seizure of the title Augustus by Clodius Albinus?" (1980, 82).

67. Chapter 2 discusses the factions in the showdown with Albinus in greater depth.

68. Cass. Dio 76.15.2.

69. "Posterity, who experienced the fatal effects of his maxims and example, justly considered him as the principal author of the decline of the Roman Empire" (Gibbon, *Decline* I.5). Campbell surveys other scholars who embraced this approach (1984, 401n1–2).

70. Among others, Campbell 2002, 115–119. "It is therefore impossible to sustain the sweeping generalizations about militarism and praetorianism in the Roman world."

71. Cass. Dio 75.1.1–2.

72. Phang 2001.

73. *RIC* 4.2–17, 92–93.

74. Cass. Dio 75.2.3. καὶ τὸ μέγιστον ὅτι μὴ ἐν τῇ τῶν συνόντων οἱ εὐνοίᾳ ἀλλ᾽ἐν τῇ ἐκείνων ἰσχύι τὴν ἐλπίδα τῆς σωτηρίας ἐποιεῖτο·

75. Haynes 1993, 7.

76. Cass. Dio 75.1.3–5.

77. Campbell 1984, 120–128. Campbell interprets this episode and the multiple acclamations, which were traditionally rewarded with donatives, as attempts to squeeze the emperors for still more money. Despite the implication of the sources that Severus had lost control over his troops, Campbell insists that he in fact maintained strict discipline (195).

78. Cass. Dio 75.1.1–2. Σεουῆρος . . . τοὺς μὲν δορυφόρους τοὺς χειρουργήσαντας τὸ κατὰ τὸν Περτίνακα ἔργον θανάτῳ ἐζημίωσε, τοὺς δὲ ἄλλους, πρὶν ἐν τῇ Ῥώμῃ γενέσθαι μεταπεμψάμενος καὶ ἐν πεδίῳ περισχὼν οὐκ εἰδότας τὸ μέλλον σφίσι συμβήσεσθαι, πολλά τε καὶ πικρὰ ὑπὲρ τῆς ἐς τὸν αὐτοκράτορά σφων παρανομίας ὀνειδίσας αὐτοῖς, τῶν τε ὅπλων ἀπέλυσε τούς τε ἵππους ἀφείλετο καὶ τῆς Ῥώμης ἀπήλασεν. ἔνθα δὴ οἱ μὲν ἄλλοι καὶ ἄκοντες τά τε ὅπλα ἀπερρίπτουν καὶ τοὺς ἵππους ἠφίεσαν, ἔν τε τοῖς χιτῶσιν ἄζωστοι ἐσκεδάννυντο· εἷς δέ τις, οὐκ ἐθελήσαντος τοῦ ἵππου ἀποστῆναι ἀλλ᾽ ἐπακολουθοῦντος αὐτῷ καὶ χρεμετίζοντος, καὶ ἐκεῖνον καὶ ἑαυτὸν κατεχρήσατο· καὶ ἐδόκει τοῖς ὁρῶσι καὶ ὁ ἵππος ἡδέως ἀποθνήσκειν.

79. Campbell notably shifts the blame for this incident on the senators who bid for the empire, not on the Praetorians who accepted the bids. "Clearly the senators were not the helpless slaves of the soldiers' greed. In such a situation ambitious men could exploit the natural tendency of the guardsmen to seek the most lucrative rewards for themselves. They had no political motives and this was the only occasion since 68 on which the guard obtruded itself forcibly into the political life of the empire" (1984, 119–120).

80. Cass. Dio 75.2.5.
81. Cass. Dio 75.2.6.
82. Some scholars do not see the jealousy in these comments and thus take them seriously, suggesting that the reforms of the Praetorians and the stationing of the Legio II Parthica in the Castra Albana somehow constituted the oppression of Italy. But as Smith 1972 demonstrated, these reforms are best explained as supplying emergency troops in the vicinity of the emperor, troops that could be mobilized quickly in case of emergency.
83. Herodian 3.10.6 explores the reasons for Severus's close relationship with Plautianus. Some accounts, he says, claimed that the two were related, while others supposed that they were lovers in their youth.
84. Levick 2007, 74–75.
85. Herodian 3.11.2. ἠμφίεστο γὰρ τήν τε πλατύσημον ἐσθῆτα, ἔν τε τοῖς δεύτερον ὑπατεύσασιν ἐτέτακτο παρῃώρητό τε τὸ ξίφος, καὶ παντὸς ἀξιώματος σχῆμα ἔφερε μόνος.
86. Cass. Dio 76.15.2a.
87. Levick 2007, 74.
88. Cass. Dio 76.15.5.
89. Cass. Dio 76.15.6.
90. Cass. Dio 76.15.6–7. πάνυ γὰρ αὐτῇ ἤχθετο, καὶ σφόδρα αὐτὴν πρὸς τὸν Σεουῆρον ἀεὶ διέβαλλέν, ἐξετάσεις τε κατ᾽αὐτῆς καὶ βασάνους κατ᾽εὐγενῶν γυναικῶν ποιούμενος. καὶ ἡ μὲν αὐτή τε φιλοσοφεῖν διὰ ταῦτ᾽ἤρξατο καὶ σοφισταῖς συνημέρευεν· ὁ δὲ δὴ Πλαυτιανὸς ἀσωτότατός τε ἀνθρώπων γενόμενος, ὥστε καὶ εὐωχεῖσθαι ἅμα καὶ ἐμεῖν, ἐπεὶ μηδὲν ὑπὸ τοῦ πλήθους τῶν τε σιτίων καὶ τοῦ οἴνου πέψαι ἐδύνατο, καὶ τοῖς μειρακίοις ταῖς τε κόραις οὐκ ἄνευ διαβολῆς χρώμενος, τῇ γυναικὶ τῇ ἑαυτοῦ οὔθ᾽ὁρᾶν τινὰ οὔθ᾽ὁρᾶσθαι τὸ παράπαν, οὐδ᾽ ὑπὸ τοῦ Σεουήρου ἢ τῆς Ἰουλίας, μήτι γε ἑτέρων τινῶν, ἐπέτρεπεν.
91. Cass. Dio 76.10.1.
92. Scholars argue over the precise identification of the "European" troops. Speidel 1984 believes that these were likely troops drawn from the garrison at Dura-Europos. Kennedy 1986 convincingly refutes the idea, proposing instead that these troops were Moesians with experience besieging Byzantium. Syrian troops were much maligned owing to Roman notions of the East as an enervating place. According to Wheeler, however, this is a literary trope and should be discarded in the face of evidence that bespeaks of the rigor of the Syrian troops (1996).
93. Cass. Dio 76.12.3–4. καὶ αὐτῷ τῶν μὲν Εὐρωπαίων τῶν δυναμένων τι κατεργάσασθαι οὐδεὶς ἔτ᾽ὀργῇ ὑπήκουσεν, ἕτεροι δὲ δὴ Σύροι ἀναγκασθέντες ἀντ᾽αὐτῶν προσβαλεῖν κακῶς ἐφθάρησαν. καὶ οὕτω θεὸς ὁ ῥυσάμενος τὴν πόλιν τοὺς μὲν στρατιώτας δυνηθέντας ἂν ἐς αὐτὴν ἐσελθεῖν διὰ τοῦ Σεουήρου ἀνεκάλεσε, καὶ τὸν Σεουῆρον αὖ βουληθέντα αὐτὴν μετὰ τοῦτο λαβεῖν διὰ τῶν στρατιωτῶν ἐκώλυσεν. οὕτως γοῦν ὁ Σεουῆρος ἐπὶ τούτοις διηπορήθη ὥστε τινὸς τῶν ἀμφ᾽αὐτὸν ὑποσχομένου αὐτῷ ἐάν γε αὐτῷ δώσῃ πεντακοσίους καὶ πεντήκοντα μόνους τῶν Εὐρωπαίων στρατιωτῶν, ἄνευ τοῦ τῶν ἄλλων κινδύνου τὴν πόλιν ἐξαιρήσειν, ἔφη πάντων ἀκουόντων "καὶ πόθεν τοσούτους στρατιώτας ἔχω;" πρὸς τὴν ἀπείθειαν τῶν στρατιωτῶν τοῦτο εἰπών.
94. Cass. Dio 76.10.2. ἵνα δη τὴν Λαουινίαν ὁ Τοῦρνος ἀγάγηται, ἡμεῖς ἐν οὐδενὶ

λόγῳ παραπολλύμεθα. The Virgilian passage is 11.371–3. This is an abbreviated exposition of an earlier argument I made (Langford 2008).

95. HA *Cl. Alb.* 3.5. Levick assesses the influence Julia Domna had in the court in terms of advising and placing her friends and allies into important positions (2007, 71–73).

96. *AE* 1984 00921. IMP(ERATORI) CAESARI DIVI SEPTIMI SEV[ERI PII FELICIS ARAB(ICI) ADIAB(ENICI) PARTHICI] / MAXIMI BRITANNICI MAXIMI [FILIO —] / [[[—]]] [DIVI M(ARCI) AVRELI] ANTO/NINI PII GERMANICI SARMATICI NEPOTI [DIVI ANTONINI PII PRON]EPOTI / DIVI HADRIANI ABNEPOTI DIVI TRAI[ANI PARTHICI ET DIVI N]ERVAE / ADNEPOTI A [[— P(VBLIO) SEPTIMIO GETAE]] ET / [I]V[LIA]E AVG(VSTAE) PIAE FELICI MATRI AVGG(VSTORVM) ET [CASTRORVM ET SENATVS] ET PATRIAE // [MILITES] / [VEXILLATIONIS] / AN[TONINIANORVM] / EVROPA[EORVM] / DEVOTI NVM[INI] / MAIESTATIQVE / EIVS.

97. For a more detailed discussion of these titles, cf. chapter 3 and Appendix C.

98. *IRT* 00408. IVLIAE AVG(VSTAE) / MATRI AVG[[G]](VSTORVM) / ET CASTRORVM / MESSIVS ATTICVS / (CENTVRIO) / COH(ORTIS) VII PR(AETORIAE) P(IAE) V(INDICIS) / V(OTVM) S(OLVIT).

99. *IRT* 00438 [[L(VCIO) S[EP]T[I]MIO GE]]/[[TAE CAES(ARI)]] / IMP(ERATORIS) CAES(ARIS) L(VCI) SEP/TIMI SEVERI PII / PERTINACIS AVG(VSTI) ARA/BICI ADIABENICI / PARTHICI MAX(IMI) / FIL(IO) ET / IMP(ERATORIS) CAES(ARIS) M(ARCI) AVRELLI / ANTONINI AVG(VSTI) FRATR/I MESSIVS ATTICVS / PRIM(VS) SACERD(OS) VOT(VM) SOL(VIT); *IRT* 00439 [[L(VCIO) S[EP]T[I]MIO GE]]/[[TAE CAES(ARI)]] / IMP(ERATORIS) CAES(ARIS) L(VCI) SEP/TIMI SEVERI PII / PERTINACIS AVG(VSTI) ARA/BICI ADIABENICI / PARTHICI MAX(IMI) / FIL(IO) ET / IMP(ERATORIS) CAES(ARIS) M(ARCI) AVRELLI / ANTONINI AVG(VSTI) FRATR/I MESSIVS ATTICVS / PRIM(VS) SACERD(OS) VOT(VM) SOL(VIT). These inscriptions can be dated between 199 and 209, after Severus had received the Parthian *siegesname* and Geta had become Caesar but not yet Augustus.

100. Herodian 3.14.9, 3.15.6.

101. Cass. Dio 76.15.

102. For a list of the hoards under investigation and the total number of coins and types found there, see Appendices A and B.

103. *RIB* 00976. IVLIAE AV[G(VSTAE)] / (M)ATRI AV[G(VSTI) / NOSTRI M(ARCI) AVR]/ELI<I> ANTON[INI] / ET CASTR(ORVM) [ET] / SENATVS ET /PATRIAE PRO |[PIETATE AC] / DEVOTIONE / [COMMVNI] / NVM(INI) EIVS / [CVRANTE G(AIO) IVL(IO)] / MARC[O] L[EG(ATO) AVG(VSTORVM)] / PR(O) PR(AETORE) COH(ORS) [I] AEL(IA) / [HISP(ANORVM) M(ILLIARIA) EQ/(VITATA)] POSVIT. *AE* 1980 00603. IVLIA[E AVG(VSTAE)] / NO[3 MATRI] / [D(OMINI) N(OSTRI) AV]/RELI ANTO[NINI AC] / CAS[TR(ORVM) AC SENAT(VS)] / AC PAT[RIAE PRO PIETATE] / AC DEV[OTIONE] / [CVRANTE C(AIO) IVL(IO) MARCO] / LEG(ATO) AVG(VSTI) PR(O) [PR(AETORE) COH(ORS) I VLPIA] / TRAIANA C[VGERNORVM] / C(IVIVM) R(OMANORVM) [POSVIT].

104. *RIB* 002298. IMP(ERATORI) CAES(ARI) M(ARCO) AVR/[ELIO A]NTONINO / [PIO FELI]CI AVG(VSTO) ARAB(ICO) / ADIAB(ENICO) P[A]RT(HICO) MAXIM/O BRIT(ANNICO) MAXIMO / TRIB(VNICIA) P[OT(ESTATE)] XVI CO(N)S(VLI) IIII / IM[P(ERATORI)] II C(AIO) IVL(IO) MARCO / LEG(ATO) A[V]G(VSTI) P[R(O)] P[R(AETORE)]. *RIB* 001202. IMP(ERATORI) CAES(ARI) [DI]V[I] L(VCI) [SEPT(IMI)

SEVERI] / [PII PERTINACIS AVG(VSTI) ARA]/BICI ADIA[BENICI PARTHICI] / MAX (IMI) FIL(IO) DIVI ANTON[INI] PI[I] G[ERM(ANICI)] / SARM(ATICI) NEP(OTI) DIVI ANTONI[NI PII] PRON(EPOTI) / DIVI HADR(IANI) ABNEP(OTI) DIVI TRAIAN[I] / PARTH(ICI) ET DIVI NERVAE ADNEP(OTI) / M(ARCO) AVRELIO ANTONINO PIO / FEL(ICI) AVG(VSTO) [P]AR[T(HICO)] M[AX(IMO) BRI]T(ANNICO) M[AX(IMO)] PONT(IFICI) MA[X(IMO)] / TR(IBVNICIA) POT(ESTATE) X[VI] IMP(ERATORI) I[I] CO(N)S(VLI) IIII P(ATRI) P(ATRIAE) / PRO PIETATE A[C] DEVOTIONE / COMMVNI CVRANTE [[[C(AIO)]]] / [[[IVLIO MARCO]]] LEG(ATO) AVG(VSTI) / PR(O) PR(AETORE) COH(ORS) II NERVIO/RVM C(IVIVM) R(OMANORVM) POS(VIT) [D(EVOTA) N(VMINI) M(AIESTATI)Q(VE) EIVS].

105. Her distance from the battlefield is confirmed in Dio's report that Julia Domna stayed in Antioch to handle the civic half of imperial business while Caracalla was campaigning in Parthia (78.18.2–3).

106. Ricciardi 2007 examines the maternal titles given to empresses of the third century. As she sees it, the Mater Castrorum title was an important indication of a close relationship between the emperor and the military, but she also envisions that the full complement of titles (Mater Castrorum, Mater Senatus, Mater Patriae, Mater Aug(g), etc.) were only given to imperial women who were actual mothers, and that the titles indicated a close relationship between the empress and whatever population of which she was designated the mother.

Chapter Two • *Romancing the Romans*

1. Cass. Dio 75.1.3–5. πράξας δὲ ὁ Σεουῆρος ταῦτα ἐς τὴν Ῥώμην ἐσῄει, μέχρι μὲν τῶν πυλῶν ἐπί τε τοῦ ἵππου καὶ ἐν ἐσθῆτι ἱππικῇ ἐλθών, ἐντεῦθεν δὲ τήν τε πολιτικὴν ἀλλαξάμενος καὶ βαδίσας. καὶ αὐτῷ καὶ ὁ στρατὸς πᾶς, καὶ οἱ πεζοὶ καὶ οἱ ἱππεῖς, ὡπλισμένοι παρηκολούθησαν· καὶ ἐγέντεο ἡ θέα πασῶν ὧν ἑόρακα λαμπροτάτη· ἥ τε γὰρ πόλις πᾶσα ἄνθεσί τε καὶ δάφναις ἐστεφάνωτο καὶ ἱματίοις ποικίλοις ἐκεκόσμητο, φωσί τε καὶ θυμιάμασιν ἔλαμπε, καὶ οἱ ἄνθρωποι λευχειμονοῦντες καὶ γανύμενοι πολλὰ ἐπευφήμουν, οἵ τε στρατιῶται ἐν τοῖς ὅπλοις ὥσπερ ἐν πανηγύρει τινὶ πομπῆς ἐκπρεπόντως ἀνεστρέφοντο, καὶ προσέτι ἡμεῖς ἐν κόσμῳ περιῄειμεν. ὁ δ' ὅμιλος ἰδεῖν τε αὐτὸν καί τι φθεγγομένου ἀκοῦσαι, ὥσπερ τι ὑπὸ τῆς τύχης ἠλλοιωμένου, ποθοῦντες ἠρεθίζοντο· καί τινες καὶ ἐμετεώριζον ἀλλήλους, ὅπως ἐξ ὑψηλοτέρου αὐτὸν κατίδωσιν.

2. Aldrete 1999, 155–159.

3. As Yavetz observes, while it was impossible to rule in Rome strictly on the basis of popular support, "it was troublesome to rule against its wishes" (1969, 135).

4. Severus also concerned himself with the well-being of the less-powerful urban plebs. He was responsible for at least a dozen citations in the *Digest* and *Code* that benefitted women, minors, and slaves (Lewis 1996).

5. Severus's autobiography was the most likely source for the *HA*'s report concerning Julia Domna's horoscope. For a fuller exploration of the ideological significance of Julia Domna's horoscope, see "Roman Matrona, Mother and Protectress" below.

6. Bryant 1996.

7. Herodian 2.15.6–8. τῆς μὲν οὖν ὁδοιπορίας τοὺς σταθμούς, καὶ τὰ καθ' ἑκάστην πόλιν αὐτῳ λεχθέντα, καὶ σημεῖα θείᾳ προνοίᾳ δόξαντα πολλάκις φανῆναι, χωρία τε ἕκαστα καὶ παρατάξεις, καὶ τὸν τῶν ἑκατέρωθεν πεσόντων ἀριθμὸν στρατιωτῶν ἐν

ταῖς μάχαις, ἱστορίας τε πολλοὶ συγγραφεῖς καὶ ποιηταὶ μέτρῳ πλατύτερον συνέταξαν, ὑπόθεσιν ποιούμενοι πάσης τῆς πραγματείας τὸν Σεβήρου βίον . . . τὰ κορυφαιότατα τοίνυν καὶ συντέλειαν ἔχοντα τῶν κατὰ μέρος πεπραγμένων Σεβήρῳ ἐν τοῖς ἑξῆς διηγήσομαι, οὐδὲν οὔτε πρὸς χάριν ἐς ὕψος ἐξαίρων, ὥσπερ ἐποίησαν οἱ κατ᾽ἐκεῖνον γράψαντες, οὔτε παραλείπων εἴ τι λόγου καὶ μνήμης ἄξιον. Swain notes that Cassius Dio needed to impress Severus not only because he wanted to protect the honors granted him by Pertinax in 193, but also because the homeland of Nicaea had thrown in their lot with Pescennius Niger (1996, 401).

8. Cass. Dio 73.23.

9. Rowan presents an excellent discussion on the challenges and benefits of quantitative analysis of hoards (2009, 33–44).

10. A demonstration is available in chapter 1, where I examine provincial hoards to determine which messages were most heavily advertised to troops on the borders. Other scholars use similar methodology; among others, Noreña 2001; Kemmers 2005, 2006, 2009; Manders 2007, 2008; Rowan 2009.

11. Cesano 1925. This and all other published hoards from the Severan period are collected in the Severan Hoard Analysis database published online as part of the Severan Database Project (http://web3.cas.usf.edu/main/other/severan/).

12. According to Duncan-Jones, coins do not reach their peak in circulation until a couple decades after their minting (1994, 106).

13. The *RIC* records fifty-three types produced for Julia Domna at the Roman mint (not counting hybrids or types used for bronze denominations) and roughly 372 for Severus (again, not counting hybrids or bronze denominations), a proportion of 1:7. In order to make the comparison between the two as meaningful as possible, I did not include coins or types of Julia Domna minted under Caracalla in these calculations. Region D has a higher proportion of Severus's to Julia Domna's coins: 1:2.52. The enormous Reka Devnia hoard in this region, with more than eighty-one thousand denarii, has surely skewed these numbers, though I am not certain how. It could be that other provincial regions would have similar proportions to the 1:2.52 if they were as well represented. It could also be that the Reka Devnia hoard was so large that it does not reflect the proportions of the other hoards in the region. I find the second explanation more convincing.

14. Cf. Appendix B.

15. From the early part of Severus's reign, *RIC* 4a.536 (VENERI VICTR) and *RIC* 4a.538 (VESTA) are the most common types in all regions; among coins minted between 195 and 211, the reverse legend PIETAS PVBLICA (*RIC* 4a.574, 170), which features Julia Domna sacrificing with her hands raised in a prayer position, was the most common or second most common type in all regions. For a full list of the most common types in zones A–E, cf. Appendix B.

16. *RIC* 4a.534–587, 165–171. I have classified maternity types as those that celebrate the literal or metaphorical motherhood of the empress as well as mother goddesses. Because Pudicitia is an important virtue ensuring the legitimacy of Severus's children, I included this type in the maternity count. Virtues such as Felicitas and Pietas (though I argue below are also related to maternity), for the sake of being conservative are not counted as maternity types. I identify the following as maternity types: *RIC* 4a.534, 537, 539–546, 549–550, 562, 565–571, 575–578, 583–586.

17. Lusnia, forthcoming, chapter 3, "Usurping History in the Roman Forum."

18. HA *Sev.* 15.7. *Cum soror sua Leptitana ad eum venisset vix Latine loquens, ac de illa multum imperator erubesceret, dato filio eius lato clavo atque ipsi multis muneribus redire mulierem in patriam praecepit.* 19.9 *Ipse decorus, ingens, promissa barba, cano capite et crispo, vultu reverendus, canorus voce, sed Afrum quiddam usque ad senectutem sonans.* Elsewhere I have explored how and why Severus's critics belittled the emperor's ethnicity, masculinity, and relationship with the gods (Langford 2008).

19. In some instances, Severus simply added his own dedication to the extant dedicatory inscriptions of earlier benefactors. Cf. the Pantheon inscription, *CIL* 06 00896 (p 3070, 3777, 4303, 4340) = *CIL* 06 31196 = *D* 00129 = *AE* 2007, +00196, and the probable inscription of the Temple of Fortuna Muliebris, *CIL* 06 00883.

20. Herodian 3.8.9. φόβῳ γοῦν ἦρξε μᾶλλον τῶν ἀρχομένων ἢ εὐνοίᾳ. τῷ μέντοι δήμῳ ἐπειρᾶτο ποιεῖν κεχαρισμένα· καὶ γὰρ θέας πολυτελεῖς καὶ παντοδαπὰς συνεχῶς ἐπετέλει, καὶ θηρίων ἑκατοντάδας ἀνεῖλε πολλάκις τῶν ἀπὸ πάσης γῆς ἡμετέρας τε καὶ βαρβάρου, νομάς τε μεγαλοφρόνως ἐπεδίδου. ἐπετέλεσε δὲ καὶ ἐπινίκιον ἀγῶνα, τοὺς πανταχόθεν μούσης τε ὑποκριτὰς καὶ ἀνδρείας μαθητὰς μεταπεμψάμενος.

21. Quint. 6.ii.27–29. *Quare, in iis quae esse verisimilia volemus, simus ipsi similes eorum qui vere patiuntur adfectibus, et a tali animo proficiscatur oratio qualem facere iudicem volet. An ille dolebit qui audiet me, qui in hoc dicam, non dolentem? Irascetur, si nihil ipse qui in iram concitat se idque exigit similia patietur? Siccis agentis oculis lacrimas dabit? Fieri non potest: nec incendit nisi ignis nec madescimus nisi humore nec res ulla dat alteri colorem quem non ipsa habet. Primum est igitur ut apud nos valeant ea quae valere apud iudicem volumus, adficiamurque antequam adficere conemur. At quomodo fiet ut adficiamur? Neque enim sunt motus in nostra potestate. Temptabo etiam de hoc dicere. Quas φαντασίας Graeci vocant nos sane visiones appellemus, per quas imagines rerum absentium ita repraesentantur animo ut eas cernere oculis ac praesentes habere videamur, has quisquis bene conceperit is erit in adfectibus potentissimus.* On the use of φαντασία to evoke emotion in the *Aeneid,* cf. Syed 2005, 26–28.

22. Emperors who violated *civilitas* were treated harshly in the literary sources and even abused with disrespectful chants within the arena (Aldrete 1999, 121–123).

23. Aldrete 1999, 103.

24. Gunderson 1996, 115–116.

25. Hopkins 1983, 14–20; Hopkins and Beard 2005, 75–121. Aldrete also notes that casual encounters in the streets and fora were far more common than splashy spectacles. These meetings were opportunities to acclaim the emperor and ask favors (1999, 113).

26. Aldrete 1999, 159–164. "Clearly there was a perception that the theater, amphitheater, circus or wherever the entertainment was taking place was a special zone in time and space in which behavior that would have been forbidden anywhere else was permitted and where the usual social hierarchy was to some degree suspended" (123).

27. Gunderson 1996, 125; Rawson 1987, 112–113.

28. Aldrete includes an excellent discussion on the mechanics of acclamations (1999, 128–147).

29. Suet. Caius. 30.2. *Infensus turbae faventi adversus studium suum exclamavit: Utinam p. R. unam cervicem haberet!*

30. Aldrete 1999, 164.

31. Yavetz recognized the usefulness of *superstitio* to politicians. "It is easy to spread false rumours among these masses (specifically, the urban plebs or the *vulgus* who attend spectacles) and their *superstitio* is liable to prove a hindrance to any ruler. The superstition can also be used for good purposes, especially if there are leaders who know how to deal with the masses and are acquainted with the *natura vulgi*" (1969, 149n3).

32. Yavetz notes that Dio was not entirely consistent in his use of derogatory terms, but gives no examples of when these instances occur (1969, 144).

33. Cass. Dio 75.1.4–5. Cf. chapter 2 note 1 for Greek text.

34. Rubin 1980, 49–51.

35. Cass. Dio 73.23.

36. Langford 2008. For a fuller discussion on the role of τύχη and *felicitas,* see below.

37. Rubin 1980, 47, 50–53.

38. In this observation, I disagree with Millar, who writes, "the same is in part true [i.e., that narrative of the events was more important to Dio than his few comments which acted merely as adornment to narrative] of the immense number of prodigies and portents which fill his pages. They could serve a literary and dramatic aim in forming a prelude to a great event, or alternatively, light relief and contrasting detail. But it is clear also that, for all the inconclusiveness of one passage where he discussed the genuineness of portents, he really believed in them [Millar backs up his claim by citing Dio's δαιμόνιον and the injunction to write history]. . . Nonetheless, it would be going much too far to say that divine intervention functions as an alternative type of historical explanation in his history . . . In sum, his use of prodigies and portents is harmless and trivial, not affecting his treatment of events, and hardly deserving the scorn which some have poured on it" (1964, 77). Elsewhere, "by contrast it is clear that he was an unquestioning adherent of traditional pagan belief and observance. His literary career began with a book, or pamphlet, on the dreams and portents by which Severus learnt that he would ascend to the throne. The purpose was no doubt diplomatic but the subject matter was to him a reality. Although he expresses himself in guarded terms on the meaning of portents, they bulk large in his work, even in the account of his own time" (179). On Dio's dream and his δαιμόνιον: "There is no special reason to doubt that Dio actually had this dream, which is of a well-known type, a χρηματισμός or *spectaculum* in which a god or prominent figure announces or prescribes what is to happen; and this being so something more is revealed—Dio could not have dreamed thus or at least would not have recorded it, if Severus had not been to him a respected and authoritative figure. Dio, in common with his time, made no attempt to rationalize his dreams; to him, they were significant events in his life whose nature required no elucidation" (180).

39. Harris 2009, 202–216; Rowan 2009, 21.

40. Cass. Dio 74.13.3.

41. Herodian 2.7.2–4.

42. Cass. Dio 74.13.4–5.

43. This passage stands in stark contrast with Dio's catalog of participants in Severus's *adventus* and Pertinax's funeral.

44. Cass. Dio 77.2.1–3. ἐν δὲ τῷ Βεσβίῳ τῷ ὄρει πῦρ τε πλεῖστον ἐξέλαμψε καὶ μυκήματα μέγιστα ἐγένετο, ὥστε καὶ ἐς τὴν Καπύην, ἐν ᾗ, ὁσάκις ἂν ἐν τῇ Ἰταλίᾳ οἰκῶ, διάγω, ἐξακουσθῆναι· τοῦτο γὰρ τὸ χωρίον ἐξειλόμην τῶν τε ἄλλων ἕνεκα καὶ τῆς ἡσυχίας ὅτι μάλιστα, ἵνα σχολὴν ἀπὸ τῶν ἀστικῶν πραγμάτων ἄγων ταῦτα γράψαιμι.

ἐδόκει οὖν ἐκ τῶν περὶ τὸ Βέσβιον γεγονότων νεοχμόν τι ἔσεσθαι, καὶ μέντοι καὶ τὰ περὶ τὸν Πλαυτιανὸν αὐτίκα ἐνεοχμώθη. μέγας μὲν γὰρ ὡς ἀληθῶς ὁ Πλαυτιανὸς καὶ ὑπέρμεγας ἐγεγόνει, ὥστε καὶ τὸν δῆμον ἐν τῷ ἱπποδρόμῳ ποτὲ εἰπεῖν· "τί τρέμεις, τί δὲ ὠχριᾷς; πλεῖον τῶν πριῶν κέκτησαι." ἔλεγον δὲ τοῦτο οὐ πρὸς ἐκεῖνον δῆθεν ἀλλ'ἄλλως, τρεῖς δὲ ἐνέφαινον τόν τε Σεουῆρον καὶ τοὺς υἱέας αὐτοῦ Ἀντωνῖνον καὶ Γέταν· ὠχρία δὲ ἀεὶ καὶ ἔτρεμεν ἔκ τε τῆς διαίτης ἣν διῃτᾶτο, καὶ ἐκ τῶν ἐλπίδων ὧν ἤλπιζε, καὶ ἐκ τῶν φόβων ὧν ἐφοβεῖτο. οὐ μὴν ἀλλὰ τέως μὲν ἤτοι ἐλάνθανε τὰ πλείω αὐτὸν τὸν Σεουῆρον, ἢ καὶ εἰδὼς αὐτὰ οὐ προσεποιεῖτο·

45. Aldrete 1999, 157.

46. Harris accepts without question Dio's report (Cass. Dio 77.3.8) that Severus suspected Plautianus because of a dream. There is no way to disprove this, but the crowd's address to Plautianus in the arena would certainly have caused jealousy and suspicion in the emperor (2009, 206).

47. Cass. Dio 75.4.2–6. συγκινουμένης οὖν διὰ ταῦτα τῆς οἰκουμένης ἡμεῖς μὲν οἱ βουλευταὶ ἡσυχίαν ἤγομεν, ὅσοι μὴ πρὸς τοῦτον ἢ ἐκεῖνον φανερῶς ἀποκλίναντες ἐκοινώνουν σφίσι καὶ τῶν κινδύνων καὶ τῶν ἐλπίδων, ὁ δὲ δῆμος οὐκ ἐκαρτέρησεν ἀλλ' ἐκφανέστατα κατωδύρατο. ἦν μὲν γὰρ ἡ τελευταία πρὸ τῶν Κρονίων ἱπποδρομία, καὶ συνέδραμεν ἐς αὐτὴν ἄπλετόν τι χρῆμα ἀνθρώπων. παρῆν δὲ καὶ ἐγὼ τῇ θέᾳ διὰ τὸν ὕπατον φίλον μου ὄντα, καὶ πάντα τὰ λεχθέντα ἀκριβῶς ἤκουσα, ὅθεν καὶ γράψαι τι περὶ αὐτῶν ἠδυνήθην. ἐγένετο δὲ ὧδε. συνῆλθον μὲν ὥσπερ εἶπον ἀμύθητοι, καὶ τὰ ἅρματα ἑξαχῶς ἁμιλλώμενα ἐθεάσαντο, ὅπερ που καὶ ἐπὶ τοῦ Κλεάνδρου ἐγεγόνει, μηδὲν μηδένα παράπαν ἐπαινέσαντες, ὅπερ εἴθισται. ἐπειδὴ δὲ ἐκεῖνοί τε οἱ δρόμοι ἐπαύσαντο καὶ ἔμελλον οἱ ἡνίοχοι ἑτέρου ἄρξασθαι, ἐνταῦθα ἤδη σιγάσαντες ἀλλήλους ἐξαίφνης τάς τε χεῖρας πάντες ἅμα συνεκρότησαν καὶ προσεπεβόησαν, εὐτυχίαν τῇ τοῦ δήμου σωτηρίᾳ αἰτούμενοι. εἶπόν τε τοῦτο, καὶ μετὰ τοῦτο τὴν Ῥώμην καῖ βασιλίδα καὶ ἀθάνατον ὀνομάσαντες "μέχρι πότε τοιαῦτα πάσχομεν;" ἔκραξαν "καὶ μέχρι ποῦ πολεμούμεθα"; εἰπόντες δὲ καὶ ἄλλα τινὰ τοιουτότροπα τέλος ἐξεβόησαν ὅτι "ταῦτά ἐστιν," καὶ πρὸς τὸν ἀγῶνα τῶν ἵππων ἐτράποντο. οὕτω μὲν ἔκ τινος θείας ἐπιπνοίας ἐνεθουσίασαν· οὐ γὰρ ἂν ἄλλως τοσαῦται μυριάδες ἀνθρώπων οὔτε ἤρξαντο τὰ αὐτὰ ἅμα ἀναβοᾶν ὥσπερ τις ἀκριβῶς χορὸς δεδιδαγμένος, οὔτ'εἶπον αὐτὰ ἀπταίστως ὡς καὶ μεμελετημένα.

48. Wiedemann 2002, 128–146.

49. Cass. Dio 73.18–21.

50. Aldrete 1999, 128–147.

51. It should be noted that Rubin's interpretation came after Millar's and, to my knowledge, he has not commented upon it. Aldrete reads the demonstration as criticizing Severus: "Several points are worth noting in this episode. First, what was clearly planned as a criticism directed at the emperor began initially with a standard acclamation of praise coupled with applause. Second, since this event occurred at the circus rather than at a theater, literally tens of thousands of people were involved . . . This performance was at least somewhat prearranged and the circus was one of the recognized sites for making such petitions. Although there was certainly a group behind this demonstration that authored the phrases to be used and may even have circulated among the public at large general knowledge of what was being planned, the chants as finally delivered in the circus involved cooperation of many tens of thousands of people" (1999, 126).

52. Cass. Dio 74.6.6–7. ταῦτά τε οὖν ἔτι καὶ μᾶλλον ἡμᾶς ἐτάραττε, καὶ πῦρ αἰφνίδιον νυκτὸς ἐν τῷ ἀέρι τῷ πρὸς βορρᾶν τοσοῦτον ὤφθη ὥστε τοὺς μὲν τὴν πόλιν ὅλην τοὺς δὲ καὶ τὸν οὐρανὸν αὐτὸν καίεσθαι δοκεῖν. ὅ δὲ δὴ μάλιστα θαυμάσας ἔχω, ψεκὰς ἐν αἰθρίᾳ ἀργυροειδὴς ἐς τὴν τοῦ Αὐγούστου ἀγορὰν κατερρύη. φερομένην μὲν γὰρ αὐτὴν οὐκ εἶδον, πεσούσης δὲ αὐτῆς ᾐσθόμην, καὶ κέρματά τινα ἀπ᾽ αὐτῆς χαλκᾶ κατηργύρωσα, ἅ καὶ ἐπὶ πρεῖς ἡμέρας τὴν αὐτὴν ὄψιν εἶχε. τῇ γὰρ τετάρτῃ πᾶν τὸ ἐπαλειφθὲν αὐτοῖς ἠφανίσθη.

53. Harris notes that "in investigating this matter, we clearly need to make some distinctions of time and place, probably also of class and gender" (2009, 123–126). In addition, "this was well appreciated by Brelich 1955, 293: 'it is not possible to talk of a general Hellenic attitude towards dreams without differentiating.' That is still more obviously true of the Roman Empire" (126n17). Harris goes on to discuss the problem of women's dreams—that is, the virtual topos of women misunderstanding dreams. In his section on "The Interpreters," Harris wisely relates that "it might possibly be argued that the literate classes, at least in Roman Egypt, were much less interested in dream-interpretation than the uneducated . . . but nothing in this chapter suggests that literacy inoculated one against dream-credulity any more than it did against palm-reading" (135).

54. Auguet 1994, 194.

55. Herodian 2.9.3. ἅπερ πάντα ἀψευδῆ καὶ ἀληθῆ τότε πιστεύεται ὅταν ἐς τὴν ἀπόβασιν εὐτυχηθῇ.

56. Cf. note 38.

57. Cic. *Leg. Man.* 28. *Ego enim sic existimo, in summon imperatore quattuor has res inesse oportere, scientiam rei militaris, virtutem, auctoritatem, felicitatem.*

58. *Scientiam rei militaris* (*RIC* 4.20–23, 93 in which VICTORIA is celebrated) and *virtus* (*RIC* 4a.24, 94 VIRT AVG TR P COS).

59. The *RIC* attests legends advertising some twelve specific legions as well as a more general claim for the *Fides* of the legions in general (*RIC* 4a.1-17, 92-3).

60. HA *Sev.* 8.5. *Rei frumentariae, quam minimam reppererat, ita consuluit, ut excedens vita septem annorum canonem populo Romano relinqueret.* I infer the timing of Severus's assumption of the *annona* on the basis of the notice's placement within the passage describing the emperor's actions while still in Rome following the *adventus* but before he left to face Niger.

61. Without other hoards to compare to the Via Tritone hoard, it is impossible to determine with any certainty that the messages on these coins were intended primarily for the populations of Rome.

62. The branch may well be a symbol for dynasty.

63. I disagree with Hill 1978, who interprets the legend as a reference to Severus's building program in which several ancient and prominent monuments were restored.

64. Pera 1979, 106–111.

65. Herodian 3.9.1.

66. Herodian 3.9.12. οὕτω μὲν δὴ Σεβῆρος, τύχῃ μᾶλλον ἢ γνώμῃ, τῇ κατὰ Παρθυαίων νίκῃ κεκόσμητο· τούτων δὲ αὐτῷ δεξιῶς καὶ ὑπὲρ πᾶσαν εὐχὴν προχωρησάντων ἐπέστειλε τῇ τε συνκλήτῳ καὶ τῷ δήμῳ, τὰς τε πράξεις μεγαληγορῶν, τὰς μάχας τε καὶ τὰς νίκας δημοσίαις ἀνέθηκε γραφαῖς.

67. Herodian 3.9.12. For the historiography on this notion, cf. Lusnia 2006, 282, who adds her own twist to the argument.

68. *Felicitas*, *RIC* 4a.73, 100 ADVENTVI AVG FELICISSIMO, an aureus; *fortuna*, *RIC*4a.77, 78, 84, and 89, 100–101. Other prominent themes in the output of the Roman mint in 196–197 were peace (*RIC* 4a.85, 88–89, 101) and the emperor's victories (*RIC* 4a.76, 86, 90, 94, 95, 100–102).

69. *Oxford Latin Dictionary*, 3rd ed., s. v. "felicitias."

70. Balsdon 1951, 2; Murphy 1986, 308; Thein 2009, 88. For Balsdon, Sulla's inclusion of dreams and *omina* in his autobiography are reason enough to doubt the dictator's sanity. Caesar uses the word felicitas only once in his memoirs, notably as proof of his ability to command and his good fortune (Murphy 1986, 308): Caes. BC 1.40. *Quod non fore dicto audientes neque signa laturi dicantur, nihil se ea re commoveri: scire enim, quibuscumque exercitus dicto audiens non fuerit, aut male re gesta fortunam defuisse, aut aliquot facinore comperto avaritiam ess convicam: suam innocentiam perpetua vita, felicitatem Helvetiorum bello esse perspectam.* For Thein, Sulla developed an unprecedented personalized definition of felicitas as reaction to his critic's charges that his success should be attributed more to *fortuna* than *virtus* (2009, 95). "The myth of Sulla's divine calling to achieve greatness and solve Rome's problems was central to his memoirs and public image" (2009, 103).

71. Most FELICITAS coins feature iconography of the goddess seated or standing with a caduceus and/or cornucopia. FELICITAS: Galba *RIC* 1.273, 246; Titus *RIC* 2.175, 139; Trajan *RIC* 2.624–626, 288; Hadrian *RIC* 2.233–237, 367–368; *RIC* 2.239–240, 368; Antoninus Pius *RIC* 3.557, 102; *RIC* 3.924, 141; *RIC* 3.1067, 156; Marcus Aurelius *RIC* 3.199–203, 229; Commodus *RIC* 3.147, 392. Lucius Verus also uses FELICITAS but with naval iconography: L. Verus *RIC* 3.1325–1340, 319–320. Most Flavian coinage celebrates FELICITAS PVBLICA rather than FELICIAS AVG: cf. Vespasian, *RIC* 2.485, 73; *RIC* 2.539–540, 78, Titus *RIC* 2.89–90, 127; *RIC* 2.138, 132, and Domitian *RIC* 2.324–325, 195. FORTVNA types show the goddess with a rudder, cornucopia, and a wheel or globe. FORTVNA: Nerva *RIC* 2.4, 223; Trajan *RIC* 2.4, 245; Hadrian *RIC* 2.41, 345; Antoninus Pius *RIC* 3.22, 28; Marcus Aurelius *RIC* 3.215, 230; Commodus *RIC* 3.166, 384; Didius Julianus *RIC* 4a.2, 15. Lucius Verus uses FORTVNA only as FORTVNA REDVCTA, *RIC* 3.341, 320; Pertinax uses Fortuna in his DIS CVSTODIBVS reverse, *RIC* 4a.2.7.

72. Scholars still hotly debate the date of the composition of the dreams. Rubin 1980 believes that they could not be completed before 202 simply because the emperor was too busy. Sidebottom 2007, 55n23 rejects the argument, pointing out that Caesar had no trouble with both composition and waging war.

73. Herodian 2.9.5. κατὰ γὰρ τὸν καιρὸν ὅν ἀπηγγέλη Περτίναξ παραλαβὼν τὴν ἀρχήν, μετὰ τὸ προελθεῖν καὶ θῦσαι καὶ τὸν ὑπὲρ τῆς Περτίνακος βασιλείας ὅρκον ἀφοσιώσασθαι ὁ Σεβῆρος ἐπανελθὼν ἐς τὴν οἰκίαν ἑσπέρας καταλαβούσης ἐς ὕπνον κατηνέχθη, μέγαν δὲ καὶ γενναῖον ἵππον βασιλικοῖς φαλάροις κεκοσμημένον ᾠήθη βλέπειν, φέροντα τὸν Περτίνακα ἐποχούμενον διὰ μέσης τῆς ἐν Ῥώμῃ ἱερᾶς ὁδοῦ. ἐπεὶ δὲ κατὰ τὴν τῆς ἀγορᾶς ἀρχὴν ἐγένετο, ἔνθα ἐπὶ τῆς δημοκρατίας πρότερον ὁ δῆμος συνιὼν ἐκκλησίαζεν, ᾠήθη τὸν ἵππον ἀποσεῖσασθαι μὲν τὸν Περτίνακα καὶ ῥῖψαι, αὐτῷ δὲ ἄλλως ἑστῶτι ὑποδῦναί τε αὐτὸν καὶ ἀράμενον ἐπὶ τοῖς νώτοις φέρειν τε ἀσφαλῶς καὶ στῆναι βεβαίως ἐπὶ τῆς ἀγορᾶς μέσης, ἐς ὕψος ἄραντα τὸν Σεβῆρον ὡς ὑπὸ πάντων ὁρᾶσθαί τε καὶ τιμᾶσθαι. μένει δὲ καὶ ἐς ἡμᾶς ἐν ἐκείνῳ τῷ χωρίῳ ἡ τοῦ ὀνείρατος εἰκὼν μεγίστη, χαλκοῦ πεποιημένη.

74. Severus's attempt to write himself into the topography of Rome is first examined by Brilliant 1967, 85–90. Lusnia explores the idea in far greater depth in *Creating Severan Rome: The Architecture and Self-Image of L. Septimius Severus (AD 193–211)* (Brussels: Latomus, forthcoming).

75. Cass. Dio 75.3.1–3. σημεῖα δὲ αὐτῷ ἐξ ὧν τὴν ἡγεμονίαν ἤλπισε, ταῦτα ἐγένετο. ὅτε γὰρ ἐς τὸ βουλευτήριον ἐσεγράφη, ὄναρ ἔδοξε λύκαινάν τινα κατὰ ταὐτὰ τῷ Ῥωμύλῳ θηλάζειν. μέλλοντί τε αὐτῷ τὴν Ἰουλίαν ἄγεσθαι ἡ Φαυστῖνα ἡ τοῦ Μάρκου γυνὴ τὸν θάλαμόν σφισιν ἐν τῷ Ἀφροδισίῳ τῷ κατὰ τὸ παλάτιον παρεσκεύασεν.

76. Treggiari 1994, 315. Goodall Powers notes, "throughout the preparations and ceremony itself she [the *pronuba*] was responsible for encouraging and guiding the bride. She was also a leader in wishing the couple perpetual harmony. Having led the bride into the bedroom, the *pronuba* prayed with her for a blessing on the marriage, helped her undress and remove her jewelry and then put her into the bed. Only then would the groom enter, either alone or escorted by others. The *pronuba* would offer a sacrifice and then leave" (1997).

77. Cass. Dio 71.31.1.

78. *HA Sev.* 3.9. *Cum amissa uxore aliam vellet ducere, genituras sponsarum requirebat, ipse quoque matheseos peritissimus, et cum audisset esse in Syria quandam quae id geniturae haberet ut regi iungeretur, eandem uxorem petiit, Iuliam scilicet, et accepit interventu amicorum. Ex qua statim pater factus est.* Severus's autobiography might have been the source for the *HA*'s report concerning Julia Domna's horoscope. My understanding of Julia Domna's horoscope and what it meant to Severus stands in contrast to the interpretations offered by Cleve and Ricciardi. Ricciardi 2007, 60 agrees with Cleve when she writes that "Julia's horoscope alone and Severus' presumed belief in its legitimacy is evidence of the impact that Julia Domna had on Septimius Severus and his political success even during his rise to power" (1982, 48). By my interpretation, Severus would be horrified to think that his use of Julia Domna's horoscope somehow indicated that he was under his wife's influence.

79. Other instances portray Severus as seeking his destiny by consulting an oracle and painting his horoscope on the ceiling of the Palace, hiding only that portion that astrologers could use to ascertain his time of death. See also Potter 1994, 146–182.

80. Pighi 1965, 157–159, IV.9–V.30.8.

81. The empress's participation in this ceremony might have been an innovation, but it seems more likely that she was following the role that the other Julia Augusta—Livia—had 110 years before. Gagé 1934 posits that Julia Domna's role was unprecedented in the Ludi Saeculares. Ghedini 1984 follows Gagé's lead. Cooley 2007 attributes the emphasis on Julia Domna's role to more complete records than were kept for Augustus's Ludi Saeculares.

82. Lusnia, forthcoming, Appendix I, "Miscellaneous and Doubtful Buildings." Lusnia reviews the history of the site and shows that the connection between the inscription and the Temple of Fortuna Muliebris is not entirely secure. Coins minted under Marcus Aurelius for Faustina also connect her to the cult of Fortuna Muliebris (*RIC* 3.683, 269).

83. Liv. *AUC* 2.40. *Non inviderunt laude sua mulieribus viri Romani—adeo sine obtrectatione gloriae alienae vivebatur—monumento quoque quod esset, templum Fortunae muliebri aedificatum dedicatumque est.*

84. *CIL* 06 00883. LIVIA [D]RVSI F(ILIA) VXSOR [CAESARIS AVGVSTI 3] / IMPP(ERATORES) C[AES]S(ARES) SEVERVS ET ANTO[NINVS AVGG(VSTI) ET GETA NOBILISSIMVS CAESAR] / ET [IVLIA] AVG(VSTAE) MATER AVG[G(VSTORVM) 3 RESTITVERVNT].

85. Kleiner 1996; Purcell 1986, 88. I take issue with this idea in my article, "The Taming of the Shrews: Septimus Severus and the Temple of Fortuna Muliebris" (forthcoming).

86. Horster 2001, 32n86, 33.

87. *CIL* 06 00997 = ILS 00324. IVLIA AVG MATER AVGG ET CASTRORVM/ MATRONIS RESTITVIT SABINA AVG MATRONIS.

88. For the historiography on the *senaculum,* cf. Lusnia, forthcoming, Appendix I. Cf. also HA *Aurelian* 49.6. *Senatum sive senaculum matronis reddi voluerat* (Paschoud 1996, 221*ff.*n6.4.3; Straub 1966, 221–240). Most recently, Hemelrijk writes that "though much of this account is mockery, ridiculing both Elagabalus and women's preoccupation with status by presenting their petty discussions in terms of senatorial decrees, it is not impossible that it refers to actual rules of precedence negotiated in the assembly of women of senatorial class. In any case, the *ordo* and *conventus matronarum,* meeting for religious and other purposes on certain festal days and on special occasions and discussing matters of importance to them, point to an organization of senatorial women in imitation of the male order" (1999, 13n24).

89. I owe this observation to James Anderson, who kindly read and commented upon my manuscript.

90. Gorrie finds that Julia Domna's coinage featuring sacrifices before the *Aedes Vestae* suggests the empress was behind the refurbishment of the House of the Vestals and the Temple of Vesta (2004, 65–68). Yet there is little firm evidence for this contention, beyond the fact that imperial women were often closely associated with Vestals. Lusnia, noting that the reconstruction of the Temple of Vesta likely was complete before the decennalia of Severus, proposes an alternate suggestion. For her, the appearance of Vesta on Julia Domna's coinage might have been meant to ward off Plautianus's charges of sexual impropriety against the empress (forthcoming, chapter 3, "Usurping History in the Roman Forum"). I think that the Pudicitia type I discuss below is a better candidate for countering these rumors.

91. Langford 2008, 130–135.

92. Almost from the moment Severus became emperor, he was engaged in a project to gloss over his African origins in favor of constructed (i.e., fictional) Roman ones (Gorrie 2004). Levick 2007, among others, shows that Julia Domna's foreign origins were ignored in state art in favor of traditional Roman depictions.

93. These comments are based upon the coin types from the *RIC.* Though they are useful in demonstrating the variety of types and legends that the imperial administration produced, they are of little help in determining the frequency or circulation of particular types. For that reason, it is difficult to claim that these types were aimed at particular audiences. As I suggested above with due caveats, these must have been circulated somewhere, and within the city of Rome seems a reasonable possibility.

94. Ghedini explores the range of divine associations attributed to Julia Domna (1984, 123–160).

95. For some, Isis was the equivalent of the Great Mother Goddess, the synthesis of all the most important mother goddesses. This is especially apparent in Apuleius's

Metamorphoses. When the goddess appeared before the still-asinine Lucius, she listed the various names that people called her, including Minerva, Proserpina, Venus, Ceres, Juno, Bellona, and Hecate. But, as she explained to Lucius, "only the Egyptians called me by my proper name, Queen Isis." *Meta.* 11.5. *Inde primigenii Phryges Pessinuntiam deum matrem, hinc autochthones Attici Cecropeiam Minervam, illinc fluctuantes Cyprii Paphiam Venerem, Cretes sagittiferi Dictynnam Dianam, Siculi trilingues Stygiam Proserpinam, Eleusinii vetusti Actaeam Cererem, Iunonem alii, Bellonam alii, Hecatam isti, Rhamnusiam illi, et qui nascentis dei Solis <et occidentis inclinantibus> inlustrantur radiis Aethiopes utrique priscaque doctrina pollentes Aegyptii caerimoniis me propriis percolentes appellant vero nomine reginam Isidem.*

96. Lucr. *DNR* 2.598–99.

97. Art historians have long noted the shift in aesthetics starting under Antoninus Pius, in which central figures are depicted frontally rather than in profile. Julia Domna's appearances on the Porta Argentarii and the Quadrifons Arch of Lepcis Magna are often cited as important markers of this shift (Budde 1957, 1–22). More than any member of Severus's immediate family, Julia Domna appears *en face* on imperial coinage—both on her own coins and those of her male relatives. For some examples, cf. *RIC* 4a.181a–c, 115; *RIC* 293a, 127; *RIC* 4a.816a–b, 202; *RIC* 4a.159, 111. I found only one likely instance of Severus in this pose (*RIC* 4a.75, 224). I have argued elsewhere (and intend to publish these findings) that in the instances where Mattingly and Sydenham 1936, 92–343 identified the *en face* figure, it is likely Julia Domna ("Under the Gaze of the Empress: Succession and Participation in Severan Coinage." Paper presented at the Annual Meeting of the Archaeological Institute of America, Boston, MA, 2005). The Frontality in Severan Coinage database is published online with the Severan Database Project at http://web3.cas.usf.edu/main/other/severan/databases/.

98. These coins seem a much better candidate for asserting Julia Domna's pudicitia than the Vesta or Vesta Mater coins (e.g., *RIC* 4a.582–586, 171) that Lusnia suggested (forthcoming, chapter 2, "Creating the Message: Elements of Severan Propaganda").

99. The same principle seems to apply to charges against Faustina the Younger. Her infidelity with a gladiator explained Commodus's behavior. HA *Marc.* 19.1–7. *Aiunt quidam, quod et veri simile videtur, Commodum Antoninum, successorem illius ac filium, non esse de eo natum sed de adulterio, ac talem fabellam vulgari sermone contexunt: Faustinam quondam, Pii filiam, Marci uxorem, cum gladiatores transire vidisset, unius ex his amore succensam, cum longa aegritudine laboraret, viro de amore confessam. Quod cum ad Chaldaeos Marcus rettulisset, illorum fuisse consilium, ut occiso gladiatore sanguine illius sese Faustina sublavaret atque ita cum viro concumberet. 4 quod cum esset factum, solutum quidem amorem, natum vero Commodum gladiatorem esse, non principem, qui mille prope pugnas publice populo inspectante gladiatorias imperator exhibuit, ut in vita eius docebitur. Quod quidem veri simile ex eo habetur quod tam sancti principis filius iis moribus fuit quibus nullus lanista, nullus scaenicus, nullus arenarius, nullus postremo ex omnium dedecorum ac scelerum conluvione concretus. Multi autem ferunt Commodum omnino ex adulterio natum, si quidem Faustinam satis constet apud Caietam condiciones sibi et nauticas et gladiatorias elegisse.*

100. Sutherland et al. 1984.

101. Clearly, the Via Tritone hoard is far less representative of what was circulated in Rome than the provincial coin hoards for the various zones. Surprisingly, the most frequent coin types of Julia Domna in Rome echo those found in the provinces. This

could simply be a product of a skewed sample, but until other hoards from Rome can be compared to those in the provinces, it is impossible to say whether the results of the Via Tritone hoard are representative of what was circulated in Rome.

102. These are important types for legitimating Julia Domna's sons and, as I will argue in chapter 3, the *pietas* of the empress was particularly useful in calming fears that the tensions between Caracalla and Geta might escalate and ultimately lead to civil war.

103. HA *Sev.* 23.1. *Sunt per plurimas civitates opera eius insignia. Magnum vero illud in vita eius, quod Romae omnes aedes publicas, quae vitio temporum labebantur, instauravit nusquam prope suo nomine adscripto, servatis tamen ubique titulis conditorum.* I cite Domitian rather than Trajan because recent scholarship recognizes much of the building attributed to Trajan was actually begun under Domitian (cf. Anderson 1981; Darwall-Smith 1996).

104. Herodian 3.8.8–9.

105. Cass. Dio 77.1.1. ὁ δὲ Σεουῆρος ἐπὶ τῆς δεκετηρίδος τῆς ἀρχῆς αὐτοῦ ἐδωρήσατο τῷ τε ὁμίλῳ παντὶ τῷ σιτοδοτουμένῳ καὶ τοῖς στρατιώταις τοῖς δορυφόροις ἰσαρίθμους τοῖς τῆς ἡγεμονίας ἔτεσι χρυσοῦς. ἐφ᾽ ᾧ καὶ μέγιστον ἠγάλλετο· καὶ γὰρ ὡς ἀληθῶς οὐδεὶς πώποτε τοσοῦτον αὐτοῖς ἀθρόοις ἐδεδώκει· ἐς γὰρ τὴν δωρεὰν ταύτην πεντακισχίλιαι μυριάδες δραχμῶν ἀναλώθησαν.

106. HA *Sev.* 18.3. *Tripolim, unde oriundus erat, contusis bellicosissimis gentibus securissimam reddidit, ac populo Romano diurnum oleum gratuitum et fecundissimum in aeternum donavit.*

107. Blázquez, interpreting evidence of Dressel 20 amphora from Monte Tessacio in Rome, demonstrated that imperial officials under Severus administered three Baetican olive oil workshops that were previously privately owned. For Blázquez, Severus's reorganization allowed "the *ratio privata* to monopolize the trade for the *annona*, to solve the problem of the rising cost of maintaining the army, and at the same time to maintain a monopoly over the exactions of the *fiscus* which had previously been carried out by the *publicani* or *conductores*" (1992, 177). HA *Sev.* 23.2. *Moriens septem annorum canonem, ita ut cotidiana septuaginta quinque milia modium expendi possent, reliquit; olei vero tantum, ut per quinquennium non solum urbis usibus, sed et totius Italiae, quae oleo eget, sufficeret.* On the surplus, cf. note 60.

108. Lo Cascio 2005, 163–164.

109. Liu 2008.

110. Daguet-Gagey has collected and commented on the inscriptions connected with the *annona* erected under Septimius Severus (2005, 502).

111. *CIL* 06 01040 (p 3071, 3777, 4319). P[RO SALVTE ET 3] / IMPERAT[ORIS CAES(ARIS) L(VCI) SEPTIMI SEVERI PII PERTINACIS AVG(VSTI) ARABICI ADIABENICI] / PAR[THICI MAXIMI PONTIF(ICIS) MAX(IMI) TRIB(VNICIA) POT(ESTATE) 3 IMP(ERATORIS) 3 CO(N)S(VLIS) 3 P(ATRIS) P(ATRIAE) PROCO(N)S(VLIS) ET] / IMPERATO[RIS CAES(ARIS) M(ARCI) AVR(ELI) ANTONINI PII FELICIS AVG(VSTI) ET P(VBLI) SEPTIMI GETAE NOB(LISSIMI) CAES(ARIS) ET] / IVLIAE AV[G(VSTAE) MATRIS AVGG(VSTORVM) ET CASTRORVM ET SENATVS ET PATRIAE] / DEND[ROPHORI. Scholars continue to discuss the actual function of the *dendrophori.*

112. Dessau 1974 dates this inscription by Caracalla's titles to 198–211. *CIL* 06 01060 (p 3071, 3896, 4321, 4351, 4493) = *CIL* 06 33858 = D 07225. IMP(ERATORI) CAESARI

M(ARCO) AVRELIO / ANTONINO AVG(VSTO) / IMP(ERATORIS) CAES(ARIS) L(VCI) SEPTIMI SEVERI PII / PERTINACIS AVG(VSTI) ARABICI ADIABEN(ICI) / PARTHICI MAXIMI P(ATRI) P(ATRIAE) FILIO / COLL(EGIVM) FABR(VM) TIGNARIOR(VM) //. The remainder of the inscription lists the names of the officers of the *collegium*.

113. Saccarii salarii: *BullCom* 1888, 83. *Acceptatores* and *terrari*: *CIL* 14 00016 (p 481) = *D* 05465. PRO [SALVTE] / IMP[ERATORIS] / CAES(ARIS) AVG[VSTI] / NOSTRI / L(VCI) SEPTIMI SEVERI PERTINACIS / HERCVLI NVMINI / SANCTO / CVM BASI MARMORATA / ACCEPTATORIBVS / ET TERRARIS / C(AIVS) SENTIVS / PORTESIS / S(VA) P(ECVNIA) D(ONVM) D(EDIT). NB: Dessau writes of the *acceptatoribus et terraris* "*incertum quae instrumenta significentur*" (1974, 369). *Argentarii* and *boarii*: *CIL* 06 01035 (p 3071, 3777, 4318, 4340) = *CIL* 06 31232 = *D* 00426 = *AE* 1993 00118 = *AE* 2002 +00148 = *AE* 2005 00183. IMP(ERATORI) CAES(ARI) L(VCIO) SEPTIMIO SEVERO PIO PERTINACI AVG(VSTO) ARABIC(O) ADIABENIC(O) PARTH(ICO) MAX(IMO) FORTISSIMO FELICISSIMO / PONTIF(ICI) MAX(IMO) TRIB(VNICIA) POTEST(ATE) XII IMP(ERATORI) XI CO(N)S(VLI) III PATRIPATRIAE ET / IMP(ERATORI) CAES(ARI) M(ARCO) AVRELIO ANTONINO PIO FELICI AVG(VSTO) TRIB(VNICIA) POTEST(ATE) VII CO(N)S(VLI) III P(ATRI) P(ATRIAE) PROCO(N)S(VLI) FORTISSIMO FELICISSIMOQVE PRINCIPI ET / IVLIAE AVG(VSTAE) MATRI AVG(VSTI) N(OSTRI) ET CASTRORVM ET SENATVS ET PATRIAE ET IMP(ERATORIS) CAES(ARIS) M(ARCI) AVRELI ANTONINI PII FELICIS AVG(VSTI) / PARTHICI MAXIMI BRITTANNICI MAXIMI / ARGENTARI(I) ET NEGOTIANTES BOARI(I) HVIVS LOCI QVI / INVEHENT / DEVOTI NVMIN(I) EORVM. According to Andreau, these *argentarii* were likely bankers, or at least carried on functions of bankers, though he posits that in the second and third centuries, the *argentarii* ceased to lend credit in auction sales (1999, 30–33, 136).

114. *CIL* 06 01872 (p 2879, 3820) = D 07266. TI(BERIO) CLAVDIO ESQVIL(INA) SEVERO / DECVRIALI LICTORI PATRONO / CORPORIS PISCATORVM ET / VRINATOR(VM) Q(VIN)Q(VENNALI) III EIVSDEM CORPORIS / OB MERITA EIVS / QVOD HIC PRIMVS STATVAS DVAS VNA / ANTONINI AVG(VSTI) DOMINI N(OSTRI) ALIAM IVL(IAE) / AVGVSTAE DOMINAE NOSTR(AE) S(VA) P(ECVNIA) P(OSVERIT) / VNA CVM CLAVDIO PONTIANO FILIO / SVO EQ(VITE) ROM(ANO) ET HOC AMPLIVS EIDEM / CORPORI DONAVERIT HS X MIL(IA) N(VMMVM) / VT EX VSVRIS EORVM QVODANNIS / NATALI SVO XVII K(ALENDAS) FEBR(VARIAS) / SPORTVLAE VIRITIM DIVIDANTVR / PRAESERTIM CVM NAVIGATIO SCA/PHARVM DILIGENTIA EIVS ADQVISITA / ET CONFIRMATA SIT EX DECRETO / ORDINIS CORPORIS PISCATORVM / ET VRINATORVM TOTIVS ALV(EI) TIBER(IS) / QVIBVS EX S(ENATVS) C(ONSVLTO) COIRE LICET S(VA) P(ECVNIA) P(OSVERVNT) // DEDIC(ATA) XVI K(ALENDAS) SEPT(EMBRES) NVMMIO ALBINO ET FVLVIO AEMILIANO CO(N)S(VLIBVS) / PRAESENTIBVS / IVVENTIO CORNELIANO ET / IVLIO FELICISSIMO / PATRONIS / QVINQVENNALIB(VS) / CLAVDIO QVINTIANO ET / PLVTIO AQVILINO / CVRATORIB(VS) / AELIO AVGVSTALE ET / ANTONIO VITALE ET / CLAVDIO CRISPO.

115. *CIL* 06 00085 (p 3003, 3755) = D 03399. M(ARCVS) AEL(IVS) M(ARCI) F(ILIVS) RVSTICVS RECT(OR) / IMM(VNIS) II HON(ORATVS) III / IN DIEM VITAE SVAE / ME(N)SORIB(VS) MACH(INARIORVM) F(RVMENTI) P(VBLICI) / QVIB(VS) EX S(ENATVS) C(ONSVLTO) COIRE LICET / CASTORES D(ONVM) D(EDIT) / ET OB

DEDICATIONE(M) / DEDIT SING(VLIS) / (DENARIOS) II / L(VCIO) FAENIO FIDELE / Q(VIN)Q(VENNALI) II / DEDIC(ATA) XV KAL(ENDAS) IVN(IAS) / SATVRNINO ET GALLO CO(N)S(VLIBVS)//.

116. The monument has been extensively studied by, among others, Andreau 1999; Benario 1958; Daguet-Gagey 2005; Elsner 2005; Haynes and Hirst 1939; Instinsky 1942; Kuhoff 1993; Pallottino 1946; Ryberg 1955. Several scholars have attested that the north face of the monument was only partially completed and probably not readily visible from the central passage.

117. Several scholars agree that the *boarii* and *argentarii* erected the porta in expectation of or as thanks for some tax breaks or other beneficia (e.g., Daguet-Gagey 2005, 504n19; Haynes and Hirst 1939, 10–11).

118. On Plautianus's titles, cf. Cass. Dio 46.46.4 and Elsner 2005. On Julia Domna's titles, cf. Daguet-Gagey 2005. Benario 1958 suggests that the Julia Domna's Mater Senatus and Mater Patriae titles were original to the monument, while Kuhoff 1993, who personally examined the inscription, dates them to 205. I reject both findings in favor of Instinsky, who dates the titles from the death of Severus to the death of Geta (1942, 211). For my own opinion on the conferring of Julia Domna's titles, cf. Appendix C. For my dating of Julia Domna's titles, cf. Appendix C.

119. Desnier finds it more likely that the figures were the consuls, one of whom happened to also be the urban praefect that year (1993, 579). Barbara Tasser finds it more likely that the figures were officials of the collegia (Daguet-Gagey 2005, 504n19). NB: Tasser's work is unpublished but cited by Daguet-Gagey.

120. Desnier 1993, 580.

121. Elsner 2005, 83.

122. There are four inscriptions erected by dedicators whom I could not identify. Either the names had been lost or there are no further testimonies of the names in literary or inscriptional evidence. Of these four inscriptions, two employed the full titles of the empress while the other two did not. *CIL* 06 03768 (p 3072, 4337, 4342) = *CIL* 06 31322; *CIL* 06 36934; *CIL* 06 00786; *CIL* 06 01048.

123. Grassi 2006.

124. Grassi 2006; Macé 2005, 316–317.

125. Wood imagines a woman's thoughts upon encountering a portrait of an imperial woman: "She might even have been able to see painted or sculptural likenesses of the ruling family without leaving her home: if her family, or the family that she served, had some personal reason for gratitude or loyalty toward imperial figures, small busts of those individuals might have a place in the *lararium*, or family shrine, of the house along with figures of household gods and ancestors. Those familiar faces would include a number of women: the mother of the emperor, perhaps; his wife, if he was married, his daughters or sisters, if he had any—people with whom, thanks to both biology and social convention, she shared a number of very personal concerns, despite their difference from her in rank, fame and status" (1999, 1).

Chapter Three • *Mater Senatus, Mater Patriae*

1. Cass. Dio 75.2.3–4. καὶ πολλὰ μὲν ἡμῖν οὐ καταθύμια ἔπραττεν, αἰτίαν τε ἔσχεν ἐπὶ τῷ πλήθει στρατιωτῶν ὀχλώδη τὴν πόλιν ποιῆσαι καὶ δαπάνῃ χρημάτων περιττῇ τὸ κοινὸν βαρῦναι, καὶ τὸ μέγιστον ὅτι μὴ ἐν τῇ τῶν συνόντων οἱ εὐνοίᾳ ἀλλ᾽ἐν τῇ ἐκείνων ἰσχύι τὴν ἐλπίδα τῆς σωτηρίας ἐποιεῖτο· I have modified Cary's excellent translation from "to the good will of his associates [in the government]" to "our good will" in order to highlight the balance that Severus had to maintain between the military and the Senate (2001, 164).

2. On the competent general, 5–6, 12–15; on *comilites* and improving military *disciplina*, 18–19; on financial responsibility, 34–41; on physical, religious, and entertainment needs, 25–33, 46–51; on lack of pretention and treatment of Senate, 24, 52, 54–79, 93; on imperial women, 83–84; on freedmen, 88.

3. Paterson 2007.

4. This did not prevent Severus from marketing himself as such just before his decennalia. Cf., e.g., *RIC* 4a.169, 113. The reverse type features Severus on horseback with the legend SPQR OPTIMO PRINC. Significantly, the types are only recorded in aureii; Severus seems to have been trying to convince the Senate that he was the Optimus Princeps for whom it pined.

5. Cass. Dio 46.46.7; HA *Sev.* 7.3–7.

6. Cass. Dio 52.19–39. See also de Blois 1998/1999.

7. Cass. Dio 46.46; 52.25.

8. I have elsewhere explored Severus's attempts to emphasize his Roman ethnicity, masculinity, and divine election and senatorial undermining of this self-presentation (Langford 2008).

9. Scholars disagree not so much on the number of senatorial positions that Severus offered to equestrians (roughly seven) but about how significant those offices were. Southern sees them as indicative of a general policy (2001, 50). Campbell, however, dismisses most of them as exigencies or the results of extraordinary circumstances (1984, 404–408). Severus was certainly not the first emperor to promote talented equestrians at the expense of senators. As the career of Pertinax demonstrates, talented equestrians could rise not only to the top of their own *cursus*, but in special cases were promoted into the senatorial ranks (Potter 2004, 74–76).

10. Cass. Dio 46.46. Levick 2007, 74–75.

11. Herodian 3.11.2. ἠμφίεστο γὰρ τήν τε πλατύσημον ἐσθῆτα, ἔν τε τοῖς δεύτερον ὑπατεύσασιν ἐτέτακτο παρῃώρητό τε τὸ ξίφος, καὶ παντὸς ἀξιώματος σχῆμα ἔφερε μόνος.

12. Herodian 1.5.6.

13. Paterson 2007, 131.

14. "The ruler's court is not the creation of the ruler alone or even his initiative. It is as much the means by which the subjects come to terms with the fact that power is now the monopoly of the ruler and the way they create a *modus vivendi* with that ruler" (Paterson 2007, 31).

15. Späth 2000 argues deftly against any "Frauenherrschaft" in the *Annales* of Tacitus. He sees Tacitus's portrayal of Agrippina as a commentary on the reigns of Claudius

and Nero and the inherent weaknesses of the principate, in general, in which the *domus Augusta* was set above all other households. In other words, the outrageous behavior of the Julio-Claudian women in Tacitus's text reflects his judgment of the emperors as weak and ineffective, unable to keep the women of their household in check according to Roman societal norms.

16. Plin. *Paneg.* 83. *Est magnificum, quod te ab omni contagione vitiorum reprimis ac revocas, sed magnificentius, quod tuos. Quanto enim magis arduum est, alios praestare, quam se: tanto laudabilius, quod, quum ipse sis optimus, omnes circa te similes tui effecisti. Multis illustribus dedecori fuit aut inconsultius uxor assumpta, aut retenta patientius: ita foris claros domestica destruebat infamia: et ne maximi cives haberentur, hoc efficiebat, quod mariti minores erant. Tibi uxor in decus et gloriam cedit . . . Eadem quam modica cultu! quam parca comitatu! Quam civilis incessu! Mariti hoc opus, qui ita imbuit, ita instituit: nam uxori sufficit obsequii gloria.* All translations of Pliny are based upon those of Radice 1997.

17. Leppin 2002, 485–486.

18. *Epist.* 3.18.2–3. *Amplecti, primum ut imperatori nostro virtutes suae veris laudibus commendarentur, deinde ut futuri principes non quasi a magistro sed tamen sub exemplo praemonerentur, qua potissimum via possent ad eandem gloriam niti. Nam praecipere qualis esse debeat princeps, pulchrum quidem sed onerosum ac prope superbum est; laudare vero optimum principem ac per hoc posteris velut e specula lumen quod sequantur ostendere, idem utilitatis habet arrogantiae nihil.*

19. Plin. *Paneg.* 7.1. *O novum atque inauditum ad principatum iter!*

20. Plin. *Paneg.* 7.4–6. *Nulla adoptati cum eo, qui adoptabat, cognatio, nulla necessitudo, nisi quod uterque optimus erat, dignusque alter eligi, alter eligere. Itaque adoptatus es, non, ut prius alius atque alius, in uxoris gratiam. Adscivit enim te filium non vitricus, sed princeps, eodemque animo divus Nerva pater tuus factus est, quo erat omnium. Nec decet aliter filium adsumi, si adsumatur a principe. An Senatum Populumque Romanum, exercitus, provincias, socios transmissurus uni, successorem e sinu uxoris accipias? Summaeque potestatis heredem tantum intra domum tuam quaeras? Non per totam civitatem circumferas oculos? Et hunc tibi proximum, hunc coniunctissimum existimes, quem optimum, quem diis simillimum inveneris? Imperaturus omnibus, eligi debet ex omnibus. Non enim servulis tuis dominum, ut possis esse contentus quasi necessario herede, sed principem civibus daturus es imperator.*

21. Liv. *AUC* 1.57.9–11. Livy's Lucretia is more a creation of Augustan moralism than a reflection of ancient women.

22. Such rhetoric might be seen as a reaction to Augustus's politicized domesticity that Milnor explored (2005, 47–93). Tacitus uses the same language in the gripping senators' discussion of the impending death of Augustus and their fears of living under Tiberius. *Accedere matrem muliebri inpotentia: serviendum feminae duobusque insuper adulescentibus, qui rem publicam interim premant, quandoque distrahant.* Tiberius is particularly impotent in the face of his mother. The senators envision themselves as slaves in this arrangement (*serviendum*) rather than corulers.

23. The *Oxford Latin Dictionary* does not include "womb" or "vagina" among the possible definitions of *sinus*. Adams, however, notes the use of the *sinus* in Tibullus and Ovid for "womb" or "vagina." "Tibullus' expression anticipates but is unconnected with,

a later medical use of *sinus,* of the vagina. The *calque sinus muliebris* is often found in Soranus' translators Caelius Aurelianus and Soran. Lat (Mustio)" (1982, 90–91).

24. Flemming 2000, 1–124.

25. The formulation of the third person and the passive and its rhetorical nature are apparent in English, too. Many children know that the phrase "It's simply not done in the better circles" is a thinly veiled imperative for "don't do that!"

26. Tac. *Hist.* 1.16. *Si immensum imperii corpus stare ac librari sine rectore posset, dignus eram a quo res publica inciperet: nunc eo necessitatis iam pridem ventum est ut nec mea senectus conferre plus populo Romano possit quam bonum successorem, nec tua plus iuventa quam bonum principem. Sub Tiberio et Gaio et Claudio unius familiae quasi hereditas fuimus: loco libertatis erit quod eligi coepimus; et finita Iuliorum Claudiorumque domo optimum quemque adoptio inveniet. Nam generari et nasci a principibus fortuitum, nec ultra aestimatur: adoptandi iudicium integrum et, si velis eligere, consensu monstratur.* All translations of Tacitus's *Histories* come from Wellesley 1988.

27. The obvious exception is Livia, upon whom the Senate heaped titles after Augustus's death. As seen in chapter 1, Livia's engagement in political or military matters embarrassed and in some cases emasculated Tiberius. Barrett outlines the difficulty Tiberius faced in honoring his mother, respecting the wishes of the divine Augustus, and running the empire according to his own judgment. Barrett interprets the Senate's honors not as an invitation to Livia to intervene in political affairs so much as an effort to follow the wishes of Augustus (2002, 146–173).

28. Cass. Dio 73.15.1–5. διά τε τἆλλα καὶ ὅτι ἠναγκάζοντο, ἅ τῷ παρτὶ αὐτοῦ κατ᾽εὔνοιαν ἐψηφίζοντο, ταῦτ᾽ ἐκείνῳ διὰ φόβον ἀπονέμειν ἐξ ἐπιτάγματος. He made similar complaints concerning Macrinus and Elagabalus, who adopted all the titles of Caracalla without waiting for senatorial approval. Cass. Dio 79.16.2 (Macrinus), 80.2.2–3 (Elagabalus).

29. Alföldy 1968, 114. See also Hammond, who accepts roughly these figures in the late second century (1957a, 77). Talbert rejects the methodology and conclusions as unfounded (1984, 31–33). More recently, Eck accepted Hammond's estimates (2000b, 218–220).

30. Though Severus is often accused of unprecedented preference for equestrians, examination of earlier emperors shows that this was a common practice (Eck 2000, 247–256; Potter 2004, xii; Talbert 1984).

31. Hoffer 1999, 5–12.

32. Through prosopographical data, scholars have determined which senators likely backed which contender. Alföldy 1968, 116–123; Birley 1999, 108–128.

33. Historians report two instances of mob demonstrations before Severus reached Rome. In the first, a mob occupied the Circus Maximus for over twenty-four hours, shouting their support for Niger (Cass. Dio 73.5; Herodian 2.7.3; HA *Nig.* 2.2). Mobs seized the circus during Julianus's bidding for the empire, and the mobs called upon Niger to be their salvation. For more on these demonstrations, cf. chapter 2. Despite Niger's low birth, he enjoyed the support of senators from the East as well as his party at Rome. It was perhaps his military exploits that made Niger so popular among the populations living in Rome.

34. All biographical information on Dio is culled from Millar 1964, 13–27.

35. Millar 1964, 29. For Swain, Cassius Dio needed to impress Severus not only because he wanted to protect the honors granted him by Pertinax in 193, but also because the homeland of Nicaea had thrown in their lot with Pescennius Niger (1996, 401).

36. Harrington 1977, 160. Rubin attributes these changes of tone to two different accounts, a propaganda pamphlet in support of Severus and a later, more critical, account written after Severus's death (1980, 49–51, 57–60).

37. Cf. Moscovich 2004 for a fuller discussion of Dio's possible sources within the palace.

38. Cass. Dio 78.8.1–9.2.

39. This assessment agrees largely with de Blois's, who sees *eunomia* as the most important quality in helping an emperor protect himself against envy and conspiracies (1998/1999, 278–279).

40. Harrington 1977, 160; Millar 1964, 29.

41. Bartsch 1994, 148–187.

42. Cf. Cass. Dio 1.3–5; HA *Sev.* 6.6–8.5, Herodian 2.14.1–2.

43. Cass. Dio 75.1.3–5. μέχρι μὲν τῶν πυλῶν ἐπί τε τοῦ ἵππου καὶ ἐν ἐσθῆτι ἱππικῇ ἐλθών, ἐντεῦθεν δὲ τήν τε πολιτικὴν ἀλλαξάμενος καὶ βαδίσας. καὶ αὐτῷ καὶ ὁ στρατὸς πᾶς, καὶ οἱ πεζοὶ καὶ οἱ ἱππεῖς, ὡπλισμένοι παρηκολούθησαν· . . . οἵ τε στρατιῶται ἐν τοῖς ὅπλοις ὥσπερ ἐν πανηγύρει τινὶ πομπῆς ἐκπρεπόντως ἀνεστρέφοντο, καὶ προσέτι ἡμεῖς ἐν κόσμῳ περιῄειμεν.

44. Severus might have been echoing the entrance of Vespasian into Rome at the end of the civil wars in 70 AD. Joseph. *BJ* 7.4.

45. Cass. Dio 75.2.12. ἐσελθὼν δὲ οὕτως ἐνεανιεύσατο μὲν οἷα καὶ οἱ πρῴην ἀγαθοὶ αὐτοκράτορες πρὸς ἡμᾶς, ὡς οὐδένα τῶν βουλευτῶν ἀποκτενεῖ. καὶ ὤμοσε περὶ τούτου, καὶ τό γε μεῖζον, ψηφίσματι κοινῷ αὐτὸ κυρωθῆναι προσετετάχει, πολέμιον καὶ τὸν αὐτοκράτορα καὶ τὸν ὑπηρετήσοντα αὐτῷ ἔς τι τοιοῦτον, αὐτούς τε καὶ τοὺς παῖδας αὐτῶν, νομίζεσθαι δογματίσας.

46. Cass. Dio 75.2.3–4.

47. Cass. Dio 46.46.7.

48. HA *Sev.* 7.3–7. *Fuitque ingressus Severi odiosus atque terribilis, cum milites inempta diriperent, vastationem urbi minantes. Aliae die armatis stipatus non solum militibus sed etiam amicis in senatum venit. In curia reddidit rationem suscepti imperii causatusque est, quod ad se occidendum Iulianus notos ducum caedibus misisset. Fieri etiam senatus consultum coegit, ne liceret imperatori inconsulto senatu occidere senatorem. Sed cum in senatu esset, milites per seditionem dena milia poposcerunt a senatu, exemplo eorum qui Augustum Octavianum Romam deduxerant tantumque acceperant. Et cum eos voluisset comprimere Severus nec potuisset, tamen mitigatos addita liberalitate dimisit.*

49. Herodian 2.14.1. This scene differs noticeably from Dio's in that the population welcoming the new emperor to Rome was not ὅμιλος—the unwashed masses—but a more respectable δῆμος. This more generous depiction of the populace perhaps reflects the humble origins of Herodian.

50. Herodian 2.14.3. τῆς δὲ ἐπιούσης κατελθὼν ἐς τὴν σύγκλητον λόγους ἐπιεικεῖς πάνυ καὶ χρηστῶν ἐλπίδων μεστοὺς ἐποιεῖτο πρὸς πάντας, καὶ κοινῇ καὶ ἰδίᾳ δεξιούμενος, λέγων ἥκειν μὲν ἔκδικος τοῦ Περτίνακος φόνου, τὴν δ᾽ἀρχὴν παρέξειν ἀφορμὴν καὶ εἴσοδον ἀριστοκρατίας, μήτε δὲ ἄκριτόν τινα φονευθήσεσθαι ἢ δημευθήσεσθαι, μήτε συκοφαντοῦντος ἀνέξεσθαι, ἀλλὰ βαρυτάτην εὐδαιμονίαν

τοῖς ἀρχομένοις παρεξεῖν, καὶ πάντα πράξειν ἐς ζῆλον τῆς Μάρκου ἀρχῆς, ἕξειν δὲ τοῦ Περτίνακος οὐ μόνον τοὔνομα ἀλλὰ καὶ τὴν γνώμην.

51. Herodian 2.14.4. ὅτι ἄρα εἴη ἀνὴρ πολύτροπός τις καὶ μετὰ τέχνης εἰδὼς προσφέρεθαι πράγμασιν.

52. HA *Sev.* 3. On the necessity of universal consensus, *alia die ad senatum venit et amicos Iuliani incusatos proscriptioni ac neci dedit.* No complaints against Severus for these executions appear in the fragments of Dio's text, which might indicate his support for such an action (Cass. Dio 75.1.3–5). More compellingly, in Maecenas's speech to Augustus, Dio has Maecenas excuse some necessary executions (52.26.7–8).

53. HA *Sev.* 8.8: *intra triginta dies quam Romam venerat est profectus.*

54. On Pertinax's adopted succession policy, see Cass. Dio 74.7.2–3.

55. Cass. Dio 75.4.4.

56. For more on this, cf. the introduction.

57. Talbert 1984, 491.

58. Dio reports that Severus never killed anyone for his property (77.16.2): καὶ διὰ τοῦτο καὶ χρήματα ἐξ ἅπαντος τρόπου, πλὴν καθ'ὅσον οὐδένα ἕνεκα αὐτῶν ἀπέκτεινε. Provincial towns and cities were fined at four times the aid they had lent to Niger, regardless of whether they had done so willingly or under compunction. Cf. Cass. Dio 75.8.4–5.

59. Cass. Dio 75.9.1–4.

60. HA *Sev.* 8.11; 9.2–3. The *HA* claims that only one senator who had sided with Niger was punished. Whittaker believes that this was a generalization from one case, Asellius Aemilianus. Aemilianus was perhaps the punished senator mentioned in the *HA* (1969, 286n1). Herodian reported that the children of Niger's generals were held hostage by Severus, who then executed them after defeating Niger (3.5.6). The *HA* suggests that he did so because of the upcoming conflict with Albinus (*Sev.* 10.1; *Niger* 6.1). The wife and children of Albinus, according to the *HA*, fared no better. Severus ordered their bodies dumped in the Rhone, while the body of Albinus was mangled, decapitated, and displayed for a time outside of his family residence in Rome, presumably as an object lesson for any of his more intransigent supporters (*Sev.* 11.9; *Albinus* 9.6–7; Herodian 3.8.1; Cass. Dio 76.7.3)

61. Date when the arch was vowed (Brilliant 1967, 92).

62. Ando 2000, 183.

63. Brilliant 1967, 91–95, 121–128, 171; de Maria 1988, 181; Lusnia 1995, 115–126; Rubin 1980, 157n118.

64. *Tab. Siar*. I, 1–21 = *ZPE* 55 (1984): 58–59, with emendations by Lebek, reads: *supraque eum ianum status Ger[manici Caesaris po]/neretur in curru triumpahli et circa latera eius statuae D[rusi Germanici patris ei]/us, naturalis fratris Ti. Caesaris Aug. et Antoniae matris ei[us et Agrippinae uxoris et Li]/viae sororis et Ti. Germanici fratris eius et filiorum et fi[liarum eius]* (Lebek 1986, 34, 67; Potter 1987, 133). de Maria, however, sees centuries-old senatorial formulae in these lines (1988, 181).

65. Alföldy 1968, 121–122. The suggestion that Albinus possibly appeared in the original decree is mine and completely speculative.

66. *CIL* 06 01033. IMP(ERATORI) CAES(ARI) LVCIO SEPTIMIO M(ARCI) FIL(IO) SEVERO PIO PERTINACI AVG(VSTO) PATRI PATRIAE PARTHICO ARABICO ET / PARTHICO ADIABENICO PONTIFIC(I) MAXIMO TRIBVNIC(IA) POTEST(ATE)

XI IMP(ERATORI) XI CO(N)S(VLI) III PROCO(N)S(VLI) ET / IMP(ERATORI) CAES(ARI) M(ARCO) AVRELIO L(VCI) FIL(IO) ANTONINO AVG(VSTO) PIO FELICI TRIBVNIC(IA) POTEST(ATE) VI CO(N)S(VLI) PROCO(N)S(VLI) P(ATRI) P(ATRIAE) ET / [[[P(VBLIO) SEPTIMIO GETAE NOBILISS(IMO) CAESARI]]] / <<OPTIMIS FORTISSIMISQVE PRINCIPIBVS>> / OB REM PVBLICAM RESTITVTAM IMPERIVMQVE POPVLI ROMANI PROPAGATVM / INSIGNIBVS VIRTVTIBVS EORVM DOMI FORISQVE S(ENATVS) P(OPVLVS)Q(VE) R(OMANVS). The grudging recognition of Severus's self-adoption (MARCI FILIO) is far less ebullient than official inscriptions erected by the imperial administration (cf. *CIL* 06 001032).

67. Brilliant cites Hasebroek 1921, 81 and *ILS* 00417 for the configuration of titles on the triumphal arch of Septimius Severus erected at Haidra in 195: "the Imperial titulature is at least in part the same as that contained in the original vote of the Senate . . . Indeed, the only occurrence of this old style titulature after 195 AD is on the Forum arch, itself evidence of the great value attributed to the original senatorial decree in establishing the proper pedigree of the monument" (1967, 92). Coins minted at Rome in all metals in 195–196 advertise Severus as DIVI M[ARCI] PII F[ILIVS] P[ONTIFEX] M[AXIMUS] TR[IBVNICIA] P[OTESTAS] III COS II P[ATER] P[ATRIAE]. *RIC* 4a.65–66, 99 (aureii) and *RIC* 4a.700–702A, 187 (denarii) and *RIC* 4a.712, 188 (dupondi).

68. Ando 2000, 183–185.

69. Rubin 1980, 157.

70. As odd as placing women on triumphal arches may sound, the Romans occasionally did: Antonia, Octavia, and Agrippina appeared on the triumphal arch of Claudius in Rome, as shown by an inscription (*CIL* 06 00921a = *ILS* 00222; Barrett 1991, 7–8). The *Tabula Sirensis* reveals that imperial women were both consulted about appropriate honors and included in the bronze attic statuary that the Senate proposed for the (never built) Arch of Germanicus (cf. note 64).

71. Campbell suggests that the rough treatment of the Senate as a whole led to individual senators becoming reticent to serve in senatorial provinces, making it necessary to appoint equestrian praefects (1984, 412).

72. Southern 2001, 40.

73. HA *Sev.* 10.2. *Albinum igitur statim hostem iudicavit et eos qui ad illum mollius vel scripserunt vel rescripserunt.*

74. HA *Sev.* 11.3. *Eo tempore lectis actis quae de Clodio Celsino laudando, qui Hadrumentinus et adfinus Albini erat, facta sunt, iratus senatui Severus, quasi hoc Albino senatus praestitisset, Commodum inter divos referendum esse censuit, quasi hoc genere de senatu posset ulcisci.*

75. Cass. Dio 76.7.4–8.4. μάλιστα δ᾽ ἡμᾶς ἐξέπληξεν ὅτι τοῦ τε Μάρκου υἱὸν καὶ τοῦ Κομμόδου ἀδελφὸν ἑαυτὸν ἔλεγε, τῷ τε Κομμόδῳ, ὅν πρῴην ὕβριζεν, ἡρωικὰς ἐδίδου τιμάς. πρός τε τὴν βουλήν λόγον ἀναγινώσκων, καὶ τὴν μὲν Σύλλου καὶ Μαρίου καὶ Αὐγούστου αὐστηρίαν τε καὶ ὠμότητα ὡς ἀσφαλεστέραν ἐπαινῶν, τὴν δὲ Πομπηίου καὶ Καίσαρος ἐπιείκειαν ὡς ὀλεθρίαν αὐτοῖς ἐκείνοις γεγενημένην κακίζων, ἀπολογίαν τινὰ ὑπὲρ τοῦ Κομμόδου ἐπήγαγε, καθαπτόμενος τῆς βουλῆς ὡς οὐ δικαίως ἐκεῖνον ἀτιμαζούσης, εἴγε καὶ αὐτῆς οἱ πλείους αἴσχιον βιοτεύουσιν . . . ἀναγνοὺς δὲ ταῦτα τριάκοντα μὲν καὶ πέντε ἀπέλυσε τῶν τὰ Ἀλβίνου φρονῆσαι αἰτιαθέντων, καὶ ὡς μηδεμίαν τὸ παράπαν αἰτίαν ἐσχηκόσιν αὐτοῖς προσεφέρετο (ἦσαν δὲ ἐν τοῖς πρώτοις τῆς γερουσίας), ἐννέα δὲ καὶ εἴκοσιν ἀνδρῶν θάνατον κατεψηφίσατο.

76. *RIC* 4a.169a–b, 113.

77. That the Senate was struggling with the question of how a Marcus could produce a Commodus is evident from the *HA*. The answer? Commodus was the issue of Faustina's sexual escapades with a gladiator, not the legitimate son of Marcus. HA *Marc.* 19.7.

78. Chastagnol 1984. On the triumph, HA *Sev.* 9.11. Hill 1979 describes a problematic but provocative method for dating undated Severan coins.

79. The reverses both of Severus and Julia Domna from this period also feature the boys individually (for Severus, see *RIC* 4a.157, 111 and *RIC* 4a.164, 112; for Julia Domna, see *RIC* 4a.542-5, 166 and *RIC* 4a.571, 169).

80. Pighi 1965, 157–159, IV.9–V.30.8; Levick 2007, 53–54.

81. The empress's participation in this ceremony might have been an innovation, but it seems more likely that she was following the role that the other Julia Augusta—Livia—had 110 years before. Gagé 1934 posits that Julia Domna's role was unprecedented in the Ludi Saeculares. Ghedini 1984 follows Gagé's lead. Cooley 2007 attributes the emphasis on Julia Domna's role to more complete records than were kept for Augustus's Ludi Saeculares.

82. There is no sign of Julia Domna's "orientalism" here. Severus downplayed Julia Domna's Syrian heritage just as he did his own African roots (Langford 2008). For more on Julia Domna in the Severan *Ludi Saeculares*, cf. chapter 2.

83. Cf. also *RIC* 4a.181a–c, 115.

84. This type is one of about seventy examples of frontality in Severan coinage, and together they represent a dramatic shift in Roman imperial numismatic and artistic aesthetics. The decision to render types frontally was clearly a conscious one. The inertia of aesthetics suggests that, if there were no thought given to the matter, numismatic figures would have continued in the profile tradition that had been established in the first century and, with few exceptions, became standard up to the reign of Severus.

85. For a more complete discussion of these types, see chapter 2.

86. An example of this iconography is the second-century bronze grouping on display at the Metropolitan Museum of Art (97.22.24), http://www.metmuseum.org/Collections/search-the-collections/130007173.

87. Herodian reports that Plautianus had been the emperor's *eromenos* (3.10.6).

88. For a fuller discussion of Plautianus, see chapter 2. Though no literary evidence places Plautianus at Hatra, it is likely that he would have been there as the head of the emperor's guard. The following year, however, his presence is attested, when Plautianus accompanied the family to Africa, where he was honored beside the imperial family (Birley 1999, 146).

89. Cass. Dio 76.15.4-5. ποτὲ γοῦν τοῦ Σεουήρου ἐν Τυάνοις νοσήσαντα αὐτὸν ἐπισκεπτομένου, οἱ στρατιῶται οἱ περὶ τὸν Πλαυτιανὸν ὄντες οὐκ εἴασαν τοὺς ἀκολουθοῦντας αὐτῷ συνεσελθεῖν· ὅ τε τὰς δίκας τὰς ἐπ' αὐτοῦ λογομένας διατάττων κελευσθείς ποτε ὑπὸ τοῦ Σεουήρου ἀργοῦντος δίκην τινὰ ἐσαγαγεῖν οὐκ ἠθέλησεν, εἰπὼν ὅτι "οὐ δύναμαι τοῦτο ποιῆσαι, ἂν μὴ Πλαθτιανός μοι κελεύσῃ."

90. Cass. Dio 76.15.6–7. καὶ οὕτω καὶ ἐς τὰ ἄλλα πάντα ὁ Πλαυτιανὸς αὐτοῦ κατεκράτει ὥστε καὶ τὴν Ἰουλίαν τὴν Αὔγουσταν πολλὰ καὶ δεινὰ ἐργάσασθαι· πάνυ γὰρ αὐτῇ ἤχθετο, καὶ σφόδρα αὐτὴν πρὸς τὸν Σεουῆρον ἀεὶ διέβαλλεν, ἐξετάσεις τε κατ' αὐτῆς καὶ βασάνους κατ' εὐγενῶν γυναικῶν ποιούμενος. καὶ ἡ μὲν αὐτή τε φιλοσοφεῖν διὰ ταῦτ' ἤρξατο καὶ σοφισταῖς συνημέρευεν. ὁ δὲ δὴ Πλαυτιανὸς ἀσωτότατός τε ἀνθρώπων γενόμενος, ὥστε καὶ εὐωχεῖσθαι ἅμα καὶ ἐμεῖν, ἐπεὶ μηδὲν

ὑπὸ τοῦ πλήθους τῶν τε σιτίων καὶ τοῦ οἴνου πέψαι ἐδύνατο, καὶ τοῖς μειρακίοις ταῖς τε κόραις οὐκ ἄνευ διαβολῆς χρώμενος, τῇ γυναικὶ τῇ ἑαυτοῦ οὔθ᾽ ὁρᾶν τινὰ οὔθ᾽ ὁρᾶσθαι τὸ παράπαν, οὐδ᾽ ὑπὸ τοῦ Σεουήρου ἢ τῆς Ἰουλίας, μήτι γε ἑτέρων τινῶν, ἐπέτρεπεν.

91. McCullough 2007, 4–6.

92. Cass. Dio 76.15.1. αἴτιος δὲ τούτων αὐτὸς ὁ Σεουῆρος μάλιστ᾽ ἐγένετο, ὅς οὕτως αὐτῷ ὑπεῖκεν ἐς πάντα ὥστ᾽ ἐκεῖνον μὲν ἐν αὐτοκράτορος αὐτὸν δὲ ἐν ἐπάρχου μοίρᾳ εἶναι.

93. McCullough 2007, 11, 13–75.

94. Cass. Dio 77.2.4.

95. Cass. Dio 77.3–4.

96. Herodian 3.11.1–12.11.

97. With all due respect to Levick, who suggests that Julia Domna was in on Caracalla's conspiracy to kill Plautianus (2007, 74–86).

98. Cass. Dio 77.4.4. καὶ αὐτόν τις τῶν τριχῶν τοῦ γενείου ἐκτίλας τῇ τε Ἰουλίᾳ καὶ τῇ Πλαυτίλλῃ προσήνεγκεν ὁμοῦ οὔσαις, πρὶν καὶ ὁτιοῦν αὐτὰς ἀκοῦσαι, καὶ εἶπεν "ἴδετε τὸν Πλαυτιανὸν ὑμῶν," κἀκ τούτου τῇ μὲν πένθος τῇ δὲ χαρὰν ἐνέβαλεν. How Dio would have known about this private scene is unclear. Moscovich posits, however, that Dio had access to information through sources in the empress's inner circle, especially Philostratus (1992, 359–361).

99. Cass. Dio 77.7.1.

100. Herodian 3.13.3–6.

101. On conquering Caledonia, Cass. Dio 77.13.1.

102. Cass. Dio. 77.11.1. ὁ δὲ δὴ Σεουῆρος ἐπὶ Βρεττανίαν ἐστράτευσε τούς τε παῖδας ἐκδιαιτωμένους ὁρῶν καὶ τὰ στρατεύματα ὑπὸ ἀργίας ἐκλυόμενα, καίπερ εἰδὼς ὅτι οὐκ ἀνακομισθήσεται.

103. Cass. Dio 77.14.1–7.

104. Cass. Dio 77.15.2. πρὶν γοῦν μεταλλάξαι, τάδε λέγεται τοῖς παισὶν εἰπεῖν (ἐρῶ γὰρ αὐτὰ τὰ λεχθέντα, μηδὲν ὅ τι καλλωπίσας)· "ὁμονοεῖτε, τοὺς στρατιώτας πλουτίζετε, τῶν ἄλλων πάντων καταφρονεῖτε."

105. Cass. Dio 78.1.4. προσεποιοῦντο μὲν γὰρ καὶ φιλεῖν ἀλλήλους καὶ ἐπαινεῖν, πάντα δὲ τὰ ἐναντιώτατα ἔδρων, καὶ ἦν οὐκ ἄδηλον ὅτι δεινόν τι παρ᾽ αὐτῶν γενήσοιτο.

106. Cass. Dio 78.1.5.

107. For Severus as peacekeeper, Cass. Dio 77.14; Herodian 3.14.1–3.

108. See Appendix C for details on dating the Mater Senatus, Mater Patriae titles.

109. Cass. Dio 79.23.

Conclusion

1. Herodian 4.1.3–5. ὡς δὲ ἀφίκοντο ἐς τὴν Ῥώμην, ὅ τε δῆμος αὐτοὺς δαφνηφορῶν ὑπεδέξατο ἥ τε σύγκλητος προσηγόρευσεν. ἡγοῦντο δ᾽ αὐτοὶ μὲν τὴν βασίλειον φέροντες πορφύραν, εἵποντο δ᾽ ὄπισθεν αὐτοῖς οἱ τὴν ὕπατον ἀρχὴν τότε διέποντες, κάλπιν φέροντες ἔνθα ἦν τὰ Σεβήρου λείψανα. οἵ τε προσαγορεύοντες τοὺς νέους αὐτοκράτορας παριόντες καὶ τὴν κάλπιν προσεκύνουν. ἐκείνην μὲν οὖν παραπέμψαντες, καὶ προπομπεύσαντες αὐτῆς, ἀπέθεντο ἐν τῷ νεῷ ἔνθα Μάρκου τε καὶ τῶν πρὸ αὐτοῦ βασιλέων ἱερὰ μνήματα δείκνυται ἐπιτελέσαντες δὲ τὰς νενομισμένας ἱερουργίας ἐπὶ ταῖς βασιλικαῖς εἰσόδοις ἀνῆλθον ἐς τὰ βασίλεια. διελόμενοι δὲ αὐτὰ ἑκάτερος

ᾤκει, παραφράττοντές τε πάσας εἰσόδους, εἴ τινες ἦσαν λανθάνουσαι, μόναις δὲ ταῖς δημοσίοις καὶ αὐλείοις ἀνέδην χρώμενοι, φρουράς τε ἐπιστήσαντες ἰδίᾳ ἑκάτερος, οὐδὲ συνιόντες εἰ μὴ πρὸς ὀλίγον, ὅσον δημοσίᾳ, εἴ ποτε, ὀφθῆναι. ἐπετέλεσαν δὲ πρὸ ἁπάντων τὴν ἐς τὸν πατέρα τιμήν.

2. Herodian 4.2.1–10.

3. Herodian 4.3.2. ἐμερίζοντο δὲ καὶ πάντων αἱ γνῶμαι, ὅσοι ἐν ἀξιώσει ἤ τιμῇ τινὶ ἦσαν κατὰ τὴν πόλιν.

4. Herodian 4.3.4. ὡς στασιάζοντας δὲ τοὺς ἀδελφοὺς ἐν ἅπασιν οἷς ἔπραττον, μέρχι τῶν εὐτελεστάτων ἔργων, ἡ μήτην συνάγειν ἐπειρᾶτο.

5. Herodian 4.3.8–9. ἡ δὲ Ἰουλία "γῆν μέν" ἔφη "καὶ θάλασσαν, ὦ τέκνα, εὑρίσκετε ὅπως νείμησθε, καὶ τὰς ἠπείρους, ὥς φατε, τὸ Πόντιον ῥεῖθρον διαιρεῖ· τὴν δὲ μητέρα πως ἂν διέλοισθε, καὶ πῶς ἡ ἀθλία ἐγὼ ἐς ἑκάτερον ὑμῶν νεμηθείην ἢ τμηθείην; πρῶτον δὴ ἐμὲ φονεύσατε, καὶ διελόντες ἑκάτερος παρ᾽ἑαυτῷ τὸ μέρος θαπτέτω· οὕτω γὰρ ἄν μετὰ γῆς καὶ θαλάττης ἐς ὑμᾶς μερισθείην." ταῦτα δὲ λέγουσα μετὰ δακρύων καὶ οἰμωγῆς, ἀμφοτέροις τε τὰς χεῖρας περιβάλλουσα καὶ ὑπὸ τὰς ἀγκάλας λαβοῦσα, συνάγειν ἐπειρᾶτο. πάντας δὲ οἴκτου καταλαβόντος διελύθη τὸ συνέδριον, ἥ τε σκέψις ἀπεδοκιμάσθη, ἑκάτερός τε ἐς τὰ ἑαυτοῦ βασίλεια ἀνεχώρησε.

6. Cass. Dio 78.2.3–6. καὶ οὕτω πιστεύσαντος τοῦ Γέτα ἐσῆλθε μὲν μετ᾽αὐτοῦ, ἐπεὶ δὲ εἴσω ἐγένοντο, ἑκατόνταρχοί τινες ἐσεπήδησαν ἀθρόοι, παρὰ τοῦ Ἀντωνίνου προπαρεσκευασμένοι, καὶ αὐτὸν πρός τε τὴν μητέρα, ὡς εἶδέ σφας, προκαταφυγόντα καὶ ἀπό τε τοῦ αὐχένος αὐτῆς ἐξαρτηθέντα καὶ τοῖς στήθεσι τοῖς τε μαστοῖς προφύντα κατέκοψαν ὀλοφυρόμενον καὶ βοῶντα· "μῆτερ μῆτερ, τεκοῦσα τεκοῦσα, βοήθει, σφάζομαι." καὶ ἡ μὲν οὕτως ἀπατηθεῖσα τόν τε υἱὸν ἐν τοῖς ἑαυτῆς κόλποις ἀνοσιώτατα ἀπολλύμενον ἐπεῖδε, καὶ τὸν θάνατον αὐτοῦ ἐς αὐτὰ τὰ σπλάγχνα τρόπον τινά, ἐξ ὧν ἐγεγέννητο, ἐσεδέξατο· καὶ γὰρ τοῦ αἵματος πᾶσα ἐπλήσθη, ὡς ἐν μηδενὶ λόγῳ τὸ τῆς χειρὸς τραῦμα ὅ ἐτρώθη ποιήσασθαι. οὔτε δὲ πενθῆσαι οὔτε θρηνῆσαι τὸν υἱόν, καίπερ πρόωρον οὕτως οἰκτρῶς ἀπολωλόντα, ὑπῆρξεν αὐτῇ (δύο γὰρ καὶ εἴκοσι ἔτη καὶ μῆνας ἐννέα ἐβίω), ἀλλ᾽ἠναγκάζετο ὡς καὶ ἐν μεγάλῃ τινὶ εὐτυχίᾳ οὖσα χαίρειν καὶ γελᾶν· οὕτω που πάντα ἀκριβῶς καὶ τὰ ῥήματα αὐτῆς καὶ τὰ νεύματα τὰ τε χρώματα ἐτηρεῖτο· καὶ μόνῃ ἐκείνῃ, τῇ Αὐγούστῃ, τῇ τοῦ αὐτοκράτορος γυναικί, τῇ τῶν αὐτοκρατόρων μητρί, οὐδ᾽ἰδίᾳ που ἐπὶ τηλικούτῳ παθήματι δακρῦσαι ἐξῆν.

7. Herodian 4.5. ἔς τε τὸν νεών, ἔνθα τὰ σημεῖα καὶ τὰ ἀγάλματα τοῦ στρατοπέδου προσκυνεῖται.

8. Herodian 4.5–6. ἐβόα δὲ πεφευγέναι κίνδυνον καὶ ἐπιβουλὴν πολεμίου καὶ ἐχθροῦ, τὸν ἀδελφὸν λέγων, μόλις τε καὶ μετὰ πολλῆς μάχης τὸν ἐχθρὸν κεκρατηκέναι, κινδυνευσάντων δὲ ἀμφοτέρων κἂν ἕνα ἑαυτῶν βασιλέα τετηρῆσθαι ὑπὸ τῆς τύχης.

9. Cass. Dio 78.3.1. ὁ δ᾽ Ἀντωνῖνος καίπερ ἑσπέρας οὔσης τὰ στρατόπεδα κατέλαβε, ιὰ πάσης τῆς ὁδοῦ κεκραγὼς ὡς ἐπιβεβουλευμένος καὶ κινδυνεύων. ἐσελθὼν δὲ ἐς τὸ τεῖχος "χαίρετε," εἶπεν, "ὦ ἄνδρες συστρατιῶται· καὶ γὰρ ἤδη ἔξεστί μοι εὐεργετεῖν ὑμᾶς."

10. Cass. Dio 78.3.3.

11. Sillar 2001, 423.

12. I interpret Caracalla's grant of universal citizenship in 212 as another of his attempts to gain support during this ideological crisis. I suspect he envisioned the provinces as a base of support and thus as an alternative to the *populus Romanus.*

13. Cass. Dio 78.12.6. ὥσπερ τινὰ ἐναγισμὸν ἐτήσιον τῷ ἀδελφῷ ποιούμενος.

14. This was the same son of Pertinax who survived his father's murder in 193. HA *M. Ant.* 10.6. *Nam cum Germanici et Parthici et Arabici et Alamannici nomen adscriberet (nam Alamannorum gentem devicerat) Helvius Pertinax, filius Pertinacis, dicitur ioco dixisse, "Adde, si placet, etiam Geticus Maximus," quod Getam occiderat fratrem, et Gothi Getae dicerentur, quos ille, dum ad orientem transiit, tumultuariis proeliis devicerat.*

15. On incest between Julia Domna and Caracalla, HA *M. Ant.* 10. On the massacre of Alexandria, cf. Herodian 4.9.3; Cass. Dio 78.22; HA *M. Ant.* 6.

16. HA *M. Ant.* 10. *Interest scire quemadmodum novercam suam Iuliam uxorem ducisse dicatur. Quae cum esset pulcherrima et quasi per neglegentiam se maxima corporis parte nudasset, dixissetque Antoninus, "Vellem, si liceret," respondisse fertur, "Si libet, licet. An nescis te imperatorem esse et leges dare, non accipere?" Quo audito furor inconditus ad effectum criminis roboratus est nuptiasque eas celebravit quas, si sciret se leges dare vere, solus prohibere debuisset. matrem enim (non alio dicenda erat nomine) duxit uxorem et ad parricidium iunxit incestum, si quidem eam matrimonio sociavit cuius filium nuper occiderat.*

17. On managing the administration in Antioch, Cass. Dio 78.18.2, 79.3; on war with the Parthians, Cass. Dio 79.1.1–3.1, Herodian 4.10.1.

18. On the wig and trousers, Cass. Dio 78.18.3; on refusing to meet the Senate, Cass. Dio 78.10.4, 78.17.

19. Cass. Dio 78.10.

20. According to Tacitus, Livia also offered much-needed advice to Tiberius. Both authors use the empress as a way of emasculating their sons. Cf. chapter 1. Cass. Dio 78.18.2–3. οὐδὲ ἐπείθετο οὔτε περὶ τούτων οὔτε περὶ τῶν ἄλλων τῇ μητρὶ πολλὰ καὶ χρηστὰ παραινούσῃ, καίτοι καὶ τὴν τῶν βιβλίων τῶν τε ἐπιστολῶν ἑκατέρων, πλὴν τῶν πάνυ ἀναγκαίων, διοίκησιν αὐτῇ ἐπιτρέψας, καὶ τὸ ὄνομα αὐτῆς ἐν ταῖς πρὸς τὴν βουλὴν ἐπιστολαῖς ὁμοίως τῷ τε ἰδίῳ καὶ τῷ τῶν στρατευμάτων, ὅτι σώζεται, μετ᾽ἐπαίνων πολλῶν ἐγγράφων. τί γὰρ δεῖ λέγειν ὅτι καὶ ἠσπάζετο δημοσίᾳ πάντας τοὺς πρώτους καθάπερ καὶ ἐκεῖνος; ἀλλ᾽ἡ μὲν καὶ μετὰ τούτων ἔτι μᾶλλον ἐφιλοσόφει, ὁ δὲ ἔλεγε μὲν μηδενὸς ἔξω τῶν ἀναγκαίων προδεῖσθαι, καὶ ἐπὶ τούτῳ καὶ ἐσεμνύνετο ὡς ὅτι εὐτελεστάτῃ τῇ διαίτῃ χρῆσθαι δυνάμενος, ἦν δὲ οὐδὲν οὐκ ἐπίγειον, οὐ θαλάττιον, οὐκ ἀέριον, ὅ μὴ οὐ καὶ ἰδίᾳ καὶ δημοσίᾳ αὐτῷ παρείχομεν.

21. Cass. Dio 78.18.2–3 on Julia Domna's extraordinary position, philosophy, and meeting delegations; Cass. Dio 78.10.4 on Julia Domna exhorting Caracalla toward restraint, especially in spending.

22. Tac. *Agr.* 42. *Sciant, quibus moris est inlicita mirari, posse etiam sub malis principibus magnos viros esse, obsequiumque ac modestiam, si industria ac vigor adsint, eo laudis excedere, quo plerique per abrupta, sed in nullum rei publicae usum <nisi> ambitiosa morte inclaruerunt.*

23. Cass. Dio 79.23.1-3 ἡ δὲ Ἰουλία ἡ τοῦ Ταραύτου μήτηρ ἔτυχε μὲν ἐν τῇ Ἀντιοχείᾳ οὖσα, καὶ οὕτω παραχρῆμα, ἅμα τῇ πύστει τοῦ θανάτου αὐτοῦ, διετέθη ὥστε καὶ πλήξασθαι ἰσχυρῶς καὶ ἀποκαρτερῆσαι ἐπιχειρῆσαι. ὅν γὰρ ζῶντα καὶ ἐμίσει, τὸν αὐτὸν τοῦτον τότε τετελευτηκότα ἐπόθει, οὐχ ὅτι ἐκεῖνον ζῆν ἤθελεν, ἀλλ᾽ὅτι αὐτὴ ἰδιωτεύουσα ἤχθετο… μνημονεύοντας, ὅπως αὐταρχήσῃ τῇ τε Σεμιράμιδι καὶ τῇ Νιτώκριδι, ἅτε καὶ ἐκ τῶν αὐτῶν πρόπον τινὰ χωρίων αὐταῖς οὖσα, παρισουμένη.

24. The nickname, Dio explains, comes from "a gladiator who was most insignificant and ugly in appearance and most reckless and bloodthirsty in spirit" (79.9).

25. Cass. Dio 79.24.1. καὶ ἡ μὲν οὕτω τε ἐκ δημοτικοῦ γένους ἐπὶ μέγα ἀρθεῖσα, κἀν

τῇ τοῦ ἀνδρὸς ἡγεμονίᾳ περιαλγῶς πάνυ διὰ τὸν Πλαυτιανὸν ζήσασα, τῶν τε υἱέων τόν τε νεώτερον ἐν τοῖς αὐτῆς κόλποις κατασφαγέντα ἐπιδοῦσα καὶ τὸν πρεσβύτερον ζῶντά τε ἀεὶ διὰ τέλους διὰ φθόνου ἔχουσα καὶ φονευθέντα οὕτω μαθοῦσα, τῆς ἀρχῆς ζῶσα ἐξέπεσεν καὶ ἑαυτὴν προσκατειργάσατο, ὥστε τινὰ ἐς αὐτὴν ἀποβλέψαντα μὴ πάνυ πάντας τοὺς ἐν ταῖς μεγάλαις ἐξουσίαις γενομένους μακαρίζειν, ἂν μὴ καὶ ἡδονή τις αὐτοῖς τοῦ βίου καὶ ἀληθὴς καὶ ἀκήρατος καὶ εὐτυχία καὶ ἀκραιφνὴς καὶ διαρκὴς ὑπάρχῃ. καὶ τὰ μὲν τῆς Ἰουλίας οὕτως ἔσχε, τό τε σῶμα αὐτῆς ἐς τὴν Ῥώμην ἀναχθὲν ἐν τῷ τοῦ Γαΐου τοῦ τε Λουκίου μνήματι κατετέθη· ὕστερον μέντοι καὶ ἐκεῖνα, ὥσπερ καὶ τὰ τοῦ Γέτα ὀστᾶ, πρὸς τῆς Μαίσης τῆς ἀδελφῆς αὐτῆς ἐς τὸ τοῦ Ἀντωνίνου τεμένισμα μετεκομίσθη.

26. *RIC* 4a.396, 275.

Appendix C

1. *RIC* 4a.380–381, 272; 588, 310. In Zone C, Italy, there are no examples of these coins. They are present in the other four zones, though poorly represented. The combined counts for *RIC* 4a.380 and 381 constitute less than 5 percent of all the regions' denarii minted at Rome under Caracalla (Zone A, 3.2 percent; Zone B, 5.6 percent; Zone D, 4.8 percent; Zone E, 4.7 percent). I can think of two possible explanations for the dearth of these types in the Italian hoards: either these types had very small issues and were targeted to areas outside of Rome, or they had regular issues and were distributed largely in Rome and Italy. The total absence of these denarii from the very small Italian hoards probably indicates that the sample size is so small as to be unrepresentative. As counterintuitive as it may sound, I think these coins were intended for Rome.

2. Cass. Dio 73.15.1–5 (Commodus), 79.16.2 (Macrinus), 80.2.2–3 (Elagabalus). Instinsky also believes that the Senate conferred these titles on Julia Domna, though he gets there with a lot less trouble than I do: Daß der Titel *mater senatus* auf ein Initiative des Senats zurückzuführen ist, besagt er durch sich selbst. Für *mater patriae* wird man dasselbe annehmen dürfen, wenn man sieht, wie sehr dies der politischen Situation entspricht, und sich ferner gegenwärtig halt, daß schon der Antrag, Livia mit diesem Titel auszustatten, im Senat seinen Ursprung gehabt hat (1942, 210).

3. Julia Domna was the first living woman to receive these titles, though both Faustinae received the titles after their deaths. They appear in her legends before Caracalla assumed the same set of titles in 213. The *RIC* dates Caracalla's PIVS FEL titles on the obverse of his coins to 213 (cf. *RIC* 4a.232–237, 245). *CIL* 14 02255 identifies Caracalla as PII FELIC. The inscription is undated, but considering that Caracalla did not advertise the Felix title until 213, it must have been modified in the wake of Geta's *damnatio memoriae.*

4. Instinsky 1942, 205; Mattingly and Sydenham 1936, 63; Williams 1902, 254.

5. Instinsky 1942, 205.

6. *CIL* 06 01035 (p 3071, 3777, 4318, 4340) = *CIL* 06 31232 = D 00426 = *AE* 1993, 00118 = *AE* 2002, +00148 = *AE* 2005, 00183.

7. Benario 1958a, 68.

8. *CIL* 06 03401 = *CIL* 14 02255 = D 02398. Dessau personally examined the inscription, however, and all these problems through erasures (1974, 480).

9. Dessau 1974, 480.

10. Benario 1958a, 70.

11. Kettenhofen, 1979, 86.
12. Private correspondence with Clay (February 25, 2005).
13. Instinsky 1942, 210.
14. Tac. *Ann.* 1.14.2

BIBLIOGRAPHY

Ancient Sources

Behr, C. A., trans. 1968. *Aelius Aristides and the Sacred Tales*. Amsterdam: Hakkert.

Behr, C. A., trans. 1986. *P. Aelius Aristides: The Complete Works*. Leiden: Brill.

Bird, H. W., trans. 1994. *Aurelius Victor: De Caesaribus*. Edited by G. Clark. Liverpool: Liverpool University Press.

Butler, H. E., trans. 1959. *The Institutio Oratoria of Quintillian*. Loeb Classical Library 3. Cambridge, MA: Harvard University Press.

Cary, E., trans. 2001. *Cassius Dio's Roman History*. Loeb Classical Library. Cambridge, MA: Harvard University Press.

Jones, C. P., trans. 2005. *Philostratus: The Life of Apollonius of Tyana*. Loeb Classical Library, 16–17. Cambridge, MA: Harvard University Press.

Magie, D., trans. 1921. *The Scriptores Historiae Augustae*. Loeb Classical Library, 139–140. Cambridge, MA: Harvard University Press.

Moore, C. H., and J. Jackson, trans. 1951. *Tacitus' Annales*. Loeb Classical Library. Cambridge, MA: Harvard University Press.

Perrin, B., trans. 1920. *Plutarch's Lives: Demetrius and Antony, Pyrrhus and Gaius Marius*. Loeb Classical Library. Cambridge, MA: Harvard University Press.

Radice, B., trans. 1969. *Pliny the Younger: Letters and* Panegyricus. Loeb Classical Library. Cambridge, MA: Harvard University Press.

Radice, B., trans. 1997. *Letters, Books VIII–X and* Panegyricus. Loeb Classical Library. Cambridge, MA: Harvard University Press.

Rolfe, J. C., trans. 1914. *Suetonius: Lives of the Caesars*. Loeb Classical Library. Cambridge, MA: Harvard University Press.

Scott-Kilvert, I., trans. 1965. *Makers of Rome: Nine Lives by Plutarch*. Baltimore: Penguin.

Wellesley, K., trans. 1988. *Tacitus: The Histories*. Baltimore: Penguin.

Whittaker, C. R., trans. 1969. *Herodian: History of the Empire from the Time of Marcus Aurelius*. Loeb Classical Library. Cambridge, MA: Harvard University Press.

Modern Collections of Ancient Evidence

Alexandridis, A. 2004. *Die Frauen des römischen Kaiserhauses*. Mainz: P. von Zabern.

Barton, I. M. 1977. "The Inscriptions of Septimius Severus and His Family at Lepcis

Magna." In *Mélanges offerts a Léopold Sédar Senghor*, 3–12. Dakar: Nouvelles Éditions Africaines.

Cagnat, R. et al., eds. 1888–. *L'année épigraphique*. Paris: Presses Universitaires de France.

Cagnat, R. et al., eds. 1975. *Inscriptiones Graecae ad res Romanas pertinentes*. Reprint, Chicago: Ares.

Collingwood, R. G., and R. P. Wright, eds. 1965. *The Roman Inscriptions of Britain*. Oxford: Clarendon Press.

de Maria, S. 1988. *Gli Archi onorari di Roma e dell'Italia romana*. Bibliotheca archaeologica 7. Rome: L'Erma di Bretschneider.

Dessau, H. 1974. *Inscriptiones Latinae Selectae*. Dublin: Weidmannos.

Fink, R. O., A. S. Hoey, and W. F. Snyder. 1940. *The Feriale Duranum*. New Haven, CT: Yale University Press.

Fittschen, K. 1982. *Die Bildnistypen der Faustina minor und die Fecunditas Augustae*. Abhandlungen der Akademie der Wissenschaften in Göttingen 3. Göttingen: Vandenhoeck & Ruprecht.

Fittschen, K., P. Zanker, and G. Fittschen-Badura. 1994. *Katalog der römischen Porträts in den Capitolinischen Museen und den anderen kommunalen Sammlungen der Stadt Rom: Band I, Kaiser- und Prinzenbildnisse*. Beiträge zur Erschliessung hellenistischer und kaiserzeitlicher Skulptur und Architektur 3. Mainz: P. von Zabern.

Glare, P. G. W. 1982. *Oxford Latin Dictionary*. New York: Oxford University Press.

Hörig, M., and E. Schwertheim, eds. 1987. *Corpus Cultus Iovis Dolicheni*. Leiden: Brill.

Hornblower, S., and A. Spawford, eds. 1996. *The Oxford Classical Dictionary*. 3rd ed. Oxford: Oxford University Press.

Keinast, D. 1996. *Römische Kaisertabelle, Grundzüge einer römischen Kaiserchronologie*. Darmstadt: Wissenschaftliche Buchgesellschaft.

Kettenhofen, E. 1979. *Die syrischen Augustae in der historischen Überlieferung*. Bonn: R. Habelt.

Klebs, E., P. von Rohden, and H. Dessau, eds. 1933–. *Prosopographia Imperii Romani*. 2nd ed. Berlin: W. de Gruyter.

Mattingly, H., and R. A. G. Carson, eds. 1923–. *Coins of the Roman Empire in the British Museum*. London: British Museum.

Mattingly, H., and E. Sydenham, eds. 1930. *The Roman Imperial Coinage: Antoninus Pius to Commodus*. Roman Imperial Coinage 3. London: Spink.

Mattingly, H., and E. Sydenham, eds. 1936. *The Roman Imperial Coinage: Pertinax to Geta*. Roman Imperial Coinage 4a. London: Spink.

Mommsen, T., O. Hirschfield, and H. Domaszewski, eds. 1863–. *Corpus Inscriptionum Latinarum*. Berlin: Reimer.

Petolescu, C. C. 1996. *Inscriptions de la Dacie romaine 1. b'Italie et les provinces occidentales*. Bucharest: Ed. Enciclopedia.

Pflaum, H.-G. 1950. *Les procurateurs équestres sous le Haut-Empire romain*. Paris: A. Maisonneuve.

Pighi, I. B. 1965. *De Ludibus Saecularibus Populi Romani Quiritum*. Amsterdam: P. Schippers.

Reynolds, J. M., and J. B. Ward Perkins, eds. 1952. *The Inscriptions of Roman Tripolitania*. Rome: British School at Rome.

Steinby, E. M. 1993–1999. *Lexicon Topographicum Urbis Romae*. Rome: Quasar.

Sutherland, C. H. V., R. A. G. Carson, H. Mattingly, I. Carradice, and T. V.Buttrey. 1984. *Roman Imperial Coinage*. London: Spink.
Waltzing, J. P. 1968. *Etude historique sur les corporations professionnelles chez les Romains depuis les origines jusqu'a la chute de l'Empire d'Occident*. Reprint, Bologna: Forni.

Modern Sources

Abzug, J. 1994. "The Portraits of Julia Domna: A Feminist Re-interpretation." MA thesis, University of Delaware.
Adams, J. N. 1982. *The Latin Sexual Vocabulary*. Baltimore: Johns Hopkins University Press.
Aja Sanchez, J. R. 1996. "Vox populi et princeps: El impacto de la opinión pública sobre el comportamiento político de los emperadores romanos." *Latomus* 55: 295–328.
Aldrete, G. S. 1999. *Gesture and Acclamations in Ancient Rome*. Baltimore: John Hopkins University Press.
Alföldi, A. 1956. "The Main Aspects of Political Propaganda on the Coinage of the Roman Republic." In *Essays in Roman Coinage Presented to Harold Mattingly*, edited by R. A. G. Carson and C. H. V. Sutherland, 63–95. London: Oxford University Press.
Alföldi, A., and J. Straub. 1970. *Bonner Historia-Augusta-Colloquium, 1964–1965*. Vol. 7, *Antiquitas. Reihe 4: Beiträge zur Historia-Augusta-Forschung*. Bonn: R. Habelt.
Alföldy, G. 1968. "Septimius Severus und der Senat." *Bonner Jahrbücher* 168: 112–160.
Alföldy, G. 1971. "Herodians Person." *Ancient Society* 2: 204–233.
Alföldy, G. 1972a. "Eine Proskriptionsliste in der Historia-Augusta." In *Bonner Historia-Augusta-Colloquium, 1970*, edited by A. Alföldi et al., 1–12. Bonn: R. Habelt.
Alföldy, G. 1972b. "Der Sturz des Kaisers Geta und die antike Geschictsschreibung." In *Bonner Historia-Augusta-Colloquium, 1970*, edited by A. Alföldi et al., 19–51. Bonn: R. Habelt.
Alföldy, G. 1977. "Reichtum und Macht der Senatoren." *Gymnasium* 84: 541–545.
Alföldy, G. 2003. "Die Repräsentation der kaiserlichen Macht in den Inscriften Roms und des Imperium Romanum." In *The Representation and Perception of Roman Imperial Power*, edited by L. de Blois et al., 3–19. Amsterdam: J. C. Gieben.
Allason-Jones, L. 1999. "Women and the Roman Army in Britain." In "The Roman Army as a Community," supplement, *Journal of Roman Archaeology* 34: 41–51.
Allison, P. M. 2001. "Using the Material and Written Sources: Turn of the Millennium Approaches to Roman Domestic Space." *American Journal of Archaeology* 105 (2): 181–208.
Allison, P. M. 2006. "Engendering Roman Spaces." In *Space and Spatial Analysis in Archaeology*, edited by E. C. Robertson et al., 343–354. Albuquerque: University of New Mexico Press.
Alston, R. 1994. "Roman Military Pay from Caesar to Diocletian." *Journal of Roman Studies* 84: 113–123.
Alston, R. 1998. "Arms and the Man: Soldiers, Masculinity and the Power in the Republican and Imperial Rome." In *When Men Were Men: Masculinity, Power and Identity in Classical Antiquity*, edited by L. Foxhall and J. Salmon, 205–223. London: Routledge.
Alston, R., and O. van Nijf, eds. 2008. *Feeding the Ancient Greek City*. Groningen-Royal Holloway Studies on the Greek City after the Classical Age. Leuven: Peeters.

Ameling, W. 1992. "Die Kinder des Marc Aurel und die Bildnistype der Faustina Minor." *Zeitschrift für Papyrologie und Epigraphik* 90: 147–166.

Anderson, G. 1993. *The Second Sophistic: A Cultural Phenomenon in the Roman Empire*. London: Routledge.

Ando, C. 2000. *Imperial Ideology and Provincial Loyalty in the Roman Empire*: Berkeley: University of California Press.

Andreau, J. 1999. *Banking and Business in the Roman World: Key Themes in Ancient History*. Cambridge: Cambridge University Press.

Auguet, R. 1994. *Cruelty and Civilization: The Roman Games*. London: Routledge.

Babelon, J., and A. von Domaszewski. 1957. *Impératrices syriennes*. Paris: A. Michel.

Baharal, D. 1989. "Portraits of the Emperor L. Septimius Severus (193–211 A.D.) as an Expression of His Propaganda." *Latomus* 48: 566–580.

Baharal, D. 1992. "Portraits of Julia Domna." *Latomus* 51: 110–120.

Baharal, D. 1996a. "The Emperor Macrinus: Imperial Propaganda and the *Gens Aurelia*." In *Gli Imperatori Severi: Storia, Archeologia, Religione*, edited by E. dal Covolo and G. Rinaldi, 47–65. Rome: LAS.

Baharal, D. 1996b. *Victory of Propaganda: The Dynastic Aspect of the Imperial Propaganda of the Severi, The Literary and Archaeological Evidence, A.D. 193–235*. Vol. 657, *BAR International Series*, edited by M. Rajka. Oxford: Tempvs Reparatvm.

Baharal, D. 2000. "Public Image and Women at Court in the Era of Adoptive Emperors (A.D. 98–180): The Case of Faustina the Younger." *Studies in Latin Literature and Roman History* 10: 328–344, plates 3–8.

Balsdon, J. P. V. D. 1951. "Sulla Felix." *Journal of Roman Studies* 41: 1–10.

Balty, J. 1966. *Essai d'Iconographie de l'Empereur Clodius Albinus*. Collection Latomus 85. Brussels: Latomus.

Barrett, A. A. 1991. "Claudius' British Victory Arch in Rome." *Britannia* 22: 1–19.

Barrett, A. A. 1996. *Agrippina*. London: Routledge.

Barrett, A. A. 2002. *Livia*. New Haven, CT: Yale University Press.

Barrett, A. A. 2005. "Aulus Caecina Severus and the Military Woman." *Historia* 54: 301–314.

Bartman, E. 1999. *Portraits of Livia: Imaging the Imperial Women in Augustan Rome*. Cambridge: Cambridge University Press.

Bartoccini, R. 1931. "L'arco quadrifronte dei Severi a Lepcis." *L'Africa Italiana* 4: 32.

Barton, C. 1992. *The Sorrows of the Ancient Romans: The Gladiator and the Monster*. Princeton, NJ: Princeton University Press.

Barton, C. 2002. "Being in the Eyes: Shame and Sight in Ancient Rome." In *The Roman Gaze: Vision, Power, and the Body*, edited by D. Frederick, 216–235. Baltimore: Johns Hopkins University Press.

Bartsch, S. 1994. "The Art of Sincerity: Pliny's *Panegyricus*." In *Actors in the Audience: Theatricality and Doublespeak from Nero to Hadrian*, 148–187. Cambridge, MA: Harvard University Press.

Bartsch, S. 2006. *The Mirror of the Self: Sexuality, Self-Knowledge, and the Gaze in the Early Roman Empire*. Chicago: University of Chicago Press.

Bastien, P. 1993. *Le Buste Monetaire des Empereurs Romains*. Wetteren: Numismatique Romaine.

Beacham, R. C. 1999. *Spectacle Entertainments of Early Imperial Rome*. New Haven, CT: Yale University Press.

Benario, H. 1958a. "Julia Domna—Mater Senatus et Patriae." *Phoenix* 12: 67–70.

Benario, H. 1958b. "Rome of the Severi." *Latomus* 17: 712–722.

Bennett, J. 2006. "New Evidence from Ankara for the *Collegia Veteranorum* and the *Albata Decursio*: In Memoriam J. C. Mann." *Anatolian Studies* 56: 95–101.

Benoist, S. 2006. "Images des dieux, images des hommes: Réflexions sur le 'culte impérial' au IIIe siècle." In *La "crise" de l'Empire romain de Marc Aurèle à Constantin: Mutations, continuités, ruptures*, edited by M.-H. Quet, 27–64. Paris: Presses de l'Université Paris-Sorbonne.

Benoist, S. 2007. "Les usages de la memoria à Rome, de la Respublica à l'Empire chrétien." In *Mémoire et histoire: Les procédures de condamnation dans l'Antiquité romain*, edited by S. Benoist and A. Daguet-Gagey, 307–315. Metz: Centre Régional Universitaire Lorrain d'Histoire.

Benoist, S. 2008. "Le pouvoir et ses représentations, enjeu de la mémoire: Rapport introductif." In *Un discours en images de la condamnation de mémoire*, edited by S. Benoist and A. Daguet-Gagey, 25–39. Metz: Centre Régional Universitaire Lorrain d'Histoire.

Benoist, S., and A. Daguet-Gagey, eds. 2007. *Mémoire et histoire: Les procédures de condamnation dans l'Antiquité romain*. Metz: Centre Régional Universitaire Lorrain d'Histoire.

Berg, R. 2002. "Wearing Wealth, Mundus Muliebris and Ornatus as Status Markers for Women in Imperial Rome." In *Women, Wealth and Power in the Roman Empire*, edited by P. Setälä et al., 15–74. Rome: Institutum Romanum Finlandiae.

Birley, A. 1969. "The Coup d'Etat of the Year 193." *Bonner Jahrbücher* 169: 247–280.

Birley, A. 1971. *Septimius Severus: The African Emperor*. London: Eyre & Spottiswoode.

Birley, A. 1987. *Marcus Aurelius: A Biography*. New Haven, CT: Yale University Press.

Birley, A. 1999. *Septimius Severus: The African Emperor*. 2nd ed. London: Routledge.

Bispham, E., G. Rowe, and E. Matthews. 2007. *Vita vigilia est: Essays in Honour of Barbara Levick*. London: Institute of Classical Studies, School of Advanced Study, University of London.

Blázquez, J. M. 1992. "The Latest Work on the Export of Baetican Olive Oil to Rome and the Army." *Greece & Rome* 39 (2): 173–188.

Boatwright, M. T. 1986. "The Pomerial Extension of Augustus." *Historia* 35: 13–27.

Boatwright, M. T. 1991. "The Imperial Women of the Early Second Century A.C." *American Journal of Philology* 112 (4): 513–540.

Boatwright, M. T. 1992. "Matilda the Younger." *Echoes de Monde Classique* 36 (11): 19–31.

Boatwright, M. T. 2003. "Faustina the Younger: 'Mater Castrorum.'" In *Les Femmes Antiques entre Sphere Privee et Sphere Publique: Actes du Diplome d'Etudes Avancees*, edited by R. Frei-Stolba, A. Bielman, and O. Bianchi, 249–268. Bern: P. Lang.

Bowersock, G. W. 1969. *Greek Sophists in the Roman Empire*. Oxford: Clarendon Press.

Brilliant, R. 1963. *Gesture and Rank in Roman Art: The Uses of Gesture to Denote Status in Roman Sculpture and Coinage*. Memoirs of the Connecticut Academy of Arts & Sciences 14. New Haven, CT: Connecticut Academy of Arts & Sciences.

Brilliant, R. 1967. *The Arch of Septimius Severus in the Roman Forum*. Memoirs of the American Academy in Rome 29. Rome: American Academy in Rome.

Brilliant, R. 2003. "Arcus: Septimius Severus." In *Lexicon Topographicum Urbis Romae*, edited by E. M. Steinby, 103–105. Rome: Edizioni Quasar.

Bryant, C. 1996. "Imperial Family Roles: Propaganda and Policy in the Severan Period." In *Gli Imperatori Severi: Storia, Archeologia, Religione*, edited by E. dal Covolo and G. Rinaldi, 23–30. Rome: LAS.

Budde, L. 1955. *Severisches Relief in Palazzo Sacchetti.* Jahrbuch des Deutschen Archäologischen Instituts 18. Berlin: W. de Gruyter.

Budde, L. 1957. *Die Enstehung des antiken Repräsentationsbildes.* Berlin: W. de Gruyter.

Burnett, A. 1987. *Coinage in the Roman World.* London: Spink.

Burnett, A. 1999. "Buildings and Monuments on Roman Coins." In *Roman Coins and Public Life under the Empire*, edited by G. M. Paul and M. Ierardi, 136–140. Ann Arbor: University of Michigan Press.

Burrell, B. 2004. *Neokoroi: Greek Cities and Roman Emperors.* Cincinnati Classical Studies, n.s., 9. Leiden: Brill.

Butcher, K. 1996. "Coinage and Currency in Syria and Palestine to the Reign of Gallienus." In *Coin Finds and Coin Use in the Roman World: The Thirteenth Oxford Symposium of Coinage and Monetary History, 25–27 March 1993—a NATO Advanced Research Workshop*. Vol. 10, *Studien zu Fundmünzen der Antike*, edited by C. E. King and D. G. Wigg, 101–112. Berlin: G. Mann.

Butcher, K., and M. Ponting. 2005. "The Roman Denarius under the Julio-Claudian Emperors: Mints, Metallurgy and Technology." *Oxford Journal of Archaeology* 24 (2): 163–197.

Butrica, J. L. 2005. "Some Myths and Anomalies in the Study of Roman Sexuality." In *Same-Sex Desire and Love in Greco-Roman Antiquity and the Classical Tradition of the West*, edited by B. C. Verstraete and V. Provencal, 209–269. Binghamton, NY: Harrington Park Press.

Buttrey, T. V. 1972. "Vespasian as Moneyer." *Numismatic Chronicle*, ser. 7, 12: 89–109.

Calabria, P. 1989. "La leggenda 'Mater Castrorum' sulla monetazione imperiale." *Miscellanea Graeca e Romana* 14: 225–233.

Campbell, D. B. 1986. "What Happened at Hatra? The Problem of the Severan Siege Operations." In *The Defence of the Roman and Byzantine East: Proceedings of a Colloquium Held at the University of Sheffield in April 1986*. Vol. 297, *BAR International Series*, edited by P. W. M. Freeman and D. L. Kennedy, 51–58. Oxford: BAR.

Campbell, J. B. 1978. "The Marriage of Roman Soldiers under the Empire." *Journal of Roman Studies* 68: 153–166.

Campbell, J. B. 1984. *The Emperor and the Roman Army 31 B.C.–A.D. 235*. Oxford: Clarendon Press.

Campbell, J. B. 2002. *War and Society in Imperial Rome 31 BC–AD 284*. London: Routledge.

Cesano, L. 1925. "Nuovi riposigli di denari di argento dell'impero romano." *Atti e Memorie dell'Istituto Italiano di Numismatica* 5: 57–72.

Chastagnol, M. A. 1984. "Les fêtes décennales de Septime-Sévère." *Bulletin de la Société nationale des Antiquaires de France* 1984: 91–107.

Christiansen, E. 1988. *The Roman Coins of Alexandria: Quantitative Studies. Nero, Trajan, Septimius Severus.* Aarhus: Aarhus University Press.

Clay, C. L. 1970. "Nilus and the Four Seasons on a New As of Septimius Severus." *Numismatic Chronicle*, ser. 7, 10: 71–87.

Clay, C. L. 1972. "The Types and Chronology of the Severan Coinage of Rome, A.D. 193–8." BA thesis, Christ Church Oxford.

Clay, C. L. 1976. "Roman Imperial Medallions: The Date and Purpose of Their Issue." In *Actes du 8eme Congres International de numismatique, New York-Washington, Septembre 1973 (A.C.I.N.)*, edited by H. A. Cahn and G. Le Rider, 253–265, plate 27. Paris: Association Internationale des Numismates Professionnels.

Clay, T. 1988. "Metallurgy and Metallography in Numismatics." *Numismatica e Antichita Classiche* 17: 341–352.

Cleve, R. L. 1982. *Severus Alexander and the Severan Women*. Berkeley: University of California Press.

Cooley, A. 2007. "Septimius Severus: The Augustan Emperor." In *Severan Culture*, edited by S. Swain, S. J. Harrison, and J. Elsner, 385–400. Cambridge: Cambridge University Press.

Corbier, M. 1995. "Male Power and Legitimacy through Women: The *Domus Augusta* under the Julio-Claudians." In *Women in Antiquity: New Assessments*, edited by R. Hawley and B. M. Levick, 178–193. London: Routledge.

Crawford, M. H. 1983. "Roman Coin Types and the Formation of Public Opinion." In *Studies in Numismatic Method Presented to Philip Grierson*, edited by C. N. L. Brooke, 47–64. Cambridge: Cambridge University Press.

Daguet-Gagey, A. 2005. "L'arc des argentiers, à Rome." *Revue Historique* 307 (3): 499–518.

dal Cavolo, E. 1989. *I Severi e il cristianesimo: Ricerche sull'ambiente storico-istituzionale delle origini cristiane tra il secondo e il terzo secolo*. Biblioteca di Scienze Religiose 87. Rome: LAS.

dal Covolo, E. 1996. "I Severi e il Cristianesimo: *Dieci anni dopo*." In *Gli Imperatori Severi: Storia, Archeologia, Religione*, edited by E. dal Covolo and G. Rinaldi, 187–196. Rome: LAS.

dal Covolo, E., and G. Rinaldi, eds. 1996. *Gli Imperatori Severi: Storia, Archeologia, Religione*. Congresso di Studi Severi 138. Rome: LAS.

Darwall-Smith, R. H. 1996. *Emperors and Architecture: A Study of Flavian Rome*. Collection Latomus 231. Brussels: Latomus.

Davies, P. J. E. 2000. *Death and the Emperor*. Cambridge: Cambridge University Press.

de Blois, L. 1998/1999. "The Perception of Emperor and Empire in Cassius Dio's Roman History." *Ancient Society* 29: 267–281.

de Blois, L., P. Erdkamp, O. Hekster, G. De Kleijn, and S. Mols. 2003. *The Representation and Perception of Roman Imperial Power: Proceedings of the Third Workshop of the International Network Impact of Empire (Roman Empire, c. 200 B.C.–A.D. 476), Netherlands Institute in Rome, March 20–23, 2002*. Impact of Empire 3. Amsterdam: J. C. Gieben.

Dench, E. 1995. *From Barbarians to New Men: Greek, Roman, and Modern Perceptions of Peoples of the Central Apennines*. Oxford Classical Monographs. Oxford: Oxford University Press.

Dench, E. 1998. "Austerity, Excess, Success, and Failure in Hellenistic and Early Imperial Italy." In *Parchments of Gender: Deciphering the Bodies of Antiquity*, edited by M. Wyke, 121–146. Oxford: Oxford University Press.

Dench, E. 2005. *Romulus' Asylum: Roman Identities from the Age of Alexander to the Age of Hadrian*. Oxford: Oxford University Press.

Desnier, J.-L. 1993. "Omina et Realia: Naissance de l'urbs sacra sévérienne (193–204 ap. J.-C.)." *Mélanges de l'École Française de Rome, Antiquité* 105 (2): 547–620.

Dixon, S. 1984. "Family Finances: Tullia and Terentia." *Antichthon* 18: 78–101.

Dixon, S. 1988. *The Roman Mother*. Norman: University of Oklahoma Press.

Dixon, S. 2001. *Reading Roman Women: Sources, Genres and Real Life*. London: Duckworth.

Donarini, D. 1974. "Tradizione ed originalità nella monetazione di Faustina Minore." *Numismatica e Antichita Classiche* 3: 147–160.

Duncan-Jones, R. 1975. "Two Possible Indices of the Purchasing Power of Money in Greek and Roman Antiquity." In *Les "devaluations" à Rome: Epoque républicaine et impériale (Rome, 13–15 nov. 1975)*, 147–158. Rome: Collection de l'École Française de Rome.

Duncan-Jones, R. 1994. *Money and Government in the Roman Empire*. Cambridge: Cambridge University Press.

Duncan-Jones, R. 1996. "Empire-Wide Patterns in Roman Coin Hoards." In *Coin Finds and Coin Use in the Roman World: The Thirteenth Oxford Symposium of Coinage and Monetary History, 25–27 March 1993—a NATO Advanced Research Workshop*. Vol. 10, *Studien zu Fundmünzen der Antike*, edited by C. E. King and D. G. Wigg, 129–138. Berlin: G. Mann.

Duncan-Jones, R. 2001. "The Denarii of Septimius Severus and the Mobility of Roman Coin." *Numismatic Chronicle* 161: 75–89.

Duncan-Jones, R. 2003. "Roman Coin Circulation and the Cities of Vesuvius." In *Credito e moneta nel mondo romano: Atti degli Incontri Capresi di Storia dell'Economia Antica, Capri, 12–14 ottobre 2000*, edited by E. Lo Cascio, 161–180. Bari: Edipuglia.

Duncan-Jones, R. 2005. "Implications of Roman Coinage: Debates and Differences." *Klio* 87 (2): 459–487.

Eck, W. 2000a. "The Emperor and His Advisors." In *The Cambridge Ancient History*. Vol. 11, *The High Empire, A.D. 70–192*, 2nd ed., edited by A. K. Bowman, P. Garnsey, and D. Rathbone, 195–213. Cambridge: Cambridge University Press.

Eck, W. 2000b. "Emperor, Senate, and Magistrates." In *The Cambridge Ancient History*. Vol. 11, *The High Empire, A.D. 70–192*, 2nd ed., edited by A. K. Bowman, P. Garnsey, and D. Rathbone, 214–237. Cambridge: Cambridge University Press.

Eck, W. 2000c. "The Growth of Administrative Posts." In *The Cambridge Ancient History*. Vol. 11, *The High Empire, A.D. 70–192*, 2nd ed., edited by A. K. Bowman, P. Garnsey, and D. Rathbone, 238–265. Cambridge: Cambridge University Press.

Ehrhardt, C. T. H. R. 1984. "Roman Coin Types and the Roman Public." *Jahrbuch für Numismatik und Geldgeschichte* 34: 41–54.

Elsner, J. 2005. "Sacrifice and Narrative on the Arch of the Argentarii at Rome." *Journal of Roman Archaeology* 18: 83–98.

Farney, G. D. 2007. *Ethnic Identity and Aristocratic Competition in Republican Rome*. Cambridge: Cambridge University Press.

Fears, J. R. 1977. *Princeps a diis electus: The Divine Election of the Empire as a Political Concept at Rome*. Memoirs of the American Academy in Rome 26. Rome: American Academy in Rome.

Fears, J. R. 1978. "Ο ΔΗΜΟΣ Ο ΡΩΜΑΙΩΝ Genius Populi Romani: A Note on the Origin of Dea Roma." *Mnemosyne* 31 (3): 274–286.

Fears, J. R. 1980. "Rome: The Ideology of Imperial Power." *Thought* 55 (216): 98–109.

Fears, J. R. 1981a. "The Cult of Virtues and Roman Imperial Ideology." *Aufstieg und Niedergang der römischen Welt* II 17 (2): 827–947.

Fears, J. R. 1981b. "The Theology of Victory at Rome: Approaches and Problems." *Aufstieg und Niedergang der römischen Welt* II 17 (1): 736–826.

Fejfer, J. 1985. "The Portraits of the Severan Empress Julia Domna: A New Approach." *Analecta Romana Instituti Danici* 14: 129–138.

Fejfer, J. 1992. "Divus Caracalla and Julia Domna." In *Ancient Portraiture: Image and Message*. Vol. 4, *Acta Hyperborea*, edited by T. Fischer-Hansen et al., 207–219. Copenhagen: Museum Tusculanum Press.

Fernandez, J. de S. 1999. "Las Emperatrices en la Moneda Romana." *Rivista Italiana di Numismatica* 100: 147–171.

Fink, R. O. 1944. "*Feriale Duranum* 1.1 and *Mater Castrorum*." *American Journal of Archaeology* 48: 17–19.

Fink, R. O. 1971. *Roman Military Records on Papyrus*. Cleveland, OH: Case Western Reserve University Press.

Fischler, S. 1989. "Social Stereotypes and Historical Analysis: The Case of the Imperial Women at Rome." In *Women in Ancient Societies*, edited by L. Archer and S. Fischler, 115–133. London: Routledge.

Fittschen, K. 1977–1978. "Two Portraits of Septimius Severus and Julia Domna." *Indiana University Art Museum Bulletin* 1 (2): 28–39.

Fittschen, K. 1982. *Die Bildnistypen der Faustina Minor und die Fecunditas Augustae* Göttingen: Vandenhoeck & Ruprecht.

Fittschen, K. 1992. "Über das Rekonstruieren griechischer Porträtstatuen." In *Ancient Portraiture: Image and Message*. Vol. 4, *Acta Hyperborea*, edited by T. Fischer-Hansen et al., 9–29. Copenhagen: Museum Tusculanum Press.

Fittschen, K. 1996. "Courtly Portraits of Women in the Era of the Adoptive Emperors (AD 98–180) and Their Reception in Roman Society." In *I, Claudia: Women in Ancient Rome*, edited by D. E. E. Kleiner and S. B. Matheson, 42–52. New Haven, CT: Yale University Art Gallery.

Flemming, R. 2000. *Medicine and the Making of Roman Women: Gender, Nature, and Authority from Celsus to Galen*. New York: Oxford University Press.

Flory, M. B. 1996. "Dynastic Ideology, the *Domus Augusta*, and Imperial Women: A Lost Statuary Group in the Circus Flaminius." *Transactions of the American Philological Association* 126: 287–306.

Flory, M. B. 1998. "The Integration of Women into the Roman Triumph." *Historia* 47: 489–494.

Flower, H. I. 2002. "Were Women Ever 'Ancestors' in Republican Rome?" In *Images of Ancestors*. Vol. 5, *Aarhus Studies in Mediterranean Antiquity*, edited by J. M. Højte, 159–185. Denmark: Aarhus University Press.

Flower, H. I. 2008. "Les Sévères et l'usage de la memoria: L'arcus du Forum Boarium à Rome." In *Un discours en images*, edited by S. Benoist and A. Daguet-Gagey, 97–115. Metz: Centre Régional Universitaire Lorrain d'Histoire.

Forbis, E. 1996. *Municipal Virtues in the Roman Empire: The Evidence of Italian Honorary Inscriptions*. Beiträge zur Altertumskunde 79. Stuttgart: Teubner.

Franchi, L. 1964. *Ricerche sull'arte di eta severiana in Roma*. Studi Miscellanei 4. Rome: L'Erma di Bretschneider.

Freyburger-Galland, M.-L. 1984. "Quelques exemples de l'emprunt linguistique du grec au latin dans le vocabulaire politique de Dion Cassius." *Ktema* 9: 330–337.

Freyburger-Galland, M.-L. 1993. "Le rôle politique des vêtments dans l'Histoire romaine de Dion Cassius." *Latomus* 52: 117–128.

Fulford, M. G. 1996. "Economic Hotspots and Provincial Backwaters: Modelling the Late Roman Economy." In *Coin Finds and Coin Use in the Roman World: The Thirteenth Oxford Symposium of Coinage and Monetary History, 25–27 March 1993—a NATO Advanced Research Workshop*. Vol. 10, *Studien zu Fundmünzen der Antike*, edited by C. E. King and D. G. Wigg, 139–152. Berlin: G. Mann.

Gagé, J. 1934. "Les jeux séculaires de 204 ap. J.-C. et la dynastie des Sévères." *Melanges de l'Ecole Francaise de Rome* 51: 33–78.

Gerding, H. 2002. *The Tomb of Caecilia Metella: Tumulus, Tropaeum and Thymele*. Lund.

Ghedini, F. 1984. *Guilia Domna tra Oriente e Occidente*. Rome: L'Erma di Bretschneider.

Gibbon, E. 2003. *The Decline and Fall of the Roman Empire*. Translated by H. F. Mueller. New York: Modern Library.

Ginsburg, J. 2006. *Representing Agrippina: Constructions of Female Power in the Early Roman Empire*. New York: Oxford University Press.

Gitler, H., and M. Ponting. 2003. *The Silver Coinage of Septimius Severus and His Family (193–211 AD): A Study of the Chemical Composition of the Roman and Eastern Issues*. Glaux 16. Milan: Ennerre.

Gitler, H., and M. Ponting. 2007. "Rome and the East: A Study of the Chemical Composition of Roman Silver Coinage during the Reign of Septimius Severus 193–211 A.D." Topoi suppl. 8, 376–397.

Gleason, M. W. 1995. *Making Men: Sophists and Self-Presentation in Ancient Rome*. Princeton, NJ: Princeton University Press.

Goodall Powers, J. 1997. "Ancient Weddings." Classics Technology Center. Last accessed August 15, 2012. http://ablemedia.com/ctcweb/consortium/ancientweddings7.html.

Gorrie, C. 2001. "The Septizodium of Septimius Severus Revisited: The Monument in Its Historical and Urban Context." *Latomus* 60: 653–670.

Gorrie, C. 2004. "Julia Domna's Building Patronage, Imperial Family Roles and the Severan Revival of Moral Legislation." *Historia* 53: 61–72.

Gorrie, C. 2007. "The Restoration of the Porticus Octaviae and Severan Imperial Policy." *Greece & Rome* 54 (1): 1–17.

Grassi, L. 2006. "Quelle Barbie dell'antichità." *Metroitaly*, June 6, 2006.

Gunderson, E. 1996. "The Ideology of the Arena." *Classical Antiquity* 15 (1): 113–151.

Hälikkä, R. 2002. "Discourses of Body, Gender and Power in Tacitus." In *Women, Wealth and Power in the Roman Empire*, edited by P. Setälä et al., 75–104. Rome: Institutum Romanum Finlandiae.

Hammond, M. 1957a. "Composition of the Senate, A.D. 68–235." *Journal of Roman Studies* 47: 74–81.

Hammond, M. 1957b. *Imperial Elements in the Formula of the Roman Emperors during the First Two and a Half Centuries of the Empire*. Memoirs of the American Academy in Rome 25. Rome: American Academy in Rome.

Harl, K. W. 1996. *Coinage in the Roman Economy, 300 B.C. to A.D. 700*. Baltimore: Johns Hopkins University Press.

Harrington, D. 1977. "Cassius Dio as a Military Historian." *Acta Classica* 20: 159–165.

Harris, W. V. 2003. "Roman Opinions about the Truthfulness of Dreams." *Journal of Roman Studies* 93: 18–34.

Harris, W. V. 2009. *Dreams and Experience in Classical Antiquity*. Cambridge, MA: Harvard University Press.

Hasebroek, J. 1921. *Untersuchungen zur Geschichte des Kaisers Septimius Severus*. Heidelberg: Winter.

Haynes, D. E. L., and P. E. D. Hirst. 1939. *Porta Argentariorum*. London: Macmillan.

Hekster, O. 2001. "Commodus-Hercules: The People's Princeps." *Scripta Classica Israelica* 20: 51–83.

Hekster, O. 2002. *Commodus: An Emperor at the Crossroads*. Dutch Monographs on Ancient History and Archaeology 23. Amsterdam: J. C. Gieben.

Hekster, O. 2003. "Coins and Messages: Audience Targeting on Coins of Different Denominations?" In *The Representation and Perception of Roman Imperial Power*. Vol. 3, *Impact of Empire*, edited by L. de Blois et al., 20–35. Amsterdam: J. C. Gieben.

Hekster, O. 2004. "Hercules, Omphale, and Octavian's 'Counter-Propaganda.'" *Babesch* 79: 159–166.

Hekster, O. 2007. "Fighting for Rome: The Emperor as a Military Leader." In *The Impact of the Roman Army*. Vol. 6, Impact of Empire, edited by L. de Blois et al., 91–106. Leiden: Brill.

Hekster, O., and E. Manders. 2006. "Kaiser gegen Kaiser: Bilder der Macht im 3. Jahrhunderts." In *Deleto paene imperio Romano Transformationsprozesse des Römischen Reiches im 3. Jahrhundert und ihre Rezeption in der Neuzeit*, edited by K.-P. Johne, T. Gerhardt, and U. Hartmann, 135–144. Stuttgart: Franz Steiner Verlag.

Hekster, O., G. de Kleijn, and D. Slootjes. 2007. *Crises and the Roman Empire: Proceedings of the Seventh Workshop of the International Network Impact of Empire (Nijmegen, June 20–24, 2006)*. Impact of Empire 7. Leiden: Brill.

Hekster, O., S. Schmidt-Hofner, and C. Witschel. 2009. *Ritual Dynamics and Religious Change in the Roman Empire: Proceedings of the Eighth Workshop of the International Network Impact of Empire (Heidelberg, July 5–7, 2007)*. Impact of Empire 8. Leiden: Brill.

Hemelrijk, E. A. 1999. *Matrona Docta: Educated Women in the Roman Elite from Cornelia to Julia Domna*. London: Routledge.

Hemelrijk, E. A. 2004. "City Patronesses in the Roman Empire." *Historia* 53: 209–245.

Hemelrijk, E. A. 2007. "Local Empresses: Priestesses of the Imperial Cult in the Cities of the Latin West." *Phoenix* 61 (3/4): 318–349.

Hemelrijk, E. A. 2008. "Patronesses and 'Mothers' of Roman Collegia." *Classical Antiquity* 27 (1): 115–162.

Hill, P. V. 1964a. "Notes on the Coinage of Septimius Severus and His Family." *Numismatic Chronicle*, ser. 7, 4: 169–88.

Hill, P. V. 1964b. *The Coinage of Septimius Severus and His Family of the Mint of Rome, AD 193–217*. London: Spink.

Hill, P. V. 1978a. "The Monuments and Buildings of Rome on the Coins of the Early Severans, A.D. 193–217." In *Scripta nummaria romana*, edited by R. A. G. Carson and C. M. Kraay, 58–63. London: Spink.

Hill, P. V. 1978b. "The Issues of Severus and His Sons in A.D. 211." *Numismatic Chronicle*, ser. 7, 18: 33–37.

Hill, P. V. 1979. "The Coin Portraiture of Severus and His Family from the Mint of Rome." *Numismatic Chronicle*, ser. 7, 19: 36–46.

Hillard, T. 1989. "Republican Politics, Women and the Evidence." *Helios* 16 (2): 165–182.

Hillard, T. 1992. "On the Stage, Behind the Curtain: Images of Politically Active Women in the Late Roman Republic." In *Stereotypes of Women in Power: Historical Perspectives and Revisionist Views*, edited by B. Garlick, S. Dixon, and P. Allen, 37–64. New York: Greenwood Press.

Hoffer, S. E. 1999. *The Anxieties of Pliny the Younger*. American Classical Studies 43. Atlanta, GA: Scholars Press.

Højte, J. M. 2002. *Images of Ancestors*. Aarhus Studies in Mediterranean Antiquity 5. Denmark: Aarhus University Press.

Holliday, P. J. 1997. "Roman Triumphal Painting: Its Function, Development, and Reception." *Art Bulletin* 79 (1): 130–147.

Hopkins, K. 1983. *Death and Renewal*. Sociological Studies in Roman History 2. Cambridge: Cambridge University Press.

Hopkins, K., and M. Beard. 2005. *The Colosseum*. Cambridge, MA: Harvard University Press.

Horster, M. 2001. *Bauinschriften römischer Kaiser: Untersuchungen zu Inschriftenpraxis und Bautätigkeit in Städten des westlichen Imperium Romanum in der Zeit des Prinzipats*. Stuttgart: Franz Steiner Verlag.

Howe, L. L. 1966. *The Pretorian Prefect from Commodus to Diocletian*. Rome: L'Erma di Bretschneider.

Howgego, C. J. 1992. "The Supply and Use of Money in the Roman World 200 B.C. to A.D. 300." *Journal of Roman Studies* 82: 1–31.

Howgego, C. J. 1993. "The Circulation of Silver Coins, Models of the Roman Economy and Crisis in the Third Century AD: Some Numismatic Evidence." *Studien zu Fundmünzen der Antike* 10: 219–236.

Howgego, C. J. 1994. "Coin Circulation and the Integration of the Roman Economy." *Journal of Roman Antiquity* 7: 1–21.

Howgego, C. J. 1995a. *Ancient History from Coins*. Approaching the Ancient World. London: Routledge.

Howgego, C. J. 1995b. "The Circulation of Silver Coins, Models of the Roman Economy." In *Coin Finds and Coin Use in the Roman World: The Thirteenth Oxford Symposium of Coinage and Monetary History, 25–27 March 1993—a NATO Advanced Research Workshop*. Vol. 10, *Studien zu Fundmünzen der Antike*, edited by C. E. King and D. G. Wigg, 219–236. Berlin: G. Mann.

Howgego, C. J. 2009. "Some Numismatic Approaches to Quantifying the Roman Economy." In *Quantifying the Roman Economy: Methods and Problems*, edited by A. K. Bowman and A. Wilson, 287–298. Oxford: Oxford University Press.

Howgego, C. J., and E. Christiansen. 1990. "Review of the Roman Coins of Alexandria: Quantitative Studies. Nero, Trajan, Septimius Severus." *Journal of Roman Studies* 80: 231–232.

Howgego, C. J., V. Heuchert, and A. Burnett, eds. 2005. *Coinage and Identity in the Roman Provinces*. Oxford: Oxford University Press.

Instinsky, H. U. 1942. "Studien zur Geschichte des Septimius Severus." *Klio* 35: 200–219.

Isrealowich, I. 2008. "The Rain Miracle of Marcus Aurelius: (Re-)Construction of Consensus." *Greece & Rome* 55 (1): 83–102.

Jones, A. H. M. 1956. "Numismatics and History." In *Essays in Roman Coinage Presented to Harold Mattingly*, edited by R. A. G. Carson and C. H. V. Sutherland, 13–33. Oxford: Oxford University Press.

Joshel, S. R. 1997. "Female Desire and the Discourse of Empire: Tacitus's Messalina." In *Roman Sexualities*, edited by J. P. Hallett and M. B. Skinner, 221–254. Princeton, NJ: Princeton University Press.

Joshel, S. R., and S. Murnaghan. 1998. *Women and Slaves in Greco-Roman Culture: Differential Equations*. London: Routledge.

Keltanen, M. 2002. "The Public Image of the Four Empresses—Ideal Wives, Mothers and Regents?" In *Women, Wealth and Power in the Roman Empire*, edited by P. Setälä et al., 105–146. Rome: Institutum Romanum Finlandiae.

Kemmers, F. 2005. "Not at Random: Evidence for a Regionalized Coin Supply?" In *TRAC 2004: Proceedings of the Fourteenth Annual Theoretical Roman Archaeology Conference, Durham 2004 Britannia*, edited by E. Swift et al., 39–49. London: Society for the Promotion of Roman Studies.

Kemmers, F. 2006. *Coins for a Legion: An Analysis of the Coin Finds from the Augustan Legionary Fortress and Flavian canabae legionis at Nijmegen*. Mainz: P. von Zabern.

Kemmers, F. 2009. "From Bronze to Silver: Coin Circulation in the Early Third Century AD." *Revue Belge de Numismatique et de Sigillographie* 155: 134–158.

Kennedy, D. L. 1986. "'European' Soldiers and the Severan Siege of Hatra." In *The Defense of the Roman and Byzantine East: Proceedings of a Colloquium Held at the University of Sheffield in April 1986*, Vol. 297, *BAR International Series*, edited by P. W. M. Freeman and D. L. Kennedy, 51–58. Oxford: BAR.

Kleiner, D. E. E. 1996. "Imperial Women as Patrons of the Arts in the Early Empire." In *I, Claudia: Women in Ancient Rome*, edited by D. E. E. Kleiner and S. B. Matheson, 28–42. New Haven, CT: Yale University Art Gallery.

Kleiner, D. E. E., and S. B. Matheson, eds. 1996. *I, Claudia: Women in Ancient Rome*. New Haven, CT: Yale University Art Gallery.

Kokkinos, N. 1992. *Antonia Augusta: Portrait of a Great Roman Lady*. London: Routledge.

Kokkinos, N. 2002. *Antonia Augusta: Portrait of a Great Roman Lady*. 2nd ed. Faringdon: Libri.

Kondratieff, E. J. 2004. "The Column and Coinage of C. Duilius: Innovations in Iconography in Large and Small Media in the Middle Republic." *Scripta Classica Israelica* 23: 1–39.

Konstan, D. 2000. "Women, Ethnicity and Power in the Roman Empire." Diotima. Last accessed August 16, 2012. http://www.stoa.org/diotima/essays/konstan1.pdf.

Konstan, D., and S. Said. 2006. *Greeks on Greekness: Viewing the Greek Past under the Roman Empire*. Cambridge Classical Journal Supplement 29. Cambridge: Cambridge Philological Society.

Kuhoff, W. 1993. "Iulia Aug. Mater Aug. n. et Castrorum et Senatus et Patriae." *Zeitschrift für Papyrologie und Epigraphik* 97: 259–271.

Langford, J. 2008. "Speaking out of Turn(us): Subverting Severan Constructions of Ethnicity, Masculinity and Felicitas." *The Ancient World* 39 (2): 125–150.

Langford-Johnson, J. 2005. "Mater Augustorum, Mater Senatus, Mater Patriae: Succession and Consensus in Severan Ideology." PhD diss., Department of Classical Studies, Indiana University.

Lebek, W. D. 1986. "Schwierige Stellen der Tabula Siarensis." *Zeitschrift für Papyrologie und Epigraphik* 66: 31–48.

Lebek, W. D. 1987. "Die drei Ehrenbögen für Germanicus: Tab. Siar. frg. I 9–34; CIL VI 31199a 2–17." *Zeitschrift für Papyrologie und Epigraphik* 67: 129–148.

Legutko, P. A. 2000. "Roman Imperial Ideology in the Mid-Third Century A.D.: Negotiation, Usurpation and Crisis in the Imperial Center." PhD diss., Classical Art and Archaeology, University of Michigan.

Leppin, H. 2002. "Rückblick und Ausblick." In *Die Kaiserinnen Roms von Livia bis Theodora*, edited by H. Temporini, 484–500. Munich: C. H. Beck.

Lévêque, P. 1947. "L'Arc des changeurs a Rome." *Revue Archéologique* 28: 52–61.

Levick, B. M. 1978. "Concordia at Rome." In *Scripta Nummaria Romana: Essays on Roman Coinage*, edited by R. A. G. Carson and C. M. Kraay, 227. London: Spink.

Levick, B. M. 1982. "Propaganda and the Imperial Coinage." *Antichthon* 16: 104–116.

Levick, B. M. 2007. *Julia Domna: Syrian Empress*. Edited by R. Ancona and S. B. Pomeroy. London: Routledge.

Lewis, N. 1996. "The Humane Legislation of Septimius Severus." *Historia* 45: 104–113.

Liu, J. 2008. "The Economy of Endowments: The Case of Roman Associations." In *Pistoi dia tèn technèn: Bankers, Loans and Archives in the Ancient World. Studies in Honor of Raymond Bogaert*. Vol. 44, *Studia Hellenistica*, edited by K. Verboven, K. Vandorpe, and V. Chankowdi-Sable, 231–256. Leuven: Peeters.

Liu, J. 2009. *Collegia centonariorum: The Guilds of Textile Dealers in the Roman West*. Leiden: Brill.

Lo Cascio, E. 2005. "The Emperor and His Administration." In *The Cambridge Ancient History*. Vol. 12, *The Crisis of Empire, A.D. 193–337*, edited by A. K. Bowman, P. Garnsey, and A. Cameron, 156–170. London: Cambridge University Press.

Lusnia, S. S. 1990. "The Public Image of Julia Domna and Her Role in Severan Dynastic Propaganda." MA diss., University of Cincinnati.

Lusnia, S. S. 1995. "Julia Domna's Coinage and Severan Dynastic Propaganda." *Latomus* 54: 119–140.

Lusnia, S. S. 1998. "The Building Program of Septimus Severus at Rome, A.D. 193–211." PhD diss., University of Cincinnati.

Lusnia, S. S. 2004. "Urban Planning and Sculptural Display in Severan Rome: Reconstructing the Septizodium and Its Role in Dynastic Politics." *American Journal of Archaeology* 108 (4): 517–544.

Lusnia, S. S. 2006. "Battle Imagery and Politics on the Severan Arch in the Roman Forum." In *Representations of War in Ancient Rome*, edited by S. Dillon and K. E. Welch, 272–299. Cambridge: Cambridge University Press.

Lusnia, S. S. *Creating Severan Rome: The Architecture and Self-Image of L. Septimius Severus (AD 193–211)*. Brussels: Latomus, forthcoming.

Macé, G. 2005. "Crepereia Tryphaena: From the Three Caskets." *Common Knowledge* 11 (2): 311–318.

Manders, E. 2007. "Mapping the Representation of Roman Imperial Power in Times of Crisis." In *Crises and the Roman Empire: Proceedings of the Seventh Workshop of the International Network Impact of Empire (Nijmegen, June 20–24, 2006)*. Vol. 7, *Impact of Empire*, edited by O. Hekster, G. de Kleijn, and D. Slootjes, 275–290. Leiden: Brill.

Manders, E. 2008. *Coinage Images of Power: Patterns in the Representation of Roman Emperors on Imperial Coinage, A.D. 193–284*. Nijmegen: Radboud Universiteit.

Marshall, A. 1975. "Roman Women in the Provinces." *Ancient Society* 6: 109–128.

Matheson, S. B. 1996. "The Divine Claudia: Women as Goddesses in Roman Art." In *I, Claudia: Women in Ancient Rome*, edited by D. E. E. Kleiner and S. B. Matheson, 182–193. New Haven, CT: Yale University Art Gallery.

McCullough, A. 2007. "Gender and Public Image in Imperial Rome." PhD diss., Classical Studies, Oxford University.

McDonnell, M. A. 2006. *Roman Manliness: Virtus and the Roman Republic*. Cambridge: Cambridge University Press.

Meadows, A., and J. Williams. 2001. "Moneta and Monuments: Coinage and Politics in Republican Rome." *Journal of Roman Studies* 91: 27–49.

Meckler, M. 1996a. "The Beginning of the *Historia Augusta*." *Historia* 45: 364–375.

Meckler, M. 1996b. "Caracalla the Intellectual." In *Gli Imperatori Severi: Storia, Archeologia, Religione*, edited by E. dal Covolo and G. Rinaldi, 39–48. Rome: LAS.

Meister, M. 1988. "Die Frauen der syrischen Dynastie in Rom." In *Frauen auf Münzen*, edited by E. Specht, 33–47. Vienna: F. Schindler.

Merino, P. E. S. 1986. "Los suenos en Dion Casio." *Estudios de Filologia Griega* 1: 83–90.

Metcalf, W. E. 1993. "Whose Libertas? Propaganda and Audience in the Early Roman Empire." *Rivista Italiana di Numismatica* 95: 337–346.

Metcalf, W. E. 1998. "Aurelian's Reform at Alexandria." In *Studies in Greek Numismatics in Memory of Martin Jessop Price*, edited by R. Ashton and S. Hurter, 268–277. London: Spink.

Metcalf, W. E. 1999. "Coins as Primary Evidence." In *Roman Coins and Public Life under the Empire*, edited by G. M. Paul and M. Ierardi, 1–17. Ann Arbor: University of Michigan Press.

Millar, F. 1964. *A Study of Cassius Dio*. Oxford: Clarendon Press.

Millar, F. 1977. *The Emperor in the Roman World, 31 BC–AD 337*. Ithaca, NY: Cornell University Press.

Milnor, K. 2005. *Gender, Domesticity, and the Age of Augustus*. Oxford: Oxford University Press.

Moscovich, M. J. 2004. "Cassius Dio's Palace Sources for the Reign of Septimius Severus." *Historia* 53: 356–368.

Murphy, P. R. 1986. "Caesar's Continuators and Caesar's 'Felicitas.'" *The Classical World* 79 (5): 307–317.

Nodelman, S. A. 1965. "Severan Imperial Portraiture, AD 193–217." PhD diss., Yale University.

Noreña, C. F. 2001. "The Communication of the Emperor's Virtues." *Journal of Roman Studies* 91: 146–168.

Noreña, C. F. 2007. "Hadrian's Chastity." *Phoenix* 61 (3): 296–317.

Oliver, J. H. 1940. "Julia Domna as Athena Polias." In *Athenian Studies Presented to W. S.*

Ferguson. Harvard Studies in Classical Philology Supplement 1, 521–530. Cambridge, MA: Harvard University Press.

Pallottino, M. 1946. *L'Arco degli argentari.* Rome: Danesi.

Paschoud, F. 1996. *Histoire auguste: Tome V.1, Vies d'Aurélien, Tacite.* Paris: Les Belles Lettres.

Paterson, J. 2007. "Friends in High Places: The Creation of the Court of the Roman Emperor." In *The Court and Court Society in Ancient Monarchies*, edited by A. J. S. Spawforth, 121–156. Cambridge: Cambridge University Press.

Patterson, J. R. 1994. "The Collegia and the Transformation of the Towns of Italy in the Second Century AD." In *L'Italie d'Auguste à Dioclétien: Actes du colloque international (Rome, 25–28 mars 1992)*, 227–238. Rome: Ècole Française de Rome.

Pera, R. 1979. "Probabili significati della scritta 'Indulgentia Augg in Cathaginem' ed 'Indulgentia Augg.'" *Rivista Italiana di Numismatica* 81: 103–114.

Phang, S. E. 2001. *The Marriage of Roman Soldiers (13 B.C.–A.D. 235): Law and Family in the Imperial Army.* Columbia Studies in the Classical Tradition 24. Leiden: Brill.

Phang, S. E. 2002. "The Families of Roman Soldiers (First and Second Centuries A.D.): Culture, Law and Practice." *Journal of Family History* 27: 352–373.

Potter, D. 1994. *Prophets and Emperors: Human and Divine Authority from Augustus to Theodosius.* Cambridge, MA: Harvard University Press.

Potter, D. 1996. "Performance, Power and Justice in the High Empire." In *Roman Theater and Society.* Vol. 1, *E. Togo Salmon Papers*, edited by W. J. Slater, 129–160. Ann Arbor: University of Michigan Press.

Potter, D. 1999. "Entertainers in the Roman Empire." In *Life, Death, and Entertainment in the Roman Empire*, edited by D. Potter and D. J. Mattingly, 256–326. Ann Arbor: University of Michigan Press.

Potter, D. 2004. "The Roman Army and Navy." In *The Cambridge Companion to the Roman Republic*, edited by H. I. Flower, 66–88. Cambridge: Cambridge University Press.

Price, S. R. F. 1984. *Rituals and Power: The Roman Imperial Cult in Asia Minor.* Cambridge: Cambridge University Press.

Purcell, N. 1986. "Livia and the Womanhood of Rome." *Proceedings of the Cambridge Philological Society* 32: 78–105.

Raepsaet-Charlier, M.-T. 1982. "Epouses et familles de magistrats dans les provinces romaines aux deux premiers siécles de l'empire." *Historia* 31 (1): 56–69.

Rawson, E. 1987. "Discrimina Ordinum: The *Lex Julia Theatralis.*" *Papers of the British School at Rome* 55: 83–114.

Ricciardi, R. A. 2007. "Where Did All the Women Go: The Archaeology of the Soldier Empresses." PhD diss., Department of Classics, University of Cincinnati.

Rose, C. B. 1997. *Dynastic Commemoration and Imperial Portraiture in the Julio-Claudian Period.* Cambridge: Cambridge University Press.

Rowan, C. 2009. "Under Divine Auspices: Patron Deities and the Visualization of Imperial Power in the Severan Period." PhD diss., Department of Ancient History, Macquarie University.

Rubin, Z. 1975. "Dio, Herodian, and Severus' Second Parthian War." *Chiron* 5: 419–441.

Rubin, Z. 1976/1977. "The Felicitas and the Concordia of the Severan House." *Scripta Classica Israelica* 3: 153–172.

Rubin, Z. 1980. *Civil War Propaganda and Historiography*. Collection Latomus 173. Brussels: Latomus.

Ryberg, I. S. 1955. *Rites of the State Religion in Roman Art*. Memoirs of the American Academy in Rome 32. Rome: American Academy in Rome.

Saavedra Guerrero, M. D. 1994. "El mecanazgo femenino imperial: El caso de Julia Domna." *L'Antiquité classique* 63: 193–200.

Sidebottom, H. 2007. "Severan Historiography: Evidence, Patterns, and Arguments." In *Severan Culture*, edited by S. Swain, S. Harrison, and J. Elsner, 52–82. Cambridge: Cambridge University Press.

Sillar, S. 2001. "Caracalla and the Senate: The Aftermath of Geta's Assassination." *Athenaeum* 89: 407–423.

Smith, R. E. 1972. "The Army Reforms of Septimius Severus." *Historia* 21: 481–500.

Southern, P. 2001. *The Roman Empire from Severus to Constantine*. London: Routledge.

Southern, P. 2007. *The Roman Army: A Social and Institutional History*. Oxford: Oxford University Press.

Späth, T. 2000. *Frauenwelten in der Antike: Geschlechterordnung und weibliche Lebenspraxis*. Stuttgart: J. B. Metzler.

Speidel, M. 1984. "'Europeans'—Syrian Elite Troops at Dura-Europos and Hatra." In *Roman Army Studies*, 301–309. Amsterdam: J. C. Gieben.

Staples, A. 1998. *From Good Goddess to Vestal Virgins: Sex and Category in Roman Religion*. London: Routledge.

Straub, J. 1966. "Senaculum, id est mulierum senatus." In *Bonner Historia-Augusta-Colloquium 1964–1965*, edited by A. Alföldi, 221–240. Bonn: R. Habelt Verlag.

Sutherland, C. H. V. 1959. "The Intelligibility of Roman Imperial Coin Types." *Journal of Roman Studies* 49: 46–55.

Swain, S. 1996. *Hellenism and Empire: Language, Classicism, and Power in the Greek World AD 50–250*. Oxford: Clarendon Press.

Swain, S., S. J. Harrison, and J. Elsner. 2007. *Severan Culture*. Cambridge: Cambridge University Press.

Syed, Y. 2005. *Vergil's* Aeneid *and the Roman Self: Subject and Nation in Literary Discourse*. Ann Arbor: University of Michigan Press.

Syme, R. 1960. *The Roman Revolution*. London: Oxford University Press.

Talbert, R. J. A. 1984. *The Senate of Imperial Rome*. Princeton, NJ: Princeton University Press.

Taylor, D. M. 1945. "The Names and Titles of Julia Domna." MA thesis, Department of Latin, Indiana University.

Temporini, H. 1978. *Die Frauen am Hofe Trajans: Ein Beitrag zur Stellung der Augustae im Principat*. Berlin: W. de Gruyter.

Temporini, H. 2002. *Die Kaiserinnen Roms von Livia bis Theodora*. Munich: C. H. Beck.

Thein, A. G. 2009. "*Felicitas* and the Memoirs of Sulla and Augustus." In *Lost Memoirs of Augustus and the Development of Roman Autobiography*, edited by C. Smith and A. Powell, 87–109. Swansea: Classical Press of Wales.

Turton, G. 1962. *The Syrian Princesses: The Women Who Ruled Rome AD 193–235*. London: Cassell.

Wallace-Hadrill, A. 1981. "Galba's Aequitas." *Numismatic Chronicle* 141: 20–39.

Wheeler, E. L. 1996. "The Laxity of the Syrian Legions." In "The Roman Army in the East," supplement, *Journal of Roman Archaeology* 18: 229–276.

Wiedemann, T. E. J. 2002. *Emperors and Gladiators*. London: Routledge.

Williams, C. A. 1999. *Roman Homosexuality: Ideologies of Masculinity in Classical Antiquity, Ideologies of Desire*. Oxford: Oxford University Press.

Williams, M. G. 1902. "Studies in the Lives of Roman Empresses." *American Journal of Archaeology* 6: 259–305.

Wood, S. E. 1999. *Imperial Women: A Study in Public Images, 40 B.C.–A.D. 68*. Leiden: Brill.

Yavetz, Z. 1969. *Plebs and Princeps*. Oxford: Oxford University Press.

Ziegler, R. 1996. "Civic Coins and Imperial Campaigns." In "The Roman Army in the East," supplement, *Journal of Roman Archaeology* 18: 119–134. Treggiari, S. 1994. "Putting the Bride to Bed." *Echos du Monde/Classical Views*, n.s., 38 (13): 311–331.

Zwalve, W. J. 2001. "*In re* Iulius Agrippa's Estate: Q. Cervidius Scaevola, Iulia Domna and the Estate of Iulius Agrippa." In *Administration, Prosopography and Appointment Policies in the Roman Empire: Proceedings of the First Workshop of the International Network Impact of Empire (Roman Empire, 27 B.C.–A.D. 406) Leiden, June 28–July 1, 2000*. Vol. 1, *Impact of Empire*, edited by L. de Blois, 154–166. Amsterdam: J. C. Gieben.

INDEX

Figure numbers in italics indicate illustrations in the gallery.